# Mestizaje

**CRITICAL AMERICAN STUDIES SERIES**

GEORGE LIPSITZ
UNIVERSITY OF CALIFORNIA–SANTA BARBARA
SERIES EDITOR

# Mestizaje

*Critical Uses of Race in Chicano Culture*

## Rafael Pérez-Torres

*Critical American Studies Series*

University of Minnesota Press

Minneapolis • London

**M
IN
NE
SO
TA**

A preliminary version of chapter 2 originally appeared as "Chicano Ethnicity, Cultural Hybridity, the Mestizo Voice," *American Literature* 70, no. 1 (1998): 153–76; copyright 1998 Duke University Press; all rights reserved; reprinted by permission of the publisher. A portion of chapter 3 originally appeared as "Mestizaje in the Mix: Chicano Identity, Politics, and Postmodern Music," in *Music and the Racial Imagination*, edited by Ronald Radano and Philip Bohlman (Chicago: University of Chicago Press, 2000), 206–30; copyright 2000 by the University of Chicago; all rights reserved. A portion of chapter 4 originally appeared as "Remapping Chicano Expressive Culture," in *Just Another Publication? Chicano Graphic Arts in California* (Santa Barbara: University Art Museum, 2001), 151–69. A brief section from chapter 6 originally appeared in "Alternate Geographies and the Melancholy of Mestizaje" in *Minor Transnationalisms*, edited by Françoise Lionnet and Shu-mei Shih (Durham, NC: Duke University Press, 2005), 317–38; copyright 2005 by Duke University Press.

"Refugee Ship" by Lorna Dee Cervantes is reprinted with permission from the publisher of *The Americas Review* (Houston: Arte Público Press—University of Houston, 1982). "Crow" is from *Emplumada*, by Lorna Dee Cervantes, copyright 1981; reprinted by permission of the University of Pittsburgh Press.

Lyrics from "La Raza" by Kid Frost with Virgin/Atlantic (ASCAP), 1990; words and music by Arturo Molina Jr., Antonio González, and Gerald Wilson; copyright 1991 EMI Virgin Songs, Inc., Too Damn, Too Brown Publishing, MI Palo Music, and Ludlow Music; all rights for Too Damn, Too Brown Publishing controlled and administered by EMI Virgin Songs, Inc.; all rights reserved; international copyright secured; used by permission. Lyrics from "Low Rider," "Runnin'," and "What Is an American?" by Latin Alliance with Far Out Music, Inc., and Universal Polygram International Publishing, Inc., 1990. Lyrics from "Tres Delinquentes" by Delinquent Habits with RCA, 1996; words and music by David Thomas, Alejandro Martínez, Ivan Scott Martin, and Sol Lake; copyright 1996 Move Something Music, Graveyard Shift Music, Keimonti Music, Memory Lost Music, and Almo Music Corp.; excerpts from "The Lonely Bull" by Sol Lake copyright 1962 Almo Music Corp.; all rights for Move Something Music, Graveyard Shift Music, Keimonti Music, and Memory Lost Music administered by Music of Windswept; all rights reserved; used by permission. Lyrics from "People of the Sun" by Rage Against the Machine with Epic, 1996. Lyrics from "Same Brown Earth" by the Latin Playboys with Slash/Warner Bros., 1994; written by Louis Pérez and David Hidalgo; copyright 1994 Chicken on Fire Music (BMI)/Hot Churro Music (BMI); administered by Bug Music, Inc.; all rights reserved; used by permission. Lyrics from "Marisela," "Manny's Bones," and "Revolution" by Los Lobos with Slash/Warner Bros., 1996. Lyrics from "Lyrical Drive-by" by Aztlán Underground with Sub-Verses, Xican Records, 1999. Lyrics from "Como Ves" by Ozomatli with Almo Sounds, 1998.

*Border Mezz-teez-o* by Victor Ochoa (1983) appears courtesy of the artist. To view his collected works, see the Web site at www.chicanozauruz.com.

Every effort has been made to obtain permission to reproduce copyright material in this book. If any proper acknowledgment has not been made, we encourage copyright holders to notify us.

Published by the University of Minnesota Press
111 Third Avenue South, Suite 290
Minneapolis, MN 55401-2520
http://www.upress.umn.edu

Library of Congress Cataloging-in-Publication Data

Pérez-Torres, Rafael.
    Mestizaje : critical uses of race in Chicano culture / Rafael Pérez-Torres.
        p.    cm. — (Critical American studies series)
    Includes bibliographical references and index.
    ISBN 13: 978-0-8166-4594-7 (hc) — ISBN 13: 978-0-8166-4595-4 (pb)
    ISBN 10: 0-8166-4594-9 (hc : alk. paper) — ISBN 10: 0-8166-4595-7 (pb : alk. paper)
    1. Mexican Americans—Race identity.    2. Mexican Americans—Ethnic identity.    3. Mexican American arts.    4. Mestizaje in art.    5. Mestizaje in literature.    6. Racially mixed people—United States.    7. United States—Race relations.    I. Title.    II. Series.
    E184.M5P425 2006
    305.868'72073—dc22

                                                                        2006000239

Printed in the United States of America on acid-free paper

The University of Minnesota is an equal-opportunity educator and employer.

12  11  10  09  08  07                                    10  9  8  7  6  5  4  3  2

*As always, for Beth*

# Contents

# Acknowledgments

There are too many people to thank for the care and kindness, intellectual and personal interest they have been kind enough to share with me, and I am embarrassed at the paucity of my ability to acknowledge them. First and foremost, I want to thank my family for their constant love, care, and support. My mother and sister especially merit more love and thanks than I could ever express. My father and late grandmother have been an inspiration, and my dear in-laws—Ted and Wilma, Judy, Jim and Jessica—have become my second family. I also wish to thank my aunts, uncles, and cousins, who are all in my heart and thoughts.

My friends, many of whom I see much too seldom, have brought insight, love, and bright laughter; I thank them all. I want especially to mention John Vasi and Nancy Willstater, Silvia Bermúdez, Ernie Chávez, Adán Griego, Ray Harris, and Chela Sandoval. My thanks go as well to Mary Pat Brady and Kate McCullough, Angie Chabram-Dernersesian, Tso-Yee Fan and Debbie Haley, Emma Pérez, Francine Masiello, Gwen Kirkpatrick, Catherine Ramírez and Eric Porter, Valerie Smith, Sonia Saldívar-Hull, María Herrera-Sobek, Larry Scanlon and Aline Fairweather, and Theresa Delgadillo. I must also offer inadequate thanks to Avery Gordon and Chris Newfield, Kum-Kum Bhavnani and John Foran, Ricardo Ortiz, Ricky Rodríguez, Dale Bauer and Gordon Hutner, José David Saldívar, Nellie McKay, Josie Saldaña-Portillo and David Kazanjian, Fernando Rocchi, Rob Casper and Matthea Harvey, Ramón

Saldívar, Fernando López-Alves and Sal Guereña. Although I do not see them often enough, Rubén Martínez and Luis Alfaro have been both generous friends and inspirational artists. I am grateful for their friendship and support.

I wish to offer an overdue thanks to George Lipsitz for his thoughtful reading and insightful suggestions, but more generally for the heroic way he has balanced exemplary intellectual work with committed political action. A particular note of gratitude goes to Deidre Freeman and Taki Kohiyama, who, along with their lovely daughters, brought light to my dark mood as this project ground to an end. I am also extremely grateful to Heloisa Buarque de Hollanda and João Horta, who for a few wonderful days managed to take my mind off this seemingly always-incomplete manuscript. And a special thanks to Lourdes Oliveira, who took care of my family and me for the past two months of writing as if we were her very own. *Saudades e beijos.*

I warmly thank my friends and colleagues at UCLA, especially Mark Seltzer and Richard Yarborough, who (though they would undoubtedly demur) have been both valued mentors and cherished friends. For many reasons, I owe a debt of gratitude to Tom Worthm, Eric Sundquist, Caroline Steeter, Max and Estelle Novak, Chon Noriega and Kathleen McHugh, Arthur Little, Françoise Lionnet, Shu-mei Shih, Rachel Lee, Tammy Ho and David Martínez, Jeff Decker and Jenny Sharpe, Kingkok Cheung, Fred Burwick, and Marla Berns. I am especially grateful to Lynn Itagaki, who suffered through an early version of this book and offered generous, insightful, and extremely useful comments that helped complete this study.

Finally, I cannot express how writing this book, as all I do, has been not just bearable but made so much sweeter because of my life's love, Elizabeth Marchant, and our beautiful boy, Caetano Julián. Words fail.

# Introduction

Mestizaje has taken on a life of its own. In discussions of Latin American and Chicana/o identity and culture, the notion of racial mixture plays a dominant role. At heart, a recognition of multiple racial and cultural influences—African, Native American, European, Asian—composes the rich and troubled story of mestizaje in the Americas. Consequently, mestizaje has become both the metaphor and the precondition for cultural production in the "New" World. Critical, visual, musical, and written arts deploy mestizaje as a thematic and formal marker of identity. The transnationality of Chicano and Chicana identity manifests the idea of mixture. The linguistic interplay between Spanish, English, and caló illustrates the synthesis of this identity in expression. The uniquely hybrid nature of Chicano culture is discussed as a correlative to the racial condition of mestizaje.

The work of Alfred Arteaga provides a useful example. He argues that the language of the borderlands "is the site of confluence in the way the Chicano body is mestizo and the homeland is international. And like the body and home, the language is hybrid and thus more than merely a sum of its parts . . . Chicano speech is like the mestizo body and the borderlands home: it simultaneously reflects multiple forces at play and asserts its hybridity" (1997, 16). This evocation of mixture in terms of race, identity, speech, and geography reflects a dominant trope in Chicano critical discourse.

Yet this interplay between race and culture has not come about easily. Perhaps because Chicanos identify as a mixed-race people, the issue of race has been one of the most vexing topics to discuss within a Chicano context.[1] I finish this book surrounded by the beauty of Salvador, Bahia, along the Atlantic coast of Brazil. This geographic point was one of the primary gateways through which enslaved Africans entered a new world where their flesh was martyred and forced to be made anew. I draw this study to a close situated in a social space that accords me—because of my skin color and hair texture—an often unspoken but always recognized racial privilege, a privilege not accorded me back home along the Pacific Coast of the United States. I am viscerally reminded, then, how racial mixture in the Americas emerges from an unequal and highly textured history of violence and conquest and cheap, inhuman exploitation. This legacy continues to run throughout the weave of social and personal development in the Americas. The flesh is the site from which arise dreams and nightmares, the elixirs and poisons of hatred and desire for both self and other. Those hatreds and desires have manifested themselves in myriad ways across the temporal and geographic expanses of the Americas both North and South.

Although not uninterested, I have no intention of here investigating the varied ways race mixing signifies defiance or acquiescence or desire across the space and time that are the Americas. I leave that intellectual history of mestizaje to more intrepid and energetic writers.[2]

Instead, my task is to trace the way race mixture within Chicano/a cultural production has helped embody both the awareness of social inequity and the contradictions those inequities have wrought. Race and issues of racialization are central to Chicano/a experiences, an observation that has informed several insightful works among the social sciences.[3] However, in cultural criticism, the tropes of the border, violence, and bilingualism rather than race have remained dominant. While the racial order in the United States has at times forced a uniform racial status on all blacks, Asians, and Native Americans, Chicanos and Chicanas remain distinct among people of color by virtue of their more ambiguous legal relationships to race. No fixed conclusion can be drawn from this ambiguity. It has, however, made Chicano culture's engagement with U.S. society consistently and self-consciously critical about the constructed-ness of social identities. This self-consciousness has produced insights and conclusions that at moments offer flashes of inspiration regarding liberation from colonial patterns of violence and exclusion. At other times, these insights have replicated forms of self-hatred that sustain racial hier-archies and colonial dispossession.

Chicano/a cultural mestizaje embodies a number of different drives. Two main ones concern me most here. One is the drive to view new and often utopian possibilities of aggregation as key to developing criti-cal sensibilities. The other reflects the contradictions and tensions that racial mixture has produced and that are incorporated in the cultural ex-pression of Chicano thought and identity. Tracing the patterns of mes-tizaje within a Chicano context, this study locates the traces of the colo-nial history from whence the term derived. Yet the uses of mestizaje by Chicana and Chicano writers, artists, critics, and scholars do not simply continue a vexed tradition in which race mixture sustains an uninspired teleology leading from the subjugated Indian, African, and Asian Other to a new, mestizo agent in history. The incorporation of mestizaje makes present a persistent oscillation between presence and absence, resistance and capitulation, agency and victimhood, power and fatigue.

As this book will illustrate, the idea of mestizaje within cultural and critical discourse has been used—at times too freely, at others too literally—in order to contend with the varying forces that tug and nudge, haul and rend the shape of Chicano culture and identity. Although the idea of mestizaje emerges from a history of essentialized and biologized racial discussions, the term has been used in Chicano/a discourse to move beyond simple ideas of identity and identity politics.

I consider the critical use of mestizaje a highly valued—though not unproblematic—conceptual tool in contemporary critical discourse. Mestizaje embodies the idea of multiple subjectivities, opening up dis-cussions of identity to greater complexity and nuance. Critical mestizaje locates how people live their lives in and through their bodies as well as in and through ideology. A disjuncture or rupture in ideology occurs through the dislocation experienced by mestizo/a bodies. Ideological constructs of subjectivity cannot always successfully hail Chicana and Chicano subjects because they undergo a dislocation of identity. Chicano mestizaje has sought to articulate the critical nature of this dislocation.

Certainly, in the United States, the one-drop rule still informs dominant constructions of a binary racial identity.[4] Thus one can discern the dislocation experienced by people who identify themselves as mixed-race.[5] This dislocation represents, I suggest, a rupture in racial ideology. Mestizaje not only marks this rupture but also signifies the embodiedness of power, the incarnation of colonial histories, the ways bodies are disciplined, formed, and deformed by ideology. The mestizaje of Chicana bodies represents the physical trace of a historical process, an often-violent encounter in which identities of race (as well as gender and sexuality, class and ethnicity) become inextricable from the material conditions of colonial and neocolonial histories.

Chicana mestizaje represents the double nature of Chicana identity. It allows for the forging of new multivalent identities *and* it embeds identity in already constraining social relations.

It is from this juncture that the following discussion springs. The chapters that compose this discussion trace some of mestizaje's contours and the differing uses to which the term has been used within a Chicano/Chicana cultural context. As will become plain, the reliance on racial mixture as a critical category in understanding and producing knowledge is neither simple nor simplistic. The temptation to simplify, however, is ever-present.

For the past two decades, Richard Rodriguez has become, as an outspoken critic of multiculturalism and bilingual education, a representative mainstream media spokesperson for ethnic—particularly Latino—identity. His views often meld well with the reactionary view that racial dialogue artificially maintains a sense of victimhood, separation, and social inequality. For example, he suggests that discourses surrounding race and ethnicity have, for the past four decades or more, demanded a purity of identity. In his collection of essays, *Brown*, Rodriguez recalls his days as a Stanford University undergraduate:

I was studying Puritanism and that, too, interested me; not least for its prohibition of impersonation.

At about this time, Malcolm X, an American puritan, discouraged African-American adolescents from hair straighteners and skin lighteners.

At about this time, ethnic studies departments were forming on some campuses. Such quorums would produce the great puritans of my age. The puritans would eventually form opinions about me, and I about them. (2002, 49)

Undoubtedly, these opinions on both sides are partial and, to a large degree, tendentious. It is clear, however, that no matter how provocative and—at moments—insightful his writing can be, Rodriguez perceives discussions of ethnicity in terms of a rather simplified (if not simplistic) notion of identity politics.

Rodriguez's observations serve as a warning that when we discuss notions of ethnicity and race it becomes too easy to assume an essence to identity. Discussions of race always run the risk of representing the body as some realm of "the real." At the same time, it is important to point out that the body has, within discussions of identity, formed a privileged site. We need to recognize that the significance of the biological body is always discursively created; yet it represents an object to which notions of identity have given priority. The discussion that follows should demonstrate, if nothing else, that the real in relation to mestizaje is as devious and elusive as it is productive in considering what it means to live on a mestizo continent.

This book is divided into three parts, each approaching the issue of Chicano mestizaje from a different angle. Part I, "Creating Mestizaje," deals with the construction of mestizaje and the manner in which notions of mestizaje have been used to engage issues of hybridity, identity, and voice. Chapter 1 considers the way mestizaje has been used critically to understand possibility and constraint in developing a new historical subjectivity. It traces the manner in which racial mixture has emerged as a discourse within the Americas and how Chicano/a critical thinking has sought to intervene in the colonial legacy of this discourse. Taking up Mary Pratt's influential discussion of transculturation and contact zones, I trace how discussions of mestizaje have informed and been informed by these key terms. I look at the doubleness in mestizaje as part of the dynamic that makes mestizo and mestiza identities multiple and relational as well as resistant to and affirmative of dominant forms of power. I consider, then, the critiques that have been offered over the uses of mestizaje and hybridity to posit identities in opposition.

Chapter 2 examines explicitly the production of a mestizo voice. How does the mestizo body gain voice, agency, and subjectivity? I trace the representation of Chicano/a subjectivity in a variety of texts, ranging from the 1956 movie *Giant* to Tino Villanueva's poetic response to the film, from Oscar Acosta's autobiographical consideration of his mestizo body to the feminist expressions of Lorna Dee Cervantes and Sandra Cisneros. This review reveals the contested sense of agency and how, through collective effort and a relational understanding of subjectivity, Chicano and Chicana bodies express their self-understanding as new subjects in history.

Part II, "Fashioning Mestizaje," addresses the role that mestizaje has played in expressive culture. There emerges a dynamic interaction between the representations of mestiza/o subjectivities within cultural objects and the mestizo forms of Chicana cultural expression. Chapter 3 traces the significance of contemporary Chicano musical expression as it both thematizes and embodies notions of mestizaje. I argue that not only is the idea of a Latino musical boom fallacious, it serves to erase a larger and continuing cultural legacy, one that calls up Chicanos and other Latinos as historical and social subjects. The chapter examines the work of musical artists who self-consciously employ a formal mestizaje, blending distinct sounds and musical influences associated with a wide variety of locations: American, African, Latin American, Afro-Cuban. Popular Chicano music responds and corresponds to musical movements of North and Latin America, yet it also seeks to articulate a distinct Chicano cultural sound. It evokes a sense of place and connection while simultaneously recasting aesthetic and semiotic codes. The aural mestizaje serves to highlight the multiple connections between Chicana culture and subjectivity and other political and social agents worldwide asserting their own new historical subjectivities. At a formal and thematic level, the music asserts a critical but productive mestizaje and acts as a powerful example of the creative mestizo voice.

Chapter 4 considers the role that Chicano public art, specifically poster art, plays in developing notions of mestizaje. I am most interested in the representations and uses of land in this public art because land has played such a key role in the development of Chicana and Chicano identities. The vexed history of land in the formation of Mexican American identity—associated with such dates as 1521, 1848, and 1965—is evoked through the visual representations of lithographic art. The visual art I examine serves to forge a connection between the mestizo body and the land it occupies. As the mestiza body is inscribed by history, so too land is revealed to be not a passive territory but a site constantly mapped and remapped. The artistic representations of Chicano public art make present not just the mestizo body in space but the interrelation between place and self.

Part III, "Challenging Mestizaje," focuses on the problematics of mestizaje made evident in the realm of literary creation. Although the hybrid dynamism of mestizaje often gets celebrated and championed as a hallmark of Chicano culture (this indeed is one of the points made in Part II), when a slipping between identities occurs to gendered and sexualized bodies, mestizaje becomes a threat. The narrative work by Emma Pérez and Gil Cuadros forms the focus of chapter 5 as they examine the ways bodies are coerced into acting out proscribed sexualized gender roles. Cuadros, in his collection of short stories *City of God*, and Pérez, with her short novel *Gulf Dreams*, provide a vision of queer mestizaje that struggles both to gain recognition within the worlds represented in their fiction and to gain voice through the narratives. In each case, the queer mestizo characters who provide the narrative focus are forced to articulate an identity that their mestizo communities can neither understand nor accept. The writing of these narratives becomes the only site where the socially impossible position of a body doubly marked—by its deviant mestizaje and its deviant sexuality—can find textual interpretation and agency. The characters try to attain an identity that incorporates both their sexual and their mestiza racial identities. Although not possible on a social level, textually the work of Cuadros and Pérez reveals that the dynamic qualities of mestizaje are manifest in a newfound hope for spiritual transformation and, if extremely tenuously, social renewal.

Chapter 6, which serves as a conclusion to this book, considers the role that the mestizo body plays as a site of knowledge. This knowledge is, ultimately, one that seems elusive or displaced. This is the reason why a sense of an ethical center in much Chicana narrative is often associated with a lost or missing member of the family. As mestizaje implies a movement between identities, there implicitly exists a space of loss. Thus the narrative of mestizaje is also a narrative of loss. I argue that the celebration of polysemic mestiza and mestizo bodies at the level of Chicano racial ideology and cultural articulation becomes a disarticulation at the level of sexuality, gender formation, and the longing for an unnameable loss. This is, ultimately, a productive loss, one imbricated in notions of nostalgia and melancholy. Yet, in considering texts by Gary Soto, Victor Martinez, and Pat Mora, it is possible to trace where the absent ethical core suggested by each narrative leads the characters to a new, though painful and uncertain, mestizo future.

The present study does not pretend to answer the difficult questions it raises regarding identity, history, subjectivity, and agency. It does attempt to open a dialogue in which the racial identities of all of America's mestizos, *indios*, and others can be understood outside of epochal binaries. In *Racial Conditions*, Howard Winant observes rather pessimistically: "None of the extant racial projects seems capable of presenting a durable and comprehensive vision of race. None can realistically address in even a minimally adequate way *both* the volatility of racial expression, meaning, and identities on the one hand, *and* the in-depth racialization of the social structure and political system in the United States" (1994, 28). I believe that the work on mestizaje undertaken by Chicana, Chicano, and other writers is beginning to address just these issues.

Mestizaje suggests the volatility and mutability of racial identity. Because it is an identity in the flesh, it is also tied in a profound way to the social structures and political systems through which the mestizo body moves. As I write in the heart of Salvador with its constant reminders of the colonial slave trade in African people, I am reminded that a deeply felt hope motivates this study. If we can better understand how mixed-race subjects in the Americas articulate agency and identity in the violent wake of their colonial histories, we may all be able to deal more productively with the weighty legacies of our unequal—though equally vexed—colonial past.

# PART I

# Creating Mestizaje

# CHAPTER 1

# The Critical Mixture of Race

Chicana/o critical discourse has privileged the role played by mestiza and mestizo bodies. These bodies serve to destabilize the unity and coherence integral to racial and gender hierarchies as these hierarchies seek to naturalize unequal relations of power; that is, mixed-race bodies undo identity formations based on purity. They thus undo ideas of simple differentiation. Similarly, Chicana culture, in claiming its mestizaje, undertakes a project of decentralization. Meaning is undone in order to forge new understandings based on the doubleness implicit in mestizaje, a doubleness that leads to a third state or condition.

Mestizaje occupies a valued position in Chicana critical discourse because, as a descriptive term and a cultural practice, it helps embody the idea of multiple subjectivities. Moreover, mestizaje signals the embodiedness of history. As such, it opens a world of possibilities in terms of forging new relational identities. At the same time, it signals how the body is tied to a colonial history of racial hierarchy whose power relations already constrain and guide the body. This is the reason Norma Alarcón, for example, has insisted in her writings that Chicana subjectivity has to be understood as a gendered and racialized as well as classed and ethnicized body. What is at stake in discussing the connection between mixed racial identities and transformative social conditions is the need to balance a sense of boundless possibility with a sense of constraint and ultimately, as I argue in the final chapter, loss. Mestizaje as a trope

3

in Chicano culture and criticism plays a complex role that signals change while simultaneously marking how institutions, ideologies, and numerous networks of power bound change.

It is the body that serves as the site of tenuous, complex, and conflicted change. Mestizaje becomes more than a powerful metaphor signaling cultural hybridity. It roots cultural production and change in the physical memory of injustice and inhuman exploitation, of desire and transforming love. This forms a critical mestizaje. The present chapter takes up the ways mestizaje has been used within a critical framework as a means of understanding possibility and constraint in the development of new historical subjectivities: Chicanos and Chicanas.

## Tabula Raza

Before turning to the main topic of this chapter, I would like to consider the terrain of racial hierarchies and racial mixture with which Chicana criticism and culture has engaged. Race mixture in the Americas emerges from a vexed history, one that has in numerous ways enforced dominant and disabling colonial racial hierarchies.[1] However, social understandings about race shift over time, changing from one epoch to another. Howard Winant in *Racial Conditions* (1994) traces the epochal nature of racial time in order to study the dynamics of race under different historical and geopolitical conditions. He writes: "we might usefully think of a racial *longue durée* in which the slow inscription of phenotypical signification took place upon the human body, in and through conquest and enslavement, to be sure, but also as an enormous act of expression, of narration" (1994, 21). Under colonial conditions, race was understood as phenotype and its significance instituted through slavery and colonialism.

The present study concerns itself with the aftermath of this history as well as with the aftermath of the next epochal moment when race was understood as an ideological rather than a biological condition.[2] I argue that Chicano culture has sought to articulate a counternarrative to the epochal signification of racial identification within a Mexican/American context by developing a sense of a critical mestizaje. This process has not taken place in a vacuum, of course, and while Chicano culture seeks to articulate a sense of an empowered mestizo agency, it simultaneously engages contending claims of racial significance.

Robert Young reminds us that the discourse of racial mixture has been a highly vexed one. The pseudoscientific cogitations of Gobineau and other thinkers in the nineteenth century inflected the way in which conceptions of race have been passed down to us. Young observes: "Until the word 'miscegenation' was invented in 1864, the word that was conventionally used for the fertile fusion and merging of races was 'amalgamation'" (1995, 9). This term, derived from metallurgy, signals a kind of passive view of mixed-race coupling. Yet it also suggests the growing anxiety about race mixing, as a term had to be invented in order to explain it. In a similar vein, in 1863, T. H. Huxley sought to differentiate between mongrels, the result of crosses between distinct races, and hybrids, which derive from crosses between distinct species (Young 1995, 10). The language developed to describe mixed-race liaisons reveals a profound anxiety of contamination. More incisively, it also betrays a desire to hide the illicit nature of race mixing by suggesting that race mixture proves unseemly not because it runs counter to the laws of man, but because it violates the laws of biology and nature.

Given this discourse of the unnatural and unseemly, it is no wonder that within a Latin American context the idea of race mixing became such a complicated issue. If racial mixture in the contexts of the United States or Europe triggered an anxiety about the possible dissolution of a social and racial order, race mixture in Latin America—because it was so pervasive—led to a complex discussion about the nature of colonial, and later national, identity. Consequently, race mixture—mestizaje—in Latin America had to play a more productive role than merely marking the decay of the social foundation.

The discourse of mestizaje, as Juan E. de Castro notes in his study tracing the history of mestizaje, has served to celebrate "miscegenation or cultural mixture as the basis for conceiving a homogeneous national identity out of a heterogeneous population" (2002, 9). Although vexed, the term gained currency within a Mexican context in the first half of the twentieth century as the result of José Vasconcelos—serving as minister of education—proposing that Mexicans view themselves as a "cosmic race." The discourse of "la raza cósmica" was an attempt in postrevolutionary Mexico to convey a pride in the mestizo heritage of a new national identity serving a new national government. The Mexican was to understand himself as a universal man who combined the racial strains and cultures of the entire world in his own person, moving away from an Indian past—glorious and tragic as it was—into a modern future. Vasconcelos deployed the idea of racial mixture in order to utilize the racial condition of Mexican society for the corporatist interest of the ruling party, the Partido Revolucionario Institucional (PRI). Advocating mestizaje served to effectively erase the presence of a contemporary indigenous identity in Mexico, relegating the Indian to the mists of a tragic and oblivious past, and it helped to erase the constructed nature of both racial and national identity. Henceforth, the idea of racial mixture would serve not to mark racial distinction but to affirm the role of the Mexican citizen-subject in the new order of modernization, technologization, and capitalist consumption.

In addition to the erasure of indigenous subjectivity, Vasconcelos's idea of the cosmic race carries with it an androcentric slant. Jean Franco points out that, though Vasconcelos himself was a proponent of women's liberation and resisted traditional restrictions of family life, his attitudes toward women were conflicted. He drew women into his campaign for literacy as minister of education to "not only create a new social space for themselves but . . . alter education itself by giving it a more maternal image" (1989, 103). Franco's analysis of Vasconcelos indicates that, despite his progressive policies, he was chained to the hero myth by which he understood his life and mission.[3] The "great man" would deliver the mestizo masses from a mythologized past—one that glorified the achievements of the Indians while simultaneously locking them away in the vaults of history—and deliver them to the world of the modern.

Thus the term "mestizaje" emerges from a conflicted past. I argue that its deployment within a resistant Chicano/a context transfigures its significance even as its use evokes this conflictual past. In part I use "mestizaje" throughout this study for precisely the reason Néstor García

Canclini rejects it in favor of the term "hybridity." For Canclini, the notion of mestizaje invokes a racial dimension, whereas hybridization "includes diverse intercultural mixtures—not only the racial ones to which *mestizaje* tends to be limited—and because it permits the inclusion of the modern forms of hybridization" (1995, 11 n. 1). As will become readily apparent, mestizaje within a Chicano context takes on numerous valences, including but not limited to racial ones. However, the racial valence is significant because it works in two contradictory ways: it embeds identity within systems of asymmetrical power relations, and it suggests mutability as mestiza and mestizo bodies enact new relational subjectivities arising from a history of racial conflict.

The legacy of mestizaje's past within a Latin American context creates an ideological dichotomy. On the one hand, racial mixture embodies a flight away from the "primitive" Indian toward the "civilized" European. The de-Indianizing body somatically manifests a social transformation that embraces hegemonic notions of progress and advancement. On the other hand, the mestizo body indexes a physical connection to a repressive colonial history of enslavement, genocide, and exploitation. The mestizo body inherits an untenable dichotomy involving numerous forms of erasure and presence.

This inheritance rests upon the varying social and historical contexts in which the term "mestizo" has been employed. These contexts produce a number of ideological connotations for mestizaje. Mexico and Brazil have embraced miscegenation as a part of their official discourse surrounding national identity. By contrast, Andean nations view the mestizo as either an individual actively denying his own ancestral roots or aspiring to shed himself of a benighted and disempowering primitive past. Priscilla Archibald notes that for this reason in the Andes, mestizos have long been figured as images of the antihero (2002, 103). And Peter Wade argues that in Mexico mestizos have occupied a central position in the national ideology while the Indian has been pushed to the margin. Thus Indians are understood as "traditional" while mestizos, though a peasant class, are seen as operating in a modern market economy (1997, 41).[4] The mestizo in both the Mexican and Andean cases represents an identity in motion moving from an ancient/authentic state into the modern. At the same time, this movement ensures an erasure of the indigenous as an actor in history.

Mestizaje thus evokes and erases an indigenous ancestry that is at once a point of pride and a source of shame. Chicanos and Chicanas receive this complex legacy of mestizaje and forge of it a nuanced strategy of self-identification. In part, the reason mestizaje has served as such a dominant trope is because of the manner in which the Chicana political and cultural body has developed within the national boundaries of the United States. By the end of the twentieth century, the United States had achieved what historian William Appleman Williams calls an "informal empire" begun in the nineteenth. Thus one of the complexities that Chicana communities face is the vexed relation to a national identity based on imperial expansion. The mestizo's racial body in the United States was born of imperial desire. The event that eventually led to Chicano consciousness was, after all, the signing of the Treaty of Guadalupe Hidalgo that ended the U.S.–Mexican War (1846–48) and ceded half of Mexico's territory to the United States, fulfilling that nation's promise of "manifest" destiny. This imperial moment creates a set of aesthetic and moral values associated with Chicano culture, in addition to a set of social and economic dynamics that have systematically disempowered Chicano communities.[5]

The events of 1848 resonate strongly. The incorporation of the Mexican Other into American national consciousness birthed the Chicano as a racial being. The racialization of the mestizo body served to make it a body under erasure and, more significantly, a body subject to the violence inherent in imperial expansion. This racialization occurred almost immediately at the moment Mexican lands were incorporated into the American nation-state. The newly forged Mexican American citizen became the object of discrimination and violence. Because of their status as of part Spanish but mostly Indian extraction, Mexican Americans assumed the role of savage Other previously played by the indigenous populations of the United States. Monika Kaup notes that the American ideology of "savage warfare—that is, relentless displacement and/or subjection of the inhabitants of the 'virgin land'—was quickly applied to the new situation. Mexicans were seen as an inferior race . . . an identification which accounts for the violent treatment of the people who became Mexican Americans following the annexation of the land" (1994, 582). Ideologically, the Mexican had no place within the logic of the growing American nation except as outsider. Thus the new Mexican American could not be seen as an "equal" among U.S. citizens because of the "deep-seated racial symbolism inherent in frontier expansion" (ibid.).

Legally, Mexican Americans were considered white. Historian Ernesto Chávez explains that when the United States annexed Mexican lands and citizens following 1848, "the U.S. government, owing to the provisions the 1790 naturalization act, made ethnic Mexicans legally white. However, socially, they were not given the privileges of whiteness and faced de facto segregation" (2002, 2). Despite the legal standing of Mexican Americans, the racial ideology of the frontier held more powerful sway than structures of social protection. Indeed, soon the force of the law would be used to ensure the subaltern position of the Mexican-descended American. Tomás Almaguer reminds us that working-class people of Mexican origin were "often denied their legal rights by being categorized as Indians" (1994, 57). The racial categorizations of nineteenth-century America on an ideological level served to constrain the mestizo body on social and economic levels.

This elision of the mestizo with the Indian body would, in another hundred years, be one of the moves that Chicano activists undertook in order to make postnational claims for identity and place; that is, the logic used in the nineteenth century to dispossess the Mexican in the United States would become one of the strategic arguments mustered to stake a claim for inclusion in the twentieth. Chicanos became Natives. Identification with the Indian gave birth to a Chicano/a critical subaltern identity in solidarity with other indigenous groups throughout the Americas. That the same logic used to disempower nineteenth-century Mexican American populations was used to empower those same populations a century later is one of the ironic legacies inherited by the mestizo body and its role in the ever-changing strategies for effecting political viability.

Although a race-based discrimination was practiced against the working classes, even those with economic advantages could find little protection in the ideological and political drive to make the Mexican a social Other in the new American empire. Mexican American families whose wealth before 1848 lay in the agricultural use of their land soon found the validity of their ownership legally brought into question. The appropriation of these lands by white Americans would very quickly become the norm as the Land Law of 1851 established the Land Commission before which disputes were brought. The purpose of the commission was to determine the validity of Spanish-Mexican grants. The burden of proof fell to the landowners whenever a dispute was brought to the commission, and the years of litigation often forced Mexican American landowners to mortgage their property to pay their legal fees. This legal trend led, as is well known, to a dispossession that forced many Mexicans into becoming part of a largely landless pool of needy laborers.

This economic and social destabilization depended on the restabilization of clearly demarcated racial distinctions. Thus there was a strong cultural project undertaken just as the mestizo body became incorporated into the national consciousness. In her study of George Lippard's 1847 book *Legends of Mexico*, Shelley Streeby notes that Lippard envisioned a new American race that "promotes a more inclusive definition of white Americanness that also welcomes, for instance, Irish immigrants, whose numbers were increasing rapidly during the 1840s" (2002, 55). Streeby draws on Lippard's text to demonstrate how popular literature helped secure national identification through more clearly delineated and (for European-descended Americans) more inclusive racial categories: "this more expansive definition of white American unity crucially depends upon the construction of Mexicans as a 'mongrel race, moulded of Indian and Spanish blood,' that is destined to 'melt into, and be ruled by, the Iron Race of the North'" (ibid.). The racialization of the mestizo (and mestiza) was meant, ultimately, to erase the mestizo from the narrative of national identity. With the consolidation of an inclusive whiteness in America, the mestizo body is meant to dissolve away into a position of subservience leading to eventual extinction.

These conditions establishing the racial identity for Mexicans formed a precondition for contemporary Chicana/o racial identity. Indeed, one of the reasons why mestizaje is contested in a U.S. context lies in the fact that the racial identity of mestizos was never legally recognized. Consequently, as Ernesto Chávez explains, "ethnic Mexicans' conquest and the manifestation of that subjugation has varied from region to region, with the result being an uneven racialization. . . . As opposed to other racialized U.S. minorities (Native Americans, African Americans, and Asian Americans), ethnic Mexicans have not encountered a unitary legal and social discrimination" (2002, 2).[6] The mixed blessing of de facto and uneven discrimination has granted the mestizo body an ambiguous role in processes of Chicana/o identification throughout history and across the nation. The mestizo body plays a role that is a part of and apart from U.S. social formations.

Suzanne Oboler makes this double role clear in her analysis of Latino identity. She argues that the conflation of race and nationality in the United States assures that the majority of the Latino population is assigned a minority status. Moreover, "racial and racialized groups as a whole live their lives in the public sphere of this society in terms of an invisibility reinforced through lack of knowledge of their respective histories. Added to this, in the case of the Latinos, are new 'invented traditions' based on a homogenized past in this country" (1995, 170). Latinos, under the regime of the sign "Hispanic," are placed in a bind, forced to assume a homogenized and homogenizing identity of difference. This identity is inevitably racialized on an ideological level and thus excluded from a "true" national identification.

In a similar vein, Arlene Dávila argues that market forces in the United States have served to promote a homogeneous vision of "Hispanic" consumers. In her study of the Latino marketing industry, she argues that the advertising world has helped propagate a sense of Hispanic identity that subsumes difference under a single and simple category of ethnic identification. One reason Hispanic advertising has been successful is because of the way it constitutes a homogeneous ethnic audience as its target group, permitting "the industry's positioning as a democratic and equalizing medium for the totality of the Hispanic population. Specifically, just as Hispanic creatives and agency owners have construed themselves as representative of all Hispanics, the industry itself has been similarly constituted as a key arena of advocacy and support for the totality of the Hispanic population" (2001, 42). Dávila points toward a dynamic in the marketplace where once again Latinos are subject to a process of identification that homogenizes difference.

Chicano culture engages with these ambiguities of nation and ethnicity and identity as it strives to function within the confines of a U.S. national culture. Mestizaje implies a doubleness experienced through the mixed-race bodies of the mestiza and mestizo, one in which a sense of belonging coexists with an awareness of exclusion. Where mestizo identity in a Latin American context simultaneously evokes and erases the place of the indigenous, mestizo identity in a U.S. context promises and denies a sense of citizenship, enfranchisement, and belonging. Racial and national (mis)identification are collapsed, effecting a simultaneous process of inclusion and exclusion. This process takes place, of course, through the body.

Critics often invoke Freud and Fanon and Foucault to explain how bodies make biological individuals subjects even as their subjectivities are born out of and through their bodies. For example, Emma Pérez, in her lucid essay "Sexuality and Discourse: Notes from a Chicana Survivor," interrogates the Oedipal arrangement that serves as a metaphor for colonial sexual and gender relations. She revisits the work of Marx, Freud, and Foucault (as well as Lacan, Irigaray, and Cixous) on issues of subjectivity and power and observes that none of these thinkers "explain colonization and its effects upon people of color" (1991, 160). She strives to reinsert the role that race plays as an integral part of Chicana identification and conflict. In her analysis, race, gender, and sexuality form relational nodes that work to subjugate Chicana experience and identity within a logic of colonial containment.

Stuart Hall undertakes an equally clear-eyed and illuminative reconsideration of Foucault, Freud, and Lacan in his introduction to the edited volume *Questions of Cultural Identity* (1996). After sketching the contours of the contemporary debate over "identity," Hall concludes that "the question, and the theorization, of identity is a matter of considerable political significance, and is only likely to be advanced when both the necessity and the 'impossibility' of identities, and the suturing of the psychic and the discursive in their constitution, are fully and unambiguously acknowledged" (1996, 16). The trope of mestizaje within Chicana discourse represents just such an attempt to suture the psychic and the discursive, just such an acknowledgment of the need for and unattainability of a stable identity. By locating the dominant metaphor of identity within the racially composed body, Chicana culture and criticism have brought to the fore the contradictory but necessary process of identity construction. This construction takes place within the context of a colonial legacy out of which mestizaje as a historical condition has developed. The complexities of mestizaje and its various ideological implications are evoked via the emphasis on race and racial memory that Chicana thought has employed in the development and articulation of Chicana and Chicano identity. This carries with it an understanding of the mestizo/a body as not just a physical being but a discursive site, a means by which Chicana culture and identity have been able to bring together both the weight of historical legacies and the hope for a transformative future.

## Indians in Aztlán

Even as mestizaje has been used to evoke both possibility and constraint, its use is fraught with the ideological baggage of its development. In her incisive study of mestizaje "Who's the Indian in Aztlán?" Josefina Saldaña argues that mestizaje served as the "biological metaphor" for the corporatist government policies of the PRI (Partido Revolucionario Institucional) in Mexico. From the mid-1930s to the 1980s, the metaphor of racial mixture served to produce a teleology of progress. This teleology posited the Indian "as an originary movement in an evolutionary Mexican history. Biologically, the Indian dissolves into the formulaically more progressive mestizo. . . . in mestizaje a third term gets produced in the mixture that subsumes previous categories" (2001, 407). This creation of a third term buries Indian identity in a static past, one that culturally serves to make references to the Indian "always citations of a noble yet tragic past: the heroic, yet inevitably unsuccessful, resistance of . . .

the Aztecs to the Spanish Conquest" (ibid.). Although a past and distant influence on racial intermixture, the Indian is rendered unimportant to current negotiations of personal and social identity.

The counterpoint to mestizaje, within Mexican national discourse, is the ideology of *indigenismo*. The central notion of *indigenismo*, as Peter Wade explains, is that "Indians needed special recognition and that special values attached to them. Very often it was a question of exotic and romantic symbolism, based more on the glorification of the pre-Cortesian Indian ancestry of the nation than on respect for contemporary Indian populations" (1997, 32). In Saldaña's analysis, this explanation means that the evolutionary logic of Mexican citizenship "subsumes the Indian as heroic past to the mestizo as heroic present" (2001, 408). The embrace of mestizo identities within a Mexican context serves to exclude Indian concerns from the contemporary, much in the way that the embrace of the romanticized Indian in a U.S. context erases the present reality of Indian subjectivity from the national consciousness.

But what of mestizaje in a Chicano context? It is important to cast a critical eye on the recasting of Chicano subjectivity as indigenous. This reconfiguration can lead to a series of complications and elisions. Issues relevant to Chicanas and Chicanos clearly are not necessarily the same as those for people who self-identify as Native Americans. Indeed, many of the mestizos who, beginning in the seventeenth century, moved north into what would become New Mexico, California, Texas, and other states were actively involved in genocidal campaigns against Native populations. The unproblematic claim by Chicanos to indigenous ancestry thus helps erase a troubling part of the Chicano past in relation to Native peoples.

Recognizing these critical points, I think it equally important to draw a distinction between mestizaje in the context of Mexican and Chicano identity formations. After all, the corporatist use of mestizaje was part and parcel of the PRI's official nationalist discourse. The role of Chicano (counter)discourse has, within U.S. culture, functioned quite differently. The mestizo and mestiza body in Chicano critical discourse has helped forge an identity that highlights the relational and political dynamics of Chicana/o identity through the recognition of race and race mixture. This is why I believe it important to emphasize race as foundational for understanding the significance of Chicano/a identity.

Saldaña suggests, by contrast, that the emphasis on mestizaje within Chicano discourse replicates the problem of erasure of the Indian by a Mexican nationalist use of mestizaje: "in our Chicano reappropriation of the biologized terms of mestizaje and indigensimo, we are also always recuperating the Indian as an ancestral past rather than recognizing contemporary Indians as coinhabitants not only of this continent abstractly conceived, but of the neighborhoods and streets of hundreds of U.S. cities and towns" (2001, 413). The erasure enacted by the trope of mestizaje in a Mexican context, she suggests, functions in precisely the same way in the Chicano deployment of racial identification. Although there is merit to this argument, there is an all too easy conflation between the nationalist cultural context in Mexico and the subnational context of Chicano/a cultural production. Although the term "Chicano nationalism" is often bandied about as shorthand for a position within Chicano thought for a rigid (and often essentialist) notion of identity and claims for national sovereignty, there is a marked and important distinction between notions of American and Chicano nationalism. Chicano discourse has generally served as a critique of American nationalist identity and its exclusivist elision of race and citizenship. A common theme throughout the development of Mexican American and Chicano culture and criticism has been the position of the Chicano as a foreigner in his own land, an issue that historian John Chávez takes up in his study *The Lost Land: The Chicano Image of the Southwest.*

Yet Saldaña's point is well taken: there have been moments in Chicano discourse that have served to romanticize images of the Indian, particularly those nationalist discourses developed in the 1960s and—as my discussion shortly addresses—reshaped in the 1980s by feminist writers such as the late Gloria Anzaldúa. However, the conditions under which this romanticization has taken place are not innocent; that is, individuals and groups, in asserting Chicano political and social identity, have strategically used notions of *indigenismo*. For example, Rodolfo Acuña notes that in the 1980s, discourses of *indigenismo* and Chicano nationalism were popular among some students in Southern California for several reasons, such as the strong segregation and intense racism in the region. Alienation, Acuña argues, drove the students "to search for an identity and an alternative vision, a void that *indigenismo* has filled. Indeed, indigenism was strong among Chicano students during this period—largely because of the failure of both society and the [political] left to attract them" (1996, 308). *Indigenismo* enabled an identity of resistance, one deployed in response to a profound sense of disempowerment and alienation. Although this particular articulation of identity is extremely problematic, it nevertheless exemplifies a type of tactical subjectivity that responds to discrimination and political exclusion. The inclusion—indeed, assertion—of indigenous ancestry within the social struggles of the United States functions quite differently than that assertion functions within the logic of a Mexican governmental regime.

If, then, mestizaje in Mexico represents a flight from the Indian, we might think of Chicana mestizaje as a race *toward* the Indian. At the very least, this race needs to be understood as a strategic assertion of racial difference in struggle against disenfranchisement. Although this does not necessarily make Indian subjectivity any more present within the cultural discourse of Chicana mestizaje, it does enable the deployment of strategic coalitions on a political level. In recognition of shared concerns within a contemporary context, groups of Chicana and Native American activists since the 1960s often have worked together in common cause. These coalitions arise as a result of the discourse of mestizaje, allowing Chicanas to recognize a shared colonial as well as racial history with Native Americans and other indigenous groups across the Americas.

Responding to this recognition of shared political goals, D-Q University in Davis, California, for example, was established in July 1971 by a group of Native Americans and Chicanos. They claimed the site of a former army communications relay station with the intention of forming a school whose management and curriculum would be determined by indigenous peoples. Their efforts were eventually successful, founding the first and only indigenous-controlled institution of higher learning located outside a reservation.[7] There are numerous other examples in which the trope of mestizaje has been used not to erase contemporary Indian concerns but, on the contrary, to foreground and address them.[8]

Within Chicano critical discourse, the mestizo body serves as a locus of identity whose refashioning foregrounds the political and relational valences of race. This body becomes a site where lines of identification get realigned. This reshaping of identity may lead, as I have noted, to political action in common cause. It may also challenge the conflation of race and nationality that in the United States assures, as Suzanne Oboler argues, a minority status for the majority of its Latino populations (1995, 170).

Nevertheless, the representation of the mestizo body has proven a complicated project within Chicano discourse. In her essay "Who's the Indian in Aztlán?" Saldaña provocatively invokes the writing of Richard Rodriguez to suggest that he makes a positive contribution in transforming the trope of mestizaje in a Mexican register. She does so to contrast Rodriguez's vision of the Indian as agent of modern Mexican history with the vision of mestizaje famously provided by Gloria Anzaldúa in *Borderlands/La Frontera*.

Saldaña's move is provocative because of the role that Rodriguez has played in debates about multicultural identity and bilingual education since the mid-1980s. Rodriguez was the recipient of a very public embrace by the conservative right as it sought a spokesman to argue for the deficiencies of bilingualism in education, in politics, and in other social spaces. José Saldívar notes the composition of Rodriguez's supporters in his reconsideration of Rodriguez's writing: "It hardly needs emphasizing (for those who followed the controversy over the author's first book, *Hunger of Memory* [1981]) that Rodriguez's admirers were once predominantly white, male editors and reviewers associated with the mainline publishing world in the northeastern United States" (1997, 146).[9] Saldívar underscores Rodriguez's bona fides among a powerful political and cultural elite, one that readily rallied behind *Hunger of Memory* and its questioning of bilingual education as the best manner by which to prepare Spanish-speaking students for a public future. One of its most controversial arguments centered on the distinction Rodriguez draws between the necessity for a "public" voice that must be articulated in English and the possibility for a "private" family voice that could be spoken in Spanish, but only behind closed doors and beyond public social spaces.

It is thus significant that Saldaña locates in Rodriguez's writing a progressive agenda vis-à-vis mestizo identity. The passage Saldaña analyzes comes from the opening essay of Rodriguez's second collection, his 1992 book *Days of Obligation: An Argument with My Mexican Father.* In "India," Rodriguez begins by pondering the significance of his own visage:

> I used to stare at the Indian in the mirror. The wide nostrils, the thick lips. Starring Paul Muni as Benito Juárez. Such a long face—such a long nose—sculpted by indifferent, blunt thumbs, and of such common clay. No one in my family had a face as dark or as Indian as mine. My face could not portray the ambition I brought to it. What could the United States of America say to me? . . . *Mestizo* in Mexican Spanish means mixed, confused. Clotted with Indian, thinned by Spanish spume.
>
> What could Mexico say to me? (1992, 1)

The passage is typical of Rodriguez's writing: the quasi-biblical description of his all too mortal flesh deflated by the allusion to Hollywood's image of Benito Juárez, the nineteenth-century national hero celebrated for expelling French imperial forces from Mexico. In the film, Juárez's dark Indian body is simultaneously enacted and erased by Paul Muni's white one. Rodriguez's evocation of the film suggests a profound sense of self-confusion. The evocation and erasure of racial identity introduces the questions central to Rodriguez's essay: What is the significance of the indigenous in the modern world? What is relevant about the mestizo face in modernity and history? And what do conceptions of race in Mexico and the United States have to say to the mestizo subject?

In her analysis of Rodriguez's writing, Saldaña explains that this opening passage reveals the inability of cultural representation to capture the significance of race. The black/white paradigm in the United States offers no means of recognition for Rodriguez. The racial model by which race can be understood in the United States has nothing to offer Rodriguez to explain his own profound awareness of racial mixture. Moreover, the ideological chaining of Indian identity to a tragic past in Mexican national discourse denies any successful future for his mestizo self. The Indian face he sees in the mirror lacks the image of ambition he understands his life to hold. Rather, it ties him to indolence, to darkness, to an impervious past.

Yet Rodriguez sees in the Indian image and and the Indian past a propensity for survival. This propensity, significantly, he associates with the Indian as a feminine figure. Thus he concludes: "The Indian stands in the same relationship to modernity as she did to Spain—willing to marry, to breed, to disappear in order to ensure her inclusion in time; refusing to absent herself from the future. The Indian has chosen to survive, to consort with the living, to live in the city, to crawl on her hands and knees, if need be, to Mexico City or L.A." (ibid., 24). Rodriguez's gendering of the Indian as female consort is, within a Mexican context, as old as the myths of Malintzín/La Malinche, the Indian translator/mistress for Hernán Corté.[10] Rodriguez suggests that the Indian continues to represent the racial, cultural, social, and political difference embodied by the mestizo, the offspring of the Indian "consort."[11] In an important turn, however, he reworks the representational trope of mestizaje. As Saldaña points out, Rodriguez refuses the erasure of the Indian "by insisting on the Indian as the primary term in the trope of mestizaje. He recognizes not only the Indian presence in the contemporary world, but the Indian as the agent of modern Mexican history" (2001, 419). However, this agent is feminized, and in his image of the feminine agent, Rodriguez casts the Indian as a breeding, crawling consort—not quite a legitimate agent in history.

Moreover, even if the Indian as female consort offers an image of some agency for Mexican mestizaje, Rodriguez's conception of racial mixture within the context of contemporary Chicano history remains another matter entirely. It is difficult to forget the vexed relationship Rodriguez has had with Chicano writers, activists, and critics who quite rightly reject his negative rendering of multiculturalism and racial identity politics, a rendering championed by an overwhelmingly white, overwhelmingly male mainstream intellectual elite. In Rodriguez's 2002 *Brown: The Last Discovery of America*, he continues to offer a vision of an increasingly racially mixed U.S. society. This mongrelization, as he conceives it, paints a picture of a new, browner America—undergoing its "last discovery." It is a picture, however, that holds little promise of agency for its racialized subjects. Indeed, this last discovery offers little more empowerment or better racial understanding than did the first. Rodriguez sees mestizo bodies increasingly populating the United States. They serve not as agents of social transformation but as a metaphor for impurity and—in a very attenuated sense—liberation.

Most simply put, Rodriguez offers an image of a multiracial and mixed-race society in which race has altogether ceased to be a focal point of conflict. Conceptions of race as Rodriguez discusses them have been completely washed clean of their colonial (and colonizing) dynamics. Significantly, he opens the preface to *Brown* with a sentence fragment:

> Brown as impurity.
>
> I write of a color that is not a singular color, not a strict recipe, not an expected result, but a color produced by careless desire, even by accident; by two or several. I write of blood that is blended. I write of brown as complete freedom of substance and narration. I extol impurity. (2002, xi)

The fragmentation suggests—beyond stylistic indulgence—the fragmented nature of his thinking. The exultation about impurity is, for Rodriguez, owing to its sense of freedom, a release from the puritanical powers that seek to enforce crisp lines of demarcation between one identity and another. However, it is also an exultation that celebrates race as free of "substance and narration"; that is, race ceases to tell a story and it ceases to contain the vexed legacy that went about creating it.

One reason he attempts to undo the story of race is, he suggests, because of its relation to narratives of victimization. In a newspaper essay, Rodriguez opines: "Now that we are a nation of sufferers and victims, the Puritans have won the day. There are, at our universities and colleges, committees of orthodoxy that decide what can and cannot be said" (2003, M1). Rodriguez's fantasy about cabalistic committees of political correctness is amusing, if not paranoid. But it is precisely against this type of puritanical control that mestizaje becomes, for Rodriguez, the metaphor for a liberatory and benign new American society. This society, marked by a messy pluralistic embrace of difference, seems to exist beyond race ("my book is about brown," he writes, "not skin, but brown as impurity" [2002, 194]).

His vision of a new impurity is another rendering of that ultimate poststructural dream, Deleuze and Guattari's ideal *body without organs* in *A Thousand Plateaus: Capitalism and Schizophrenia.* Rodriguez's version is much more accessible, pleasant, reassuring, even entertaining, but it eviscerates agency as surely as Deleuze and Guattari's erasure of the body. He offers us a vision of "brown"—as complete freedom of substance and narration—that disembodies (one might say disembowels) the meaning of brown. Rodriguez's ruminations about a new America offer little insight into how racialized bodies negotiate and contest relations of power, much less the role that Indian subjectivity will play in the future of Chicano agency. And it certainly does not add much to our understanding of how mestizo bodies transform the face of U.S. society.

In a similar way, Josefina Saldaña suggests that Gloria Anzaldúa's evocation of pre-Cortesian identity fails to address the concerns of indigenous people in the present and serves to silence them: "Once again mestizaje is deployed to produce a biological tie with pre-Aztec Indians rather than a political tie with contemporary U.S. Native Americans or Mexican Indians. Consequently, in this system of representation, indigenous subjectivity is once again put under erasure" (2001, 415). In Saldaña's view, Anzaldúa's work does not challenge Mexican nationalist uses of mestizo discourse as it serves the corporatist interests of the state. Rather, its association of the Chicano/a with pre-Cortesian cultures thwarts any possible reorientation of Chicano positionality in relation to the indigenous. Saldaña concludes: "Ultimately, Anzaldúa's model of representation reproduces liberal models of choice that privilege her position as a U.S. Chicana: she goes through her backpack and decides what to keep and what to throw out, and she chooses to keep signs of indigenous identity as ornamentation and spiritual revival" (ibid., 420). Anzaldúa's position—even as a marginal identity—within a First World context grants her a privileged position. Anzaldúa is not forced into a position of disempowerment based on her indigenous—as opposed to Chicana—identity even as she chooses which elements of indigenous identity she will employ and in what manner she will use them.

On a rhetorical level, Saldaña's pitting Rodriguez against Anzaldúa is an astute move. It allows Saldaña to measure cleverly the way they each employ mestizaje and the varying levels of Indian agency their different views offer. However, when discussing the idea of mestiza consciousness and the uses of indigenous cultural identity within a contemporary Chicano framework—one that recognizes the importance of both feminist and queer insights into our understanding of Chicana/o identity—it is absolutely necessary to recognize the contributions Anzaldúa has made in viewing Chicano culture as racialized, relational, and hybrid. The vision of mestizaje Anzaldúa proffers—while controversial—must be a part of the dialogue.

Although I do not want to posit Anzaldúa's *Borderlands/La Frontera* as a primary text in our understanding of Chicana mestizaje, I do think it important to consider both why her text has been so highly influential and what Chicana and Chicano critics have had to say about her understanding of relational identities and hybrid cultures. I believe the manner in which her critics have viewed her contributions provides a critical map of Chicana mestizaje, how it is currently perceived, and what dynamics prevail in its present construction. More important, perhaps, is the manner that Anzaldúa's insights have served to illuminate critical fields beyond Chicana/o studies and to reveal the influence that Chicana/o studies have had and the transformations it has wrought in the broader interdisciplinary arena of American studies.

## The Anzaldúa Code

In *Borderlands/La Frontera*, Gloria Anzaldúa posits mestiza identity as a privileged site of marginality, one that allows for decentering and deconstructing energies to emerge as a response to modern and postmodern conditions of displacement. In this sense, the mestiza body moves through and becomes the borderlands as a site in transition: between Spanish-speaking and English-speaking, between the Third World and the First, between the resilience of the disempowered and the domination of the technological, between Us and Other.

This transition is triggered by cultural, social, and economic disruption. As Anzaldúa notes, "For many mexicanos *del otro lado*, the choice is to stay in Mexico and starve or move north and live" (1987, 10). The dream of national unity and neatly demarcated citizenry is disrupted by the unequal distribution of resources and opportunities that drive so many workers out of Mexico in search of jobs. Large transnational, corporate decisions premised upon an increasingly globalizing economic structure disrupt the choices individuals can make in response to their conditions of living.

An economic dimension, José Saldívar argues, is central to the analysis Anzaldúa offers in her work: "At the heart of her dissent from racialist purity and patriarchal postmodernity is her deep hostility to the process of late capitalism. . . . she exposes the primordial crime of capitalism—not so much wage labor but the gradual displacement of the older forms of collective life from a Borderland now seized and privatized" (1991, 83). The destructive economic and political disruptions inflicted by the needs of capitalism and nationalism generate a painful but productively disruptive response in the mestiza body.

Anzaldúa asserts that the mestiza undergoes a disruption at the level of identity. She cherishes this disruption as a type of creative power. Thus she famously appropriates the imagery of pre-Cortesian religious iconography to signal and symbolize processes of creative rupture. This appropriation is a rhetorical move meant to mirror the valorization of Aztec culture in dominant visions of Chicano and Mexican nationalisms. These nationalist scripts served, as Anzaldúa and other Chicana writers make clear, to silence women's voices in the formation of Mexican and Chicana identities. Anzaldúa's evocation of Aztec goddesses, for example, is part of a strategic counterdiscourse contesting male-identified notions of Chicano identity.

The resurrection of indigenous religious iconography also represents an attempt to reclaim spirituality in the face of ceaseless Western technological advancement. Because she identifies the syncretic transformation of Coatlalopeuh—the Aztec creator goddess evocative of sexuality and power—with the desexed Virgen de Guadalupe, Anzaldúa invokes the pre-Cortesian goddess in order to posit an image of rupture and change. She locates the roots of Guadalupe's iconic power in a figure associated with a powerful sexuality, disrupting the placid image of the virginal mother. Guadalupe, the potent religious, political, and cultural image of the Chicano/Mexicano, becomes for Anzaldúa "the symbol of ethnic identity and of the tolerance for ambiguity that Chicanos-Mexicanos, people of mixed race, people who have Indian blood, people who cross cultures, by necessity possess" (1987, 30). She creates out of Guadalupe an image of ambiguity and creative transformation.

Of course, not all Chicanos or Mexicanos possess a tolerance for ambiguity, above all as regards gender and sexuality. Yet Anzaldúa claims that the racial position of the mestiza/o translates into possibilities for liberating social and cultural transformation. Her use of pre-Cortesian religious imagery becomes an iconic measure of how Chicana/o creative and critical production seeks to transform the self-hating that is one legacy of colonial encounters. To move from hatred toward a constructive change requires that an emotional alteration take place: "Those activities or Coatlicue states which disrupt the smooth flow (complacency) of life are exactly what propel the soul to do its work: make soul, increase consciousness of itself. Our greatest disappointments and painful experiences—if we can make meaning out of them—can lead us toward becoming more of who we are. Or they can remain meaningless. The Coatlicue state can be a way station or it can be a way of life" (ibid., 46). Anzaldúa associates this state with a painful but creative psychic disruption. She evokes a critical vocabulary that simultaneously valorizes the deployment of pre-Cortesian iconography beyond a nationalist script and makes present a psychological and philosophical insight that may not otherwise be clearly present for her readers.

For example, Chela Sandoval associates the Coatlicue state with what in his writing Roland Barthes in *A Lover's Discourse* calls a "punctum": that which breaks the subject free from repressive emotional conditions (Sandoval 2000, 141ff.). This disruption leads to an "abyss beyond dualisms" where, temporarily, "political weapons of consciousness are available in a constant tumult of possibility" (ibid., 141). In her own writing on political consciousness, Emma Pérez describes this rupture as a "liberatory, amorphous, transitory, translational, trans-identity state for anyone, not just women of color, who desires communication among differences" (1999, 145 n. 97). The potential for transformation is what Pérez sees as the affirming project of the new mestiza:

> *la nueva mestiza*, the mixed-race woman, is the privileged subject of an interstitial space that was formerly a nation, and is now without borders, without boundaries. The concept-metaphor woman, formerly known as "worker" in Chicano nationalist discourse, is challenged by Anzaldúa, who critiques that discursive "nation" as a space that negates, dismisses, and occludes feminists, queers (*jotas y jotos*), and anyone who is not of "pure" Chicano blood and lineage. Mestizaje, for Anzaldúa, is redefined and remixed into an open consciousness. (Ibid., 25)

Pérez derides the essentializing qualities of the Chicano nationalist discourses that Anzaldúa also critcizes. Rather, the borderlessness particular to the Coatlicue state serves to open up the possibility for a new consciousness.

In a similar vein, Angie Chabram-Dernersesian argues that Anzaldúa's writing moves Chicana/o discourse into a realm that allows for new relational understandings of identity. She argues that Anzaldúa takes us "light years ahead of patriarchal nationalist narratives that plot Chicano histories of expropriation along a unidimensional racial line" (1997, 124). This opening is also a quality that Arturo Aldama examines and champions in his study of Anzaldúa in *Disrupting Savagism*. He argues that through her work Anzaldúa emerges as a "speaking subject-in-process" who grounds her "enunciatory discourse to the materiality of women's bodies traumatized by poverty and colonial, racial, and sexual violence and to the materiality of dispossessed territories to articulate the psychic processes of recovery and decolonization" (2001, 128). Aldama thus envisions Anzaldúa's emancipatory literature as one that brings together the body and the land in a project of decolonial liberation.

In general, the responses to Anzaldúa split along two lines. Either she is championed—as exemplified by these critics—for her vision of oppositional consciousness, articulated from a site of specificity, locality, and resistance, or she is criticized for her overly utopian (and perhaps facile) blending and bridging of borders.

José Limón provides a good example of the negative reaction Anzaldúa's work elicits. In his brief discussion of her writing, he rejects the view that she provides a strong sense of specificity and locality. He does not see her work as "a tightly localized, specific, richly ethnographic assessment of one specific part of the border, what [Américo] Paredes has called the Lower Border." Instead, he sees her work has having "been converted from a provocative literary work into the example *par excellence*" of an unproductive and empty abstraction of border theory (1998, 157). There is some merit to Limón's observation, which is really more a critique of the way Anzaldúa's work has been used rather than of her text itself. Yet one can understand the danger of collapsing into vacuity and abstraction when teasing out the radical possibilities and ample vision of transgressive identities that *Borderlands* seems to articulate.

In his essay "In the Borderlands of Chicano Identity, There Are Only Fragments," Benjamin Sáenz provides a similar point of attack. He is dismissive of Anzaldúa's reclamation of pre-Cortesian god figures as a process of personal and social transformation. Her invocation of a dislocated past leaves one constructing identity based upon an essential loss:

> To return to the "traditional" spiritualities that were in place before the arrival of Cortés and company makes very little sense. The material conditions that gave rise to the Aztec's religion no longer exist. Anzaldúa's language, her grammar, her talk are ultimately completely mortgaged to a nostalgia that I find unacceptable. The resurrection of the old gods (be they "white" or "indigenous") is a futile and impossible task. To invoke old gods as a tool against oppression and capitalism is to choose the wrong weapon. (1997, 86–87)

Although he is a novelist, Sáenz seems to take Anzaldúa's spiritual journey rather literally. Nevertheless, he correctly questions the efficacy of spiritual transformation on a social and political level. From this perspective, the mestizaje that Anzaldúa champions as a strategy of personal development does seem very distant from the actual racialized conditions Chicanos and Chicanas endure in systems of social exchange. More specifically, what is lacking in her vision of spiritual transformation is how to negotiate power relations in order to achieve real contemporary social and political transformation. This transformation must, at some level, address the manner in which Chicana and Chicano subjects struggle with the vexing conditions of race and racialization. At a metaphorical level, Anzaldúa calls for the embrace of the dark Other within oneself. Although this might suggest a personal embrace of a racialized identity, a negotiation with racial politics and its complex dynamics does not form a central part of Anzaldúa's path to personal regeneration.

In defense of Anzaldúa, we should recognize the manner in which many critics take up her work as a statement of new possibilities. Monika Kaup, for one, considers Anzaldúa's book "the most sophisticated attempt by a mixed-race American writer to celebrate *mestizaje* as relation-identity, countering both Paz's closed model of the tragic mestizo and the North American negation of race mixture. *Borderlands/La Frontera: The New Mestiza . . .* is as much about women as it is about *mestizaje*; we cannot separate her poetics of syncretism from her poetics of Chicana feminism" (2002, 193). These blended "poetics" allow Anzaldúa to embrace the "utopian potential of her hybrid identity" (ibid., 195). Her hybrid identity as a mixed-race mestiza and lesbian (Anzaldúa often insisted on the term "dyke Chicana") forms an integral part of her relational identity.

Yet, as empowering as this relational identity seems to be, its utopian potential does need to be understood within the highly uneven relations of power in which that identity exists. Given the constraints of the borderlands in terms of economic exploitation, political disenfranchisement, state and personal violence, violation, and erasure, it would be a mistake to believe that any potential utopia could easily be realized. There is a tendency on the part of Kaup and other critics to overstate the utopian potential of Anzaldúa's vision. This is the point at which those who accuse Anzaldúa of overly romanticizing notions of borders tend to abandon her project.

There is much in Anzaldúa's vision, however, that serves to inspire and motivate those who seek an empowered and empowering understanding of Chicana mestizaje. The emphasis on reconfigured community and family that forms such a prominent part of her vision has inspired critics and writers to seek alternative spaces for women's communities. Also, Anzaldúa's examination of the border region highlights the complex and varied way that power circulates through communities and subjectivities. Her emphasis on transformation is significant because the circulation of power she studies does not trace a closed and static system. Her vision highlights the transformative possibilities ever at work in repressive networks of power.

For example, Mary Pat Brady in *Extinct Lands, Temporal Geographies* sees the dual nature of the border as it is discussed in Anzaldúa's text. The border represents simultaneously a site of potential transformation and a seriously entrenched system of meaning and power:

> If, as Chicana border-crossing narratives point out, the U.S.–Mexico border is both a system with multiple and slippery meanings and symbologies and a state-sponsored aesthetic project whose crossing and ongoing production involve contradictory and ambivalent historical narratives, family memories, desires, and national(ist) fantasies, then to meditate on "borders" is no simple, naïve, or clichéd task. Gloria Anzaldúa's *Borderlands/La Frontera* further underscores this point through a theoretical discussion of borders that moves, from multiple vantage points and through shifting genres, to tackle the sliding tensions between border meanings and effects. (2002, 83)

Brady notes that numerous projects function simultaneously at the border. Multiple semiotic systems, vying historical narratives, and personal family stories all are at work. Anzaldúa's intervention into these contending meanings not only serves to demonstrate the way these meanings are internalized (the borders that move) but reflects the fractured nature of how the border and its various meanings shape and fragment the borderlands. In many ways, the relation of the reader to borders influences what one takes away from *La Frontera*.

Where Sáenz finds nostalgia, Limón abstraction, and Saldaña erasure in Anzaldúa's text, Sonia Saldívar-Hull finds politically committed feminist writing. Saldívar-Hull highlights the cultural locatedness of Anzaldúa: "As a Chicana 'totally immersed' in her culture, she can choose to reject the crippling aspects of traditions that oppress women and silence homosexual men and women. . . . The feminista that Anzaldúa presents is a woman comfortable with new affiliations that subvert old ways of being, rejecting the homophobic, sexist, racist, imperialist, and nationalist" (2000, 73). This perspective focuses on those aspects of Anzaldúa's writing that offer a politically engaged critique of identity within Chicano/a culture.

Saldívar-Hull does not highlight, as do others, Anzaldúa's nostalgic waxing for a lost Indian identity nor her grossly generalized theories of borderness. Instead, Anzaldúa along with other Chicana theorists "insist on illuminating the complications and intersections of the multiple systems of exploitation: capitalism, patriarchy, heterosexism, and White supremacy" (ibid., 36). This illumination of a variety of interconnected exploitative discourses explains why Anzaldúa's work has been so informative. The relational and transformational qualities of identity that *Borderlands/La Frontera* seems to offer have served to make it an influential expression of cultural and personal mestizaje. Although it may fall short of connecting the visionary with the worldly or the Indian subject with the mestizo body, Anzaldúa's text amplifies the sense of possibility within Chicano discourse. Finally, it provides a vision—mediated, incomplete, fractured—of the disrupted terrain that is Chicana/o mestizaje.

## Mestizo Transculturation

Anzaldúa has played a very prominent role in the intellectual development of contemporary Chicana/o critical thought, but an equally powerful—though much more mediated—force is the work of Cuban critic Fernando Ortiz from the 1940s. In *Cuban Counterpoint*, Ortiz writes: "The real history of Cuba is the history of its intermeshed transculturations" (1947, 98). For Ortiz, transculturation names the process by which a subjugated group simultaneously incorporates and transforms the culture of a dominant group. The colonial process, in which a dynamic of subjection and domination is at play, does not imply a simple top-down process of control and erasure. Rather, subjugated constituencies maintain a tenuous, though nonetheless real, agency in the development of thought, belief, and action.

Ortiz's work is significant because, as Fernando Coronil notes, it provides a prefiguration of concerns central to postcolonial and ethnic studies regarding agency and representation.[12] His work thus forms an important dialogue with scholars interested in the dissemination of and resistance to dominant power. Ortiz provides a touchstone for the study of aggrieved communities in the Americas. Moreover, his work has been key in developing contemporary models by which to understand the dynamics of culture in terms of accommodation, incorporation, acquiescence, and resistance.

For example, in the introduction to her 1992 study on travel writing, *Imperial Eyes*, Mary Louise Pratt incorporates Ortiz's model of cultural transformation. She discusses how ethnographers have used the term "transculturation" "to describe how subordinated or marginal groups select and invent from materials transmitted to them by a dominant or metropolitan culture. While subjugated peoples cannot readily control what emanates from the dominant culture, they do determine to varying extent what they absorb into their own, and what they use it for. Transculturation is a phenomenon of the contact zone" (1992, 6). Citing Fernando Ortiz (and Ángel Rama's later incorporation of the term into literary studies), Pratt notes that transculturation takes place in what she has famously termed "contact zones." These are "Social spaces where disparate cultures meet, clash, and grapple with each other, often in highly asymmetrical relations of domination and subordination—like colonialism, slavery, or their aftermaths as they are lived out across the globe today" (ibid., 4). Pratt's view of transculturation depends on the relation between cultures that occupy different positions of power. The aftermath of colonialism, slavery, and other conditions associated with European expansion into the Americas fosters the unequal relations of domination and subordination that characterize contact zones.

Pratt's framework for analyzing travel writing under imperialism articulates a compelling model that a number of critics employ in their analyses of the asymmetrical relations of power between Chicana communities and the broader U.S. society. Contemporary critical writing leaves no doubt that articulations of Chicana/o subjectivity must still contend with the legacy of colonial relations in more or (many times) less mediated ways. Both Chela Sandoval in *Methodology of the Oppressed* and Emma Pérez in *The Decolonial Imaginary* invoke ideas of coloniality and decolonialization in order to articulate their theories of resistant subjectivities. As Emma Pérez explains, "The decolonial imaginary embodies the buried desires of the unconscious, living and breathing in between that which is colonialist and that which is colonized. Within that interstitial space, desire rubs against colonial repressions to construct resistant, oppositional, transformative, diasporic subjectivities that erupt and move into decolonial desires" (1999, 110). These desires that rub against colonial repressions drive the unsettling powers that compose Pratt's contact zones, zones of contestation and struggle. Although her analysis centers on cosmopolitan representations of the Other in centuries past, her study of empire abroad is informed by a quite contemporary concern for conditions at home. In her essay "Criticism in the Contact Zone"— based on a talk she gave in 1990, two years before the publication of *Imperial Eyes*—she considers the significance of unequal contact within a North American context. She notes that U.S. ethnic literatures

> are often conceptualized as expressions of particular communities or identities. But within ethnic (especially Chicano) studies, this perspective is being complemented by another point of view that regards ethnic cultures not in terms of their autonomy and discreteness but as something quite different: as borderlands, site of ongoing critical and inventive interaction with the dominant culture, as permeable contact zones across which significations move in many directions. (1993, 89)

Pratt looks to Chicano/a writing for an articulation of what it means to be in "contact" with different and differentiating modes of power. Ethnic criticism negotiates the demands of an elementary identity politics as well as the demands of dominant cultural formations. This negotiation represents a kind of supplement—both an addition to and a replacement of—normative ideas behind identity and community and resistance to dominant power.

Pratt goes on to note that the idea of permeable contact zones "was dramatically explored by Gloria Anzaldúa in her influential book *Borderlands/La Frontera: The New Mestiza*. Writing as a Chicana lesbian working-class philosopher, Anzaldúa refused to locate herself within any single identity or community. She adopted a mestiza perspective from which she advances [an] agenda for the whole society" (ibid.). Pratt adopts the elision of culture/race in considering the mestiza perspective of Anzaldúa's work. The (metaphorical) borderlands become the site where contact is made among subnational communities even as the asymmetrical relationships of race-/gender-/class-based distinctions take place. For Pratt, this "permeable, borderlands perspective is not expected to replace the constructs of autonomy, authenticity, and community which often legitimate minority discourses. It rather adds a relational optic, specifically a way of making claims for the inventiveness and ongoing criticalness of ethnic cultures and minority perspectives. It brings into relief their engagement with other occupants of the contact zone, and their *availability to* reception outside the subnational community" (ibid., 89–90). The experience in contact zones is a double one: commonplace notions of community in terms of autonomy and authenticity coexist with a critical sense of relational engagement. The doubleness of mestizaje meets its correlative in the critical terrain of the borderlands.

This is not quite a classic case of Western double-consciousness, as the borderlands relationship is not based entirely on a Hegelian master–slave dialectic. Rather, the relational condition of the Chicano contact zones is multiple. And, most important for Pratt, the contacts within these zones decenter established social order: "In a contact perspective, borders are placed in effect at the center of concern while homogeneous centers move to the margins. Interestingly, that is pretty much how the world looks from [a] 'minority' or subaltern perspective: economic and civic life is likely to be conducted in contact zones, ongoingly comprising struggles to operate in institutions made by others" (ibid., 88). For almost two decades, ideas about borderlands, mestizaje, transculturation, and contact zones have been instrumental in the development of Chicano/a

cultural criticism. An emphasis has been placed on the mutually constituted character of "American" and "Chicano" and "Mexican" cultures.[13]
An emphasis on culture as mutually constituted finds in hybridity not a
simple mélange or a passive mixture but a volatile, contested, contestatory, and endlessly innovative dynamic.

The doubling implicit in mestizaje suggests that a productive ambivalence underlies Chicana and Chicano identity. Several critics have
asserted the imperative role that a racial/cultural confluence represents
in understanding the contemporary condition not just of Chicanos, but
of the Americas as a whole. Earl Fitz asserts that race mixture presents
a challenge to our understanding of culture in a hemispheric context:
"Although in the Americas we have long tended to interpret it narrowly,
as an issue of biology alone, miscegenation may well be more germane to
our collective New World experience if considered in its larger cultural
context, a perspective that allows us to view it as being profoundly and
inextricably linked to the diverse social, economic, and political structures that guide and align our various American cultures" (2002, 243).
Fitz offers a Pan-American vision of race and culture. The impetus behind his critical perspective is, ultimately, informed by a sense of political and social potentiality and possibility. He argues that miscegenation
should be thought of as a cultural issue rather than as an exclusively
racial one, allowing us

> to see not only our past and present more clearly but, more importantly,
> our future as well, the people and societies that we ought to be. Should this
> come about, the issue of miscegenation, understood in a larger, more cul-
> tural context, might well help us begin at long last to realize what was one
> of the driving myths that led the Eurpeans to our shores hundreds of years
> ago—the vision of the New World as an edenic paradise. (Ibid., 244)

Fitz is correct in identifying the impetus that led so many explorers to
the shores of the Americas, but his utopian hope (perhaps overstated) of an
earthly paradise serves to remind us what is at stake. Although the bloody
and tragic colonial history of the Americas provides the context for contemporary social inequities both north and south of the U.S.–Mexico

border, it is at the site of culture that the most productive and empowering consequences of this history emerge.

This emphasis on the geopolitical site of cultural production is the point that Karen Mary Davalos makes in her study of museum exhibits that display Chicano art. She argues that the experiences of diaspora and mestizaje are key in understanding the significance of Chicano/a artistic practices, because these experiences "help to produce complex representational practices by people of Mexican descent. A long history of intercultural mixing makes it nearly impossible (or at least improbable) to contain Mexican-origin representational practices within binary models of 'us' or 'them'" (2001, 7). The productive ambivalence of mestizaje undoes on a cultural level the distinction between self and other, as several critics have observed. Davalos adds to the discussions about Chicano identities a critical distinction between a diasporic and mestizo/a sensibility. As opposed to the decentering impetus inherent to mestizaje, "Diaspora requires geographic and temporal specificity and thus can contradict a cultural identity that is not dependent on space or time. Some Mexican-origin people in the United States create profound ties to Mexico and the United States, living in deterritorial communities and creating concurrent binational representational practices. In addition, diaspora implies an authentic place, whereas mestizaje rejects authenticity" (ibid., 27). The geopolitical implication of diaspora, from Davalos's point of view, is that a site of origin—and thus of some "authentic" identity—has been abandoned. Mestizaje, by contrast, implies the constant and dynamic construction of the new, the weaving of cultural formations drawn from complex and evolving relations.

I believe that the doubleness of mestizaje may not reject altogether the power behind notions of authenticity, but its doubleness does problematize the idea. Moreover, although mestizo identity is elusive and mutable, for Davalos to suggest that it is independent of space or time overstates the case.[14] However, her analysis of Chicano representational practices does offer a provocative contrast between models of dispersal and models of mixture in considering how culture expresses and influences Chicano/a subjectivity.

In considering the position of Chicana identity in culture, Davalos makes the important observation that mestizaje is a doubling process: "We cannot consider mestiza/o experience from one perspective for it always originates from at least two places. Mestizaje is thus both an expression of affirmation and self-determination and a result of domination. It is the combination of these expressions and results that gives rise to the hybrid forms in representation" (ibid.). The double-edged sword of mestizo subjectivity—subject in and subject to history—is marked on the body. The doubleness is within. Although diaspora suggests a kind of doubleness, it is ultimately one that implies dispersal—from place, from origin, from culture, from language, from nation. A process of transculturation takes place as a result of diaspora, of course, yet the productive ambiguity implicit in mestizaje suggests a different dynamic. Rather than dispersal or flight, the mestizo self is one living in doubleness or, in Stuart Hall's phrase, living identity through difference.

The politics of living identity through difference is, according to Hall, "the politics of recognizing that all of us are composed of multiple social identities, not of one. That we are all complexly constructed through different categories, of different antagonisms, and these may have the effect of locating us socially in multiple positions of marginality and subordination, but which do not yet operate on us in exactly the same way" (1991b, 58). The critical use of mestizaje highlights this idea of being located in multiple positions of marginality and subordination (but also at times of centrality and power). From different perspectives and for different purposes, Fitz, Davalos, and Hall all consider the effect of mixture on social and cultural identities.

We can see how this mixture on a social level leads to a type of productive hybridity in popular cultural practices. For example, the refashioning of the American luxury sedan into stylized lowrider cars is a form of transculturation. The automobile—representing the technological power of American capitalism—evokes associations of freedom and individuality, the assertion of a powerful American self speeding toward a utopian future on the road. The transformation into a lowrider undercuts the car's intended use: it becomes an object meant to disrupt accepted norms of decency and utility. The re-formation of cultural goods not only marks distinct ethnic identification, it also challenges the ways public space gets defined as ethnic or racialized subjects reshape and occupy that space.

Another example of an ethnic reclamation of the public sphere is the transformation of the classic American business suit into the "reet pleat" of the zoot suit. Chon Noriega's essay "Fashion Crimes" addresses how clothing has served as the material of transculturation, marking out a distinctive Chicano identity engaged in asymmetrical relations of power. "With Chicano fashion," Noriega writes, "the ornamental is utilitarian because it advertises a social conflict, yet it also disguises an identity from the state. It is strategic" (2001a, 7). The power of the zoot suit lies in its ability to signify and obfuscate at the same time. The zoot suit signals a crisis within a public space by advertising social dislocation while at the same time hiding identity from state power. All zoot-suiters, in the eyes of the state, are equally criminal. The need to disguise individual identity while asserting ethnic distinction is linked precisely to the degree that the zoot-suiters stand in a position of inequality. By transforming the uniform of the businessman—and by flouting the fabric rationing imposed during World War II—the zoot-suiter constructed a position of doubleness for himself (and, at times, herself). Pachuco and pachuca cultural expression asserts a distinct yet blended identity that matches the racial doubleness of the mestizo body.

This doubleness is intimately connected to the violence of national politics and social change. The so-called Zoot-Suit Riots serve as a culturally and politically crystallizing moment that led, in the 1960s and 1970s, to the rearticulation of a politically engaged Chicano subjectivity. In June 1943, thousands of servicemen stationed in ports along the Southern California coast, along with a significant number of civilians, formed squads to track down and punish zoot-suited youths. They marched through the streets of Los Angeles, beating every zoot-suiter they came across. Running riot through the streets, they halted streetcars while Mexicans, Filipinos, and African Americans were pushed into the streets and beaten. At one point, the servicemen hired taxi cabs (other taxi drivers volunteered their services) and drove through the Mexican barrio stripping and beating youths at random.[15]

In his extensive study *The Zoot-Suit Riots*, Mauricio Mazón suggests that the zoot-suiter, in his sartorial splendor, represented the antithesis of the serviceman who was forced to give up his own sense of individuality in the service of his nation. The violence was an expression of the antiauthoritarianism of the new servicemen. Having no other outlet, they sought members of a visible subculture in order to vent their own frustrations. (It should be noted that the riots were part of a larger anticivilian wave of violence being committed by newly inducted servicemen.)

Against this historical backdrop, Catherine Ramírez, in her essay "Crimes of Fashion," considers fashion's strategic use in reshaping the social terrain for Chicanas/os. Ramírez seeks to reinsert into Chicano identity discourse the role that Mexican American women played in establishing the zoot subculture. She finds that pachucas developed a distinctly Chicana-style politics, an expression of difference via style that employed fashion commodities in order to subvert their intended use-value. By subverting the clothing and fashion items meant to signal specific social roles, "pachucas pointed to the constructedness of gender and class categories (among both Anglo-Americans and Mexican Americans); rejected middle-class definitions of feminine beauty and decency; and redefined U.S. citizenship by claiming a right to collective goods, including not only coats, trousers, and lipsticks, but public space" (2002, 25). The pachuco and pachuca expression of personal identity provides a key example of transculturation within a Chicana/o context. These cultural players asserted a distinct yet blended cultural identity that parallels the mixed racial identity of the mestizo self.

The function of mestizaje within the critical framework I have been evoking here is to foreground the condition of multiple identities. This condition of multiplicity does not negate an identification with a community or a strategic use of authenticity in order to name identity. It adds, as Pratt notes, an optic by which the mestizo/a self can open itself to new relations. Indeed, Chicano subjectivity is often premised on the idea of a transnational (as opposed to binational) identity. The movement through national identifications, rather than from one to another, becomes an operational means by which new relational conditions are fostered. Yet these conditions are not entirely free of the constraints surrounding mixed-race peoples.

Mestizo bodies within transnational movements of global capital assert the troubling conditions that have produced those bodies. The mestizo body, marked as a product of colonial history and moving in often coercive systems of globalized labor, makes present its own position in uneven relations of power. In their study of economic development and migration in Los Angeles, Victor Valle and Rodolfo Torres assert, "the globalized economy and its impact on transnational cultural formations has theoretical and political significance for an understanding of the concept of mestizaje as a transcultural style of Latino border crossing" (2000, 7). This style of border crossing manifests the power behind movements across national boundaries. Valle and Torres employ the term "mestizaje" to convey how, implicit in a category of racial identity, a social category emerges, one associated with both geopolitical border crossings and the transcultural nature of those crossings. The notion of mestizaje in this register evokes multiple levels of identification and disidentification.

Local cultures often struggle to maintain symbolic orders that stand in contradistinction to globalizing culture. Similarly, the mestizo body is drawn away from the local, called upon in service of the global movement of capital. Valle and Torres observe that "the globalization of capital, with its power to penetrate and dominate regional markets and undermine native economies, obliges the Mexican peasant or Guatemalan worker to ignore certain rules and boundaries in order to survive" (ibid., 189). Valle and Torres locate mestizo agency as a response to geopolitical power. Consequently, "[s]entimental loyalty to a particular nation-state and, by extension, that state's idealized 'traditional' culture becomes an impoverishing, even life-threatening luxury. To this extent, then, the lived transcultural experience of mestizaje must also be considered transnational and potentially postnational" (ibid., 189–90). This is not to argue that mestizos in transnational circulation then discard all national allegiance or faith in idealized notions of "traditional" culture. These allegiances and faiths are often compelling factors in maintaining transnational flows of labor. However, the maintenance of a national identity must be negotiated and inevitably transformed in the face of transcultural experiences.

Mestizo transculturation does not take place in a free-form (nor in an entirely liberating) fashion. Rather, the push and pull of globalizing powers create fissures along which mestizo bodies move and through which mestizo culture is produced. Thus, Valle and Torres observe, "The lived experience of cultural mestizaje is not schizoid, nor does it lack the boundedness to produce identity. Instead, Latinos have evolved a countertradition, or anti-aesthetic, of juggling languages, music, clothing, styles, foods, gender, anything with which to fashion a more meaningful social and cultural coherence" (ibid., 190). The meaningful coherence is, of course, one sutured from the varying influences encountered in transnational movement. In sum, the "'styles' of mestizo cultural construction evolve dialectically, generating adaptive responses to changing material conditions and forms of cultural representation. Contrary to the musings of some European postmodernists, who see the multicultural Americas as an orgy of limitless conjunctions, heterodoxy in this hemisphere occurs within materially and cultural defined combinatory systems" (ibid.). As will become evident in the chapters that follow, the process of mestizo/a cultural formation is a contested and ever-evolving one. An area in which that contestation occurs, as the next section discusses, has to do with the function of the mestiza/o body in terms of difference and sameness.

## The Hybrid Fantasy

The role of diversity within state institutions (and the cover term "multiculturalism") may indeed seek to foster the illusion of harmonious conviviality. The rhetoric of multiculturalism has been used to replicate the ideology of the melting pot, suggesting that all racial/ethnic groups in the United States stand in equal positions of power. This neotraditional vision of the multicultural erases the unequal distribution of power among diverse constituencies. What is called for is a resistant understanding of multiculturalism—the kind I argue a critical mestizaje represents. Chicano critical practices—in dialogue with other oppositional critiques—underscore a basic inequality within the mosaic of multi-cultural America. From this perspective, it is possible to illuminate the discontinuous and contradictory terrain negotiated by those groups whose identity is premised on the ability to move through different cultural configurations, simultaneously at home and yet foreign within the scope of these configurations.

At this level, the idea of mestizaje at once suggests change and permanence. The tension between the fluid and the fixed evident in the uses of the term "mestizaje" finds parallels (though not necessarily simultaneity) with critical discourses that range from the poststructural to the postcolonial to the postmodern. The polarities of fluid and fixed partially form the horizon by which critical notions of mestizaje can be understood. At its most celebratory, an embrace of mestizaje equates the processes of racial mixture (inscribed by a legacy of colonial inequality and perpetuated by the violence of enforced globalization) with a free-for-all of decentered and endlessly developing subject formations.

The recurring use of mestizaje as a trope signaling processes of transformation (cultural, political, ideological) has opened it to the charge that it serves as a weak fantasy of completion. Within Latin American literary studies, Antonio Cornejo Polar expresses skepticism over the usefulness of mestizaje as a metaphor to explain the Latin American literary tradition. He argues that the metaphor of mestizaje fails because of its entrenchment within biological discourses:

> It is evident that categories like mestizaje and hybridity take root in disciplines alien to cultural and literary analysis, basically in biology, aggravated by the fact—in the case of mestizaje—that it deals with a concept ideologized in the extreme. (1998, 7)[16]

The suturing of a biologized (and ideologized) term onto literary studies, Polar argues, is at best an artificial imposition of one disciplinary term onto another. At its worst, mestizaje is the actualization of an ideological position regarding the benign multiracial nature of Latin American society.[17]

The evocation of mestizaje, as either a biologized or an ideologized term, serves to erase conditions of difference and struggle constitutive of the literary production in Latin America:

> the concept of mestizaje, in spite of its tradition and prestige, is what dramatically falsifies the condition of our culture and literature. In effect, what it does is offer harmonious images of what is obviously torn apart and belligerent, proposing figurations that are at bottom only pertinent to those to whom it is convenient to imagine our societies as smooth and not at all conflictive spaces of cohabitation. (Ibid., 7–8)[18]

The evocation of mestizaje serves not a useful literary critical function, Polar suggests, but merely an ideological one. The term weakens one's understanding of the specificity of Latin American literature.

Although mestizaje is critiqued within the frame of Latin American studies, Polar's discussion is still crucial to our present considerations. He situates his argument in the debate over the form of Latin American literary criticism within a U.S. academic context. The main target of his attack is the desire within the academy to evoke a benign vision of literary production. For this he blames Ángel Rama, who, as Mary Louise Pratt notes, appropriated Fernando Ortiz's idea of transculturation. In actuality, Polar says,

> the idea of transculturation is being converted more and more into the most sophisticated cover for the category of mestizaje. After all, the symbol of Fernando Ortiz's "stew" that Rama takes up may very well be the major emblem of the false harmony deriving from a process of multiple mixings. (Ibid., 8)[19]

The deployment of transculturation in order to understand literary development in Latin America masks the false harmony of mestizaje. The dream of racial equality and the passive cultural blending merge in an ideological (which is to say false) image of literary harmony.

Polar seems most concerned with the manner that mestizaje has been used within a U.S. rather than a Latin American context. At the same time, he expresses reservations about the way the idea of mestizaje has served to advance particular ideological projects in various locations within Latin America. Thus the championing of hybridity, transculturation, or radical mestizaje in the U.S. academy serves, as Polar's position implies, to deform the true, discontinuous, and contested condition of culture in a Latin American context. The failure of mestizaje as an adequate metaphor for literary studies lies in the numerous discourses in which mestizaje is already imbricated.

However, because of the manner in which mestizaje has come to be used, the very vestiges of its ideological uses serve to make of mestizaje a critical category within a Chicano context. The transplantation of foreign ideology into the United States transforms the significance of mestizaje, especially as Chicano/a writers and critics have attempted to wrest from it a way to articulate the contradictory and multiple subjectivity of today's U.S. mestizos and mestizas.

Polar's argument is premised on an understanding of Latin America as an ontological category, a knowable and unified field whose literature has been misread owing to a critical myopia. This has led Alberto Moreiras to critique Polar's analysis of the Latin American condition. Although he applauds Polar's call for a new paradigm by which to study the discontinuities of literary production, Moreiras refuses to view Latin America as a discrete site of what, borrowing from Fredric Jameson, he terms a critical regionalism. He argues that Latin America cannot be reduced to an area that stands in contradistinction to modernity, globalization, or any other totalizing conceptualization currently at play in the formation of geopolitical meaning, and that "all attempts to circumscribe the local are bound to run into their conceptual impossibility, even when the local is understood as a contradictory instance" (2001, 60). The local, he says, cannot stand as some privileged site at odds with and in resistance to globalizing consumer capitalism. Within the contemporary logic of globalized economies, there is no escape from the all-absorbing and appropriating powers of consumption. As a result, "any supposed resistance to consumption is nothing but a ploy of consumption, a coy niche-marketing of the product for a more or less elite segment of the consumer population" (ibid., 65). The assertion of critical difference or resistance (what Moreiras calls the "dreamed alternative singularizations of thinking" [ibid., 69]) may seek to assume a kind of locality within global discourse. This effort ultimately proves to be just another manifestation of the very globality it seeks to escape.

Of particular interest to Moreiras is Chela Sandoval's theory of differential consciousness. Sandoval seeks to identify those tactics employed by the oppressed in their struggle for agency and resistant power. She notes that mestizos and mestizas, as new "citizen-subjects," employ technologies of "a differential mode of oppositional consciousness" as they articulate a subjectivity that works in resistance to enfolding regimes of power. This oppositional consciousness represents

> a concomitant microphysics of power capable of negotiating this newest phase of economic and cultural globalization. . . . people of color in the United States, familiar with historical, subjective, and political dislocation since the founding of the colonies, have created a set of inner and outer technologies to enable survival within the developing state apparatus, technologies that will be of great value during the cultural and economic changes to come. (2000, 79)

Mestiza/o bodies have experienced the often-repressive technologies of the state apparatus and, consequently, developed in response technologies of survival and struggle. These are technologies of the local (Sandoval's microphysics of power) that, in a contemporary context, provide a means by which to continue articulating subjectivity *in* and *against* globalizing forces of homogenization.

Thus differential consciousness represents the tactical movement between ideologies in order to make manifest the desire for oppositional ideological commitment. Moreiras rejects Sandoval's view that this tactical movement leads to genuine subjectivity: "Sandoval's theory reveals, in spite of itself, a constitutive lack of closure. It is perhaps not so much a theoretical inconsistency or flaw as rather itself an expression of how tactical singularization is a reactive practice against homogenization: nothing but an alternative consumptive move from within consumption" (2001, 70–71). Again, the attempt to articulate a position not necessarily outside but against the logic of global consumption is doomed to find itself "(re)producing local difference for the sake of a merely regionally diversified consumption of sameness" (ibid., 57). The global assumes many local forms as it undertakes its project of absorption.

From Moreiras's point of view, the tactical singularization oppressed constituencies employ to gain some sense of agency renders a critical subjectivity illusory. Under these conditions, an oppositional subjectivity can only stand on the weak grounds of negation: "A radically tactical subjectivity, whose content can only be mimetic negation even as it seems to be affirming something or other, comes close to no subjectivity at all. The negativity of differential consciousness cannot but preempt the very possibility of its affirmative emergence" (ibid., 72). As a reactive strategy, oppositional consciousness cannot provide the grounds on which to mount a genuine subjectivity, an "affirmative emergence." Sandoval's analysis does indeed recognize that oppositional subjectivity functions as "a *tactical subjectivity* with the capacity to recenter depending upon the kinds of oppression to be confronted" (ibid., 14). Given the powerful consumptive logic of globalization, the question seems to be one of degree: in what manner can subjectivities in difference exist? Can regionalism (locality) stand in opposition to global systems and consumer capitalism? Can mestizaje as a critical category-under-construction in Chicano cultural discourse serve as a kind of critical regionalism?

The answer I explore in this book is a conditional yes. Critical positions of difference can serve as sites from which to articulate opposition and even resistance. Despite the extensive insights about the power of globalization and its relation to the local that Moreiras's work offers, I believe there is problem with the point of view on which it relies. Moreiras's position presupposes the impossibility of contesting the global in any meaningful way. Arguing that the local can only be constructed in response to and within the global and then suggesting that the local thereby has no identity in and of itself is tautological. Beyond this logical dilemma, the essay's analytic point of view presents a difficulty. Moreiras argues that dreams of singular difference within totality

are not only the dreams of urban squatters and Third World feminists, of U.S. queers or Muslim fundamentalists, of neo-Zapatista guerrilla leaders or German cyberpunks, of Catalán greenheads, Galician rockers, or Bangkok S&M practitioners: they are also the dreams of (former) academic area-studies intellectuals as they resist their reconversion into corporate intellectuals at the very instant of their absorption by the global university. (Ibid., 70)

Any belief in a singular difference within totality is, for Moreiras, nothing but a dream.[20] The notion of critical individuation is an illusion. Thus he can collapse all these iconic instances of subjectivity as difference—urban squatters, First World queers, Third World feminists, religious fundamentalists, guerrilla leaders, punk rockers, sadomasochists, university professors—and consider them indices of one and the same desire. Within the logic of his argument, all these differences look identical. However, these different identities and positionalities are most assuredly not the same. The specificity of difference is, finally, not reducible to a simple philosophical category. The lived practices of subjectivities in difference are not simply "choices" or "styles," each equally interchangeable with the other. They are, rather, the source of differential forms of knowledge and epistemologies.

Moreiras's discussion does not adequately take into account how different positionalities create new epistemologies and subjectivities. His study reflects less on the "hallucination" of difference and more on the dream of a critical totality. The critic himself becomes the totalizing ground, the globalizing position of privilege that does, indeed, consume all it contains. There is, I would suggest, a theoretical overconfidence—reflective not of the author but of the position the authorial voice assumes in relation to his object of study. All differences are radically leveled, except that of the authorial position standing dispassionately beyond identity positions. The authorial voice thus becomes the transcendent field of totality.

## Dubious Gifts

A critical consideration of other subjectivities can recognize the contested terrain in which new subjectivities articulate their position as agents and objects of hegemony, even as they assert—contra Moreiras—a difference that matters. As Stuart Hall observes, "Hegemony is not the disappearance or destruction of difference. It is the construction of a collective will through difference. It is the articulation of differences which do not disappear" (1991b, 58). Rather than attempt to consider how subjectivity in opposition stands outside hegemony, Hall and others suggest that differences within hegemony are not constantly under erasure, nor do they always serve the totalizing forces of late-capitalist consumption. Rather, these differences can form a locus for political change. Hall argues that a political game that "increasingly is able to address people through the multiple identities which they have—understanding that those identities do not remain the same, that they are frequently contradictory, that they cross-cut one another, that they tend to locate us differently at different moments, conducting politics in the light of the contingent, in the face of the contingent—is the only political game that the locals have left at their disposal" (ibid., 59). The local as an always-contingent site provides a limited space in which differences that matter, made visible through the recognition of multiple identity formations, allow for a difference in opposition.

Clearly, competing and compelling forces pull the mestizo body—and its sociocultural significance—in different directions. Or, perhaps more aptly, the mestizo body moves in multiple directions as it enacts numerous, frequently contradictory, discourses of identity. Just as mestizo bodies are at times produced as the object of contending dynamics of social, economic, and political power, so too mestizos and mestizas within a Chicano context serve as agents hailed by the pull of different ideological forces.

The betweenness of mestizaje represents not a simple space in which the wish fulfillment of difference can magically or marginally be enacted. Mestizaje rather stands as a site of contentious and sometimes violent social transformation. In his consideration of subalternity in an American context, Walter Mignolo notes this when he states that the celebration of "bilanguaging" is "precisely the celebration of the crack in the global process between local histories and global designs" (2000, 250). Mignolo asserts that the breakdown in global processes takes place at that point where local histories slip away from the machinations of global design. He employs the term "languaging" in order to take us "to what makes language possible: without languaging, no language is possible. Languaging is . . . a 'way of life,' engaging needs and desires to enact the politics and ethics of liberation" (ibid., 265). This strategy recalls Mary Pratt's view that marginal communities in the United States began asserting their histories and lifeways—different from officially recognized ones—*as part of their citizenship*, as the very mode of their membership in the national community (1993, 86). Mignolo sees in these assertions an enactment of liberation politically and aesthetically. Although I suggest that we keep in mind the constrained realm of this liberation, it is important to assert that this liberation is very real and, perhaps, the only kind possible given the global ramifications of colonial legacies.

Lifeways enacted between languages, between established ways of life, and between polarities of power serve as practices of liberation. Mignolo notes: "since languaging is interacting *in* language and language is what allows for describing and conceiving languaging, bilanguaging then would be precisely that way of life between langauges: a dialogical, ethic, aesthetic, and political process of social transformation" (2000, 265). Mignolo's idea of bilanguaging places the speaker between cultures engaged in a process of change premised upon dialogue and action. As such, the speaker's actions and experiences are embedded in the way of life associated with each language. Subjectivity does not arise as an act of independent social transformation. More centrally, this social transformation is not the willed euphoria or willful dream of difference that Moreiras suggests is the inevitable result as the local differentiates itself from the global. Rather than be absorbed by the global, "bilanguaging in certain situations and in certain colonial legacies could lead the way toward a radical epistemological transformation" (ibid., 267).

The conditions of this transformation are shaped by the diverse colonial legacies that go into making contemporary epistemologies and hegemonies. Not all colonial legacies are the same. Moreover, the place the nation occupies in relation to colonial and imperial structures varies geographically and temporally. All these conditions circumscribe the situation of bilanguaging. Ultimately, the production of meaning and identity in a new register emerges: "Bilanguaging acquires a new dimension, not just the dimension of the linguistic per se, or of dialogical thinking, but languaging in the sphere of sexuality, race, and human interactions. Bi-languaging is no longer idiomatic (Spanish, English) but is also ethnic, sexual, and gendered" (ibid., 269). The languaging of identity is the enactment of new subjectivities, the coming into being of new communities staking a claim in the making of history and civilization.

Although Mignolo's conceptualization suggests a teleological program, I think it is unavoidable to believe that progress, though not inevitable, is possible. The power of Mignolo's argument is its insistence on the variable conditions that go into making the bilanguaging experience. Cultural mixture—premised on the lived practices of racial mixture—serves to achieve a change in the lifeways of those people and communities involved. The site of "bilanguaging" becomes a place where different modes of living and understanding come together in a transformative process. Thus Mignolo's discussion allows us to consider the ways in which epistemic changes are part and parcel of a critical Chicano mestizaje, a site of divergent lifeways lived through both the body and ideology.

This journey from Ortiz to Ramos to Polar, Moreiras, Sandoval, Hall, and Mignolo indicates the vivid awareness of mixture, both racial and cultural, as dominant and problematic in comprehending the significance of Latin American/Latino/Chicano ways of knowing. In articulating what I see as a critical mestizaje in Chicana/Chicano intellectual work, the discussions by these critics help to delineate the issues pertinent to discussion of racial mixture. What is at stake in discussing the role of race in American and Latin American studies generally (and in Chicana/o studies specifically) is how to articulate a body of knowledge that stands in a critical position to dominant epistemologies. More important, perhaps, is how this body of knowledge stands in a critical position to itself. The relational and contingent nature of mixed-race identities opens up a critical realm where the doubling dynamics of locality and globality, resistance and affirmation, belonging and alienation as central components of identity can be most plainly seen.

I would like to close this part of my discussion with a brief observation about transculturation. It is significant that within American cultural criticism there has been a profound process of mutual transformation between Chicana/o thinkers and dominant academic thought. While the academy has transformed the way Chicano scholars, writers, intellectuals, and critics live and think, Chicano critical and cultural thought has influenced the development of academic thought and practice. We have seen that Mary Louise Pratt's notion of contact zones derives from her engagement with the writing of Gloria Anzaldúa. Donna Haraway has incorporated the work of both Anzaldúa and Chela Sandoval in her development of cyborg thought. Emma Pérez has clearly influenced the thinking—if not the writing style—of Homi Bhabha, with whom she has studied and who praises her work on the cover of *The Decolonial Imaginary*. Mary Pat Brady inflected the thought of Edward Soja, who finds utopian possibility in the idea of a mestiza Third Space. Janice Radway's key insights about *Reading the Romance* are influenced by the work of José Limón, Lisa Lowe's *Immigrant Acts* followed collaborative teaching and speaking with Norma Alarcón, and many urban cultural studies scholars owe a debt to the work of George Sánchez. Indeed, from the work of Américo Paredes on borderlands culture in the 1950s through José Limón's studies on Chicano humor, dance, and folklore in the 1980s to the exemplary interdisciplinary monographs of Gloria Anzaldúa, José David Saldívar, Rosa Linda Fregoso, and Angie Chabram-Dernersian, Chicano/a studies has provided a key grammar and vocabulary for cultural studies in the United States. I sketch out these intellectual interactions not to claim a primacy of thought for Chicana writers and critics, but rather as examples of the kind of transculturation that has taken place in one locale of the U.S. cultural landscape.

I do not mean to imply that transculturation is an easy, or even benign, process. But these examples help to illustrate the dynamic nature of culture as it shifts beneath our feet. Nor is this discussion meant to elide transculturation and mestizaje. Mestizaje is a critical category for understanding Chicano/a identity and culture as double-valenced: both embedded in a legacy of colonial struggle and moving through new configurations of resistant identities. It is situated in unitary notions of community and it opens itself to new relational configurations of identity. Difficult questions regarding mestiza identity and history, Chicana/o subjectivity and agency, remain open to discussion, as the following chapters illustrate.

Clearly, there is no single satisfactory position from which to approach the complexities that Chicana mestizaje as a critical category engenders. Equally clear, however, is the influence that Chicana thought has had on recent discussions of difference and sameness. The nature of difference within and/or against totality must inevitably engage critics struggling with the significance of difference in the Americas. Chicana subjectivity has held, for some, an influential position because it seems to embody the very conditions of difference within sameness that I here seek to associate with mestizaje. In part, this influence has to do with the privileged position Chicanos and Chicanas have come to assume. Chicanos function as members of an imperial nation with social resources dispersed to them as a grudging but necessary strategy of containment. The formation of Chicano intellectuals has been a limited, unintended, yet powerful result of new contact zones formed out of the U.S. imperial project. A critical self-awareness is, I argue, part of the multiple and relational condition of Chicano mestizaje.

The privileged position of Chicano subjectivity comes at a heavy cost. It does not come in terms of lost authenticity or lost identity—though at times the loss of a critical mestizo identity is one of the preconditions for success in the highly racialized national economy of the United States. Rather, the cost has been to those racialized and marginalized bodies that believed in the future well-being of their descendants. This perspective gives the term "privilege" a different valence. The privilege of Chicano and Chicana mestizaje is twofold: it benefits from its position within a nation-state that consolidates power as a result of colonial legacies and continued imperial projects, yet it benefits as well from the constructed memories of its colonial legacies, legacies marked by the body and carried forward as a dubious gift into an uncertain future.

CHAPTER 2

# The Mestizo Voice

In the beginning and unto the end was and is the lung: divine afflatus,
baby's first yowl, shaped air of speech, staccato gusts of laughter, exalted
airs of song, happy lover's groan, unhappy lover's lament, miser's whine,
crone's croak, illness's stench, dying whisper, and beyond and beyond
the airless, silent void.

A sigh isn't just a sigh. We inhale the world and breathe out meaning. While we can. While we can.

—Salman Rushdie, *The Moor's Last Sigh*

The embodiment of mestizo subjectivity calls up a historical consciousness, one that can empower Chicanas and Chicanos or replicate colonial
dislocations of racial inequalities. The doubleness of mestizaje represents
not just a decentering racial mixture but the doubled roles mestizos have
played as agents and subjects in a colonial and imperial history. Chicano
cultural production gives voice to these manifestations of doubleness.
The construction of mestizo subjectivity and the formation of mestiza
cultural practices represent—at their most productive—twin strategies
by which audiences are gathered, fluid subjectivities enacted, political alliances forged, ethnic identities affirmed. This dynamism has served to
make mestizaje durable as both cultural strategy and ethnic identification.

As the preceding chapter illustrates, within Chicana/o critical discourse, mestizaje has been used to articulate multiple and relational identity positions. Critical mestizaje embodies the struggle for power, place,
and personhood arising from histories of violence and resistance. As
vying social discourses have produced Chicano/a identities and cultural
formations, so too have they given rise to a series of different significances ascribed to the mestizo. In tracing these differences, patterns of
appropriation and misrepresentation emerge.

The present chapter addresses how, at the level of culture, Chicano and Chicana expression affirms the idea of strategic reconfigurations, the formation of historical memory as well as the transculturation necessary for the voicing of subaltern identities. Mestizaje becomes a means to articulate subjectivity otherwise, to consider ways of expressing a reworking of the self in a minor key that negotiates dominant majoritarian paradigms of subjectivity.

Mestizaje within a Chicano/a context represents a strategy by which counterhegemonic identities can be articulated. Simultaneously, it stands as a condition engendered through historical processes. The following discussion suggests that in considering the historical and political exigencies of mestizaje, the voice of the mestizo in Chicano culture emerges as an attempt to articulate an empowered and empowering ethnic identity. The mestizo voice acts to enunciate a historical consciousness inexorably tied to the body.

## Conundrums of Mixture

Where critical mestizaje has been used to envision a radical challenge to a unitary sense of identity, the sense of mixture inherent to the mestizo condition also carries a sense of assimilative possibility; that is to say, the mestizo can be made to fit into a pluralist paradigm of benign difference. We might think of Chandra Mohanty's meditations on the significance of race and difference. She argues that the challenge of race

> resides in a fundamental reconceptualization of our categories of analysis so that differences can be historically specified and understood as part of larger political processes and systems. The central issue, then, is not one of merely *acknowledging* difference; rather, the more difficult question concerns the kind of difference that is acknowledged and engaged. Difference seen as benign variation (diversity), for instance, rather than as conflict, struggle, or the threat of disruption, bypasses power as well as history to suggest a harmonious, empty pluralism. (1989/90, 181)

Mohanty articulates a key dilemma posed by the management of race and difference, particularly in the U.S. academy. Difference becomes celebrated as an inclusive sign of benign liberalism, an empty gesture of acceptance that erases the enduring asymmetry characteristic of social difference.

The problem of a critical versus assimilative difference-within-sameness is certainly not new to Chicano and Chicana experience. Within a post–World War II context, the 1956 film *Giant* offers a prime example of how the mestizo body can be used to affirm a vision of empty pluralism. Although the movie was striking in its time for the inclusion of mestizo bodies as part of the American social landscape, I provide a counterreading of the film that questions its ostensibly progressive agenda. *Giant* presents to a mass audience previously absent affirmative images of Mexicans, but ultimately the film serves to subordinate mestizo/a figures. They become part of a post–World War II racial hierarchy rather than a significant challenge to the power imbalance enacted by that hierarchy. Although the manifest content of the film bespeaks a vision in which racial difference is subsumed beneath the national signifier "America," in actuality a white patriarchy retains its privileged position as sole agent in writing a new American history.

In posing this argument, I am drawing on the work of Tino Villanueva, who responds to the film and its politics of (dis)empowerment. Villanueva's 1993 poem *Scene from the Movie Giant* is a direct response to the voicelessness imposed on the mestizo by the film. The genesis of the poem is precisely the lack of mestizo agency in the film. It examines the feelings of the poet as he recollects his responses upon first seeing the film as a boy seated in a dark movie theater in Texas. As the speaker notes in the poem, the movie deals with social struggle but leaves him feeling as though he can "carry nothing to the fight" (1993, 36). Thus Villanueva's poem, as a voicing of mestizaje, embodies some of the liberatory qualities desired by mestizo subjects.

Missing from Villanueva's rendering is a sense of the political and social struggles involved in the formation of Chicano identity that, for example, serves as the focus of Oscar Acosta's novels *The Autobiography of a Brown Buffalo* (1972) and *The Revolt of the Cockroach People* (1973). Acosta's Chicano nationalist version of mestizaje highlights a sense of collectivity and political project implicit in the development of mestizo consciousness. However, in giving voice to a masculinist mestizo discourse, his articulation serves to devalue numerous voices seeking to broaden notions of mestizaje beyond a racial/national paradigm. Within Acosta's narratives, mestizo consciousness is tied directly to a masculinist desire and an affirmation of mestizo agency at the cost of a liberated *mestiza* subjectivity.

While Acosta's voicing of mestizaje serves to silence mestiza voices, the work of poststructural critics in their rush to assert the deconstructive qualities of mestizaje at times erases the historical-material specificity of the term. In response to the potential elisions and illusions involved in conceptualizing mestizaje as the apogee of *différance*, a feminist poetics of mestizaje seeks to reembody and rehistoricize mestizaje. The processes of mestizaje are often occluded by American pluralist, masculinist, nationalist, or poststructuralist valorizations of an all-too-evasive borderland. The poetry of Lorna Dee Cervantes helps crystallize the salient issues in her poetics of mestizaje. Her work suggests a vision of mestizaje as a tactical subjectivity, one that gives voice to subjectivity both inscribed by and opposed to dominant systems of power.

This position of double-voicedness is evident as well in the widely read short story "Woman Hollering Creek" by Sandra Cisneros. Cisneros's narrative enacts a rewriting of gendered scripts for Mexicana/Chicana subjects within a violent patriarchal society. The story famously recasts the coupling of popular legends about La Llorona and La Malinche, transforming these stories in which women are portrayed as betrayers of nation and family into a story of new gendered possibilities. The new mestiza is empowered to claim a voice through the collective efforts of women in common cause.

Expanding on a key point made by Chela Sandoval, I argue that the term "mestiza" is not just a fixed signifier but also serves as "a *tactical subjectivity* with the capacity to de- and recenter, given the forms of power to be moved" (Sandoval 2000, 59). The capacity for change through mestizaje is perpetually negotiated given the systems of power—discursive, repressive, militarized, ideological—that mestizos contest. The terrain crossed by mestizo and mestiza bodies forms a topos overlaid by strategies of survival and triumph. Mestizaje thus becomes a means of weaving together the traces of a historical-material legacy with the vision of a potential—and potentially resistant—subjectivity.

## Curious Guardians and Inscrutable Minions

Gayatri Spivak reminds us that in undertaking social transformation, it is imperative to ignore that the starting point is shaky and that the end will be inconclusive. Uncertainty needs to be placed in the margin. Simultaneously, and most importantly, it is the margins, the space of uncertainty, of aporia, that "haunt what we start and get done, as curious guardians" (1991, 158). An endless vigilance is necessary as we construct relations with and pose challenges to the worlds of power around us. Responsibility lies in interrogating the uses to which we put notions such as hybridity and mestizaje, and a lack of vigilance leads to a return of repression. To forget this critical function of the margin results in a conservative hailing of established practices and "a masquerade of the privileged as the disenfranchised, or their liberator" (ibid., 159). Clearly, throughout the contested histories of, on the one side, an Anglo-American United States and, on the other, a mestizo Mexico, the privileged feel themselves either disenfranchised from their own sense of well-being owing to the threatening presence of oppressed Others or as the privileged feel called upon to act as liberators. A reliance on well-scripted roles (rather than on their critical interrogation) leads again and again to a reinscription of unequal relations of power.

This imbalance most clearly reveals itself in moments of crisis, when culture responds to moral and political anxiety. The 1956 film *Giant* represents such a case. Filmed the same year as the landmark Supreme Court decision *Brown v. Board of Education*, the movie recounts the triumphs and tribulations of the Benedict family.[1] Jordan "Bick" Benedict, the native Texan played by Rock Hudson, manages a fortune produced from the cultivation of cattle on vast Texas grange lands. These lands are populated and worked by a large Mexican American community that lives a life, separate but unequal, segregated from the white Texans who own the land. Bick woos Leslie, the fey and spoiled eastern girl, played by Elizabeth Taylor, and she valiantly adapts to the tough demands of life in the Wild West. In his last role, James Dean portrays Jett Rink, the antihero who parlays a small plot of inherited land into a vast oil fortune that ultimately drives him to despotism, drink, and degradation. Bick and Leslie Benedict work through their marital difficulties and social differences, expand their wealth, and raise a family. *Giant* becomes a representation of postwar America as a (notably heterosexual) national giant whose virile West and refined East come together in a productive union of power and growth. The film gives voice to a new America, one that struggles with discourses of inclusion and pluralistic liberalism.

The movie reveals a critical fault line in terms of the growth that the central character undergoes. The main conflict of the movie revolves around Bick Benedict's behavior toward the Texan Other: Mexicans. As a white man whose ancestors built their fortune on the systematic dispossession of Mexicans, Bick views Mexicans as inscrutable minions who have their own mysterious ways and generally keep to themselves. (Early in the film, Leslie—earnestly but innocently—reminds a stiff-backed Bick that Texas "stole" its land from Mexico. Despite her faux pas, Bick is still taken with her.) Although her own childhood home is run by black servants who cook, clean, and care for her patrician family, Leslie proves more accepting of the Mexican Other than her husband. A good liberal easterner, she is ready to lend some kindness to her humble mestizo servants. Real racial trouble arises only when their eldest son, Jordie, decides to marry a Mexican woman—named, unimaginatively, Juana. Bick is less than thrilled at the choice his son has made. His daughter Judy, in contrast, elopes with the humble—but white—ranch hand Bob Deitz. Each union produces a son. One is a blonde, blue-eyed toddler. Significantly, it is the other, the dark mestizo baby boy, who is destined to carry on the Benedict name.

Several critics have praised the movie for its liberal and inclusive vision of a new postwar America. José Limón, for example, suggests that there must be a "historically specific appreciation of how *radical* the film was in including such a Mexican presence as it did in the 1950s, and how precisely sophisticated . . . it was in ensuring that the audience knew that Mexican-Americans had a real active presence in American life" (1998, 123). Along the same lines, Charles Ramírez Berg calls *Giant* "one of the most enlightened of all of Hollywood's wide-screen epics" (1992, 43). While acknowledging these points, I nevertheless offer the following reading in response to the notable lack of agency manifested by the Mexican presence. This lack of agency is powerfully articulated in Tino Villanueva's poem *Scene from the Movie Giant*.

Villanueva's poem alludes primarily to the climactic scene of the film. In it, Bick, Leslie, youngest daughter Lutz, daughter-in-law Juana, and the mestizo grandchild—little Jordie Benedict—are on their way back home from attending the ill-fated grand opening of Jett Rink's resort hotel. They stop for a bite in a roadside hamburger joint named Sarge's Place. The hostility toward Juana and little Jordie, whose somatic presence marks them "Mexican," is immediately palpable as the plump blonde waitress first stares at them and then grudgingly serves the Benedicts water. Sarge, the owner, is likewise unhappy, but he backs down from confronting the Benedicts after insulting Juana and little Jordie, who Juana says wants ice cream ("Ice cream?" Sarge asks. "I thought he'd want a tamale").

Things come to a head when an elderly Mexican man and woman with their daughter take a table by the door. This proves too much for Sarge, who unceremoniously attempts to eject the unwelcome customers. The old man futilely holds out to Sarge a wad of dollar bills proving his ability to pay—which is to say, proving his economic worth. Bick intervenes, suggesting that Sarge should treat these people with more respect, reminding him: "The name Benedict has meant something to people around here for a considerable time." Sarge backs down and jerks a thumb at little Jordie and asks if "that little papoose back there, he a Benedict too?" As if for the first time, it dawns on Bick that, indeed, a mestizo child is the bearer of both his own Christian and family name: Jordan Benedict III. When Bick acknowledges his mestizo grandson, Sarge backs down and tells him to forget the question. Nevertheless, he proceeds to eject the Mexican family. At this point Bick throws the first punch, stuns Sarge, and assumes a position as liberator of the oppressed.

The fight scene that follows bespeaks a battle of epic proportions. As Richard Meyer observes in his analysis of Rock Hudson's film roles,

Hudson's body—which stood six feet four inches—assumes a great significance. Hudson represents largeness and strength: even his name, taken from the Rock of Gibraltar and the Hudson River, provides an "expansive landscape of the masculine" (1991, 260). Hudson's name ultimately proved ironic, given his vexed position as a gay man repeatedly called upon to represent idealized heterosexual males and who, toward the end of his life, acknowledged that he was HIV positive and suffering from AIDS.[2]

In this climactic scene, Hudson plays the role of the great white father. The low camera angles accentuate the height and vastness of the titanic combatants. Adding to the sense of epic battle, the militaristic drumbeat of "The Yellow Rose of Texas" plays prominently as the sound track for the showdown.[3]

Bick loses the fight. The battle is nevertheless significant as a representation of the battles America has come to wage in terms of race and an emerging pluralistic vision of inclusion. As a metaphor for this greater America, Bick is forced to accept a different relationship to racial identity. The catalyst for this epic battle is, after all, Bick's acknowledgment of his racialized grandson, Jordie. In a sense, the moment of recognition offers a patriarchal blessing by Bick's admitting finally the familial links to "that little papoose." The mestizo body is claimed in the film, admitted into the national family, and in being admitted ultimately erased within a discourse of benign racial difference.

It should be noted that two other mestizos play significant roles in the movie: the young Mexican named Angel, played by Sal Mineo, and Dr. Guerra. Early in the film, Angel proves himself to be the cowboy Bick's own son never wants to be. Unfortunately, he is killed fighting for the United States during World War II. At Angel's funeral, Bick, in a gesture of national reconciliation, carries the Texas flag to Angel's family. The other mestizo, Dr. Guerra, sets up a clinic in the Mexican shantytown where the workers on Bick's ranch live. He serves as the inspiration for Jordan Jr. to become a doctor. Significanly, once Jordan makes this decision, Dr. Guerra never again appears in the film. In both cases, the mestizo disappears behind a white presence.[4] In the logic of the film, mestizos quite literally cease to have need of existence as individual agents. When the white characters champion them or their humanity, white liberalism effectively assimilates mixed-race bodies and washes out representations of the mestizo. Only whiteness is left.

Mestizaje cannot provide an empowered subjectivity, cannot offer agency in the film's epic battle over the racial and national redefinitions the film represents. The titanic white father must stand up for the Mexicans, represented by an ineffectual old man, helpless youngsters, and sobbing women. It is the white father who must claim his (grand)son, bestow legitimacy, and defend the family name—even if it belongs to a mestizo child he would under other circumstances scorn. The film thus provides, evocative of Spivak's discussion, an image of the privileged as savior.[5] A benign, pluralistic vision incorporates difference within its own grand discourse of sameness. The somatically marked Other cannot speak for himself or herself. Instead, Bick does the speaking with his fists, fighting for the inclusion of all subjects. But those subjects are left voiceless, incorporated into a discourse of equality that ensures again erasure.

The final scene of *Giant* underscores the fact of subalternity owing to racial difference. Following the fight, domestic calm returns: Bick recovers from his battle wounds; Leslie affirms her love, support, and respect for her man. The couple speak as they watch over their two grandchildren—one racially "pure," one multiracial—and reminisce over the years spent together. The film presents a teleological national narrative by asserting a final triumph, a sense of arrival, an affirmation of progress in relation to human rights. As Leslie tells Bick, until that moment when he stood up for the downtrodden and the excluded, she had been thinking: "Jordan and I and all the others behind us have been failures." This moment in which Bick fights for the inclusion and rights of the dispossessed represents for Leslie a moral victory, a culmination of the hundred-year Benedict family history.

Yet that inclusion does not prevent Bick from bemoaning the fact "my own grandson don't even look like one of us. I swear, honey, he looks like a little wetback." Although difference in *Giant* becomes part of a discourse of liberal humanism and pluralistic democracy, difference still marks alterity and inferiority. There is still an "us" who stand at the center of discourse, agent and subject of history, and a second constituency composing "them," the Others who are not yet (and may never be) "us."

Moreover, the final scene illustrates how images may overpower words. The discourse of inclusion and equality that Leslie and Bick speak is belied by the mise-en-scène of the closing shot. The grandchildren stand side by side in their crib, cousins, fruit of the same family tree. Behind the white child stands a white lamb; behind the brown child stands a brown calf. While the image suggests that the brown little Jordie will inherit the family's cattle ranch, the image is also a metonymic representation of the way different colors bespeak a difference in species. It is a representation of unbroachable racial difference. Where the dialogue between Bick and Leslie bespeaks equality, the mise-en-scène underscores difference. Although one might be tempted to read this scene as a moment of triumph or a vision of pastoral peace—a representation of a world where the calf lies down with the lamb—it is difficult not to read the significance of the final image in a more sinister light.

The closing moments of *Giant*, suggesting that different races represent different species, evokes a dominant strain of nineteenth-century racial theory. This other species, embodied by the mestizo, is acceptable only insofar as it fits within an overarching authoritative discourse: in this case, one of benign pluralism and liberal democracy. Yet the implicit difference, that which is unvalued and undesirable, is simultaneously maintained and erased in a double movement of acceptance and repugnance. The mestizo body ostensibly serves as the guarantor of postwar American equality. Yet it remains not more than the "little wetback," long an object of racism and repression. Although upheld as an equal within the postwar American family, the mestizo sinks beneath the weight of prejudice, derision, and disgust.

In this register, the mestizo body serves a discourse that remains deaf to the particularities of how that body gives voice to its experiences. In the climactic scene, silently holding his money up to Sarge—attempting to assure his legitimacy as an agent in economic exchange—the old Mexican man becomes an image of a voiceless body, an inarticulate symbol within other systems of meaning through which only Sarge and Bick are able to speak. It is this voicelessness in relationship to mestizaje that drives Tino Villanueva to respond to the film in *Scene from the Movie Giant* (1993).

## A Breath Not Fully Breathed

Villanueva's autobiographical poem examines the effect the film has had on the poet's sense of self and voice. As a sixteen-year-old boy in a darkened Texan movie theater, the poet feels himself made marginal as the fight scene between Bick and Sarge unfolds and "a small dimension of a film . . . became the feature of the whole" (1993, 11). Villanueva emphasizes the significance that this one scene holds for him. His experience of the movie is one of objectification and marginalization represented by Juana, the mestiza figure who becomes the scopic object of the plump blonde waitress. More important, the waitress's gaze objectifies little Jordie, the "child, half-Anglo, who in Juana's womb / Became all Mexican just the same" (18). Interpellated by the ideology of race, the poet too feels subjected as he remembers himself "[l]ocked into a back-row seat" (12) watching the film. The sense of impotence and silence that is underscored by his position in a segregated movie theater makes the poet feel sharply his situation, aware that he must sit "shy of speech, in a stammer / Of light, and breathe a breath not fully breathed" (19). Mestizaje becomes a site of disempowerment within the very cultural object—the film *Giant*—that seeks to affirm new racial attitudes in the United States. Villanueva's poem helps reveal the incongruities of a mestizaje that becomes both subject of and subject to a liberal discursive inclusion. The poet makes clear that these contradictions produce a position of disempowerment: "I am on the side / Of Rock Hudson, but carry nothing to the fight" (36).

Empty-handed, the speaker comes to find through poetry a voice by which to articulate his sense of outrage and silence. The poem becomes a means of contestation, a site of an empowering counterdiscourse that asserts a hitherto silent voice: "Now I am because I write: I know it in my heart / and know it in the sound iambics of my fist that / mark across the paper with the sun's exacting rays" (50). Through the poet's words and rhythms, the pale flickering light of the movie house becomes transformed into the exacting rays of the sun. The power of Sarge's fist is transformed into the fist of the poet writing out his verses. By thematizing the importance of language in identity ("I am because I write"), the poet asserts his own sense of subjectivity: "At this moment of being human / (when the teller is the tale being told), / the ash of memory rises that I might speak" (52). Thus the teller and the tale, the writing and the writer, the speaker and his voice emerge as one out of the ashes of memory. A fiery future is created in which a new voice and a new subject arise. The voice, significantly, is mestizo, one that speaks in English as well as Spanish: "O life, this body that speaks, this / repetitive self drawn out from *la vida revivida,* / *vida sacada de cada clamor* [renewed life, life extracted from each uproar]" (ibid.). The poem affirms an other self, one that interweaves on a linguistic level the sense of mestizaje it addresses on a thematic level as a site of conflict. This melding envisions mestizaje as a means of speaking, an affirmation of voice.

A nagging silence persists, however. What enables the speaker to leap from silent subjected observer to speaking participant in subjectivity remains unspoken. No mention is made how the speaker moves from standing "on the side / Of Rock Hudson, but [carrying] nothing to the fight" (36) to being an agent able to extricate his life from this battle. The poet seems to arise sui generis as a new subject, speaking and making up for what could not be previously spoken. The self that emerges from the poem stands alone, one dissociated from history, seemingly free of those (historico-/politico-)racialized constituencies who sought to intervene against the silencing of *Giant.* The poem rejects dominant forms of thought and does contest the silence imposed upon the disempowered and dispossessed. But an invocation of a very significant material history remains absent.

*Scene from the Movie Giant* seems to represent the grandeur of individual achievement and a story of personal—not collective—growth. Ironically, the poem offers a vision of the poet rising majestically above adversity as a type of new giant finally able to speak. Yet the poet's assertion of an articulate Chicano ethnicity—an assertion manifested clearly in the bilingualism of the poem's closing lines—becomes dissociated from the political and historical struggles of the 1960s and 1970s that did, indeed, give the mestizo some voice. This observation is not meant as a critique of Villanueva as a poet, as a subject, or as an agent in the development of Chicanismo. Anybody familiar with the history of Chicano culture knows well the role he played as one of the groundbreaking writers to articulate Chicano identity, first in Spanish and later

English, through his poetry. His commitment and sincerity cannot be questioned. Rather, my goal is to understand the means by which mestizo agency is manifested within *Scene*. Historically, the construction of Chicano ethnicity functions both as an agent moving toward political engagement and as a product resulting from political activity. There is a double movement in which ethnicity becomes a subject of and subject to social forces. Mestizaje interpellates new subjects in history. Ultimately, Villanueva's poem obscures this process of subjectivization and remains silent about the conditions that enabled Chicano and Chicana social visibility.

## Mestizaje in the Margins

In contrast to Villanueva's poem, the work of Oscar "Zeta" Acosta is incessantly concerned with the political processes pushing and pulling mestizo identity. Part of Acosta's concern centers on the strongly racialized quality of Chicano ethnic identity. Although there is within both Mexican and Chicano nationalist discourses a clear affirmation of the indigenous, one need not search hard to encounter social values that often reject the autochthonous. Acosta's memoir *The Autobiography of a Brown Buffalo* (1972) dwells at length on the devaluation of his indigenous identity. The book covers Acosta's coming-of-age and his later experiences with the counterculture of the 1960s, the anti–Vietnam War movement, and (most centrally) the rise of Chicano nationalism. Reminiscing about his childhood in the San Joaquin Valley, Acosta argues for the importance of race within his community: "Everyone in the Valley considers skin color to be of ultimate importance. The tone of one's pigmentation is the fastest and surest way of determining exactly who one is" (1989, 86). He goes on to illustrate:

> My mother, for example always referred to my father as *indio* when he'd get drunk. . . . If our neighbors got drunk at the baptismal parties and danced all night to *norteño* music, they were "acting just like Indians." Once I stuck my tongue in my sister Annie's mouth—I was practicing how to French kiss—and my ma wouldn't let me back in the house until I learned to "quit behaving like an Indian." (Ibid.)

As promiscuity, licentiousness, drunkenness are taught to be Indian traits, Acosta learns cultural stereotypes that encode moral qualities into racialized physical features. The conflation of race and culture is complete. Acosta is thus taught to desire those somatic qualities most unlike his. The passage reflects a Mexican nationalist ideology that envisions a progressive form of identity, one that moves away from the Indian and toward the civilized European. The mestizo body as a body in racial transition represents a site in conflict, a body taught to desire against itself.[6]

In the fourth grade, for example, Acosta experiences a crush on Jane Addison, the blonde, shy, pigtailed "American" girl with red acne "all over her beautiful face" (ibid., 89). His infatuation with Jane Addison's beautiful face arises from a desire for white bodies that extends to even his grade school teacher, Miss Rollins. She reads *Robinson Crusoe* to the class while Acosta sits in the front row: "from this frontline position I could stare as long as I wanted at the long, creamy legs of the most beautiful teacher I ever had" (ibid.). These desires for Jane Addison and Miss Rollins (who most appropriately reads the *opus classicus* of colonization, *Robinson Crusoe*) represent the conflicted colonized condition of the mestizo subject.

Out of his desire for creamy thighs, blonde pigtails, and blue eyes Acosta recognizes his own self negatively cast: "I grew up a fat, dark Mexican—A Brown Buffalo" (86). In contrast to these white female bodies, his mestizo body is a source of torment and disgust, a site of disdain and emotional torture. When the blonde Jane Addison ridicules Acosta before the entire fourth grade class, he realizes:

> My mother was right. I am nothing but an Indian with sweating body and faltering tits that sag at the sight of a young girl's blue eyes. I shall never be able to undress in front of a woman's stare. I shall refuse to play basketball for fear that some day I might have my jersey ripped from me in front of those thousands of pigtailed, blue-eyed girls from America. (95)

Because of the way his mother defines "Indian," Acosta views the mestizo body as a signifier of all that diminishes him before the blonde, blue-eyed

American girls imagined as the source of some pervasive scopic power. Desire for the (white/colonizing/female) Other leads to an identification in which his own (mestizo/colonized/male) body becomes wholly Other. Acosta's desire demarcates a colonized desiring against his self.[7]

In the various Chicano and Mexicano communities from which ethnic identities emerge, the devaluation of the indigenous, of the racial Other, carries with it a potent charge. The struggle against this devaluation represents one of the sources of Chicano antiauthoritarian contestation. To a degree, the anti-indigenous trajectory of Mexicano/Chicano practice is dismissed as so much false consciousness in Acosta's second book, *The Revolt of the Cockroach People* (1973).

At a central point of the novel, Acosta participates in a three-day fast protesting the arrest of twenty-one Chicano demonstrators in Los Angeles. During the fast, three teenage Chicanas approach Acosta and crawl into his tent under his blanket. Soon political solidarity turns to something else:

> I caress a leg and it holds still, waiting for my hand. It is firm and soft and warm. I reach for a soft arm. It comes into mine easily. There is no hesitation. And then a moist lip to my ear. . . . I reach for a breast. It is small. Wonderfully small and firm. It fits into my palm. A brown pear in my hand. God Almighty! *This* is the revolution. (1987, 89)

The reclamation of the mestizo (more significantly, *mestiza*) body initiates a simultaneous process of liberation and containment. Acosta identifies the revolution in a transformation of sexual desire reflected in his exclamations of appreciation for the mestiza body. The mestiza body returns as a site not of repugnance but of longing. At the same time, the reclamation of the mestiza body enacts simple objectification. The narrative itself highlights the disassembled body parts that compose Acosta's objects of desire: a leg, an arm, a lip, a breast.

Reasserting ties to the mestizo represents not just an objectification of the body, but also a reinscription of impoverished social roles. As the night wears on, Acosta's thoughts turn from the revolutionary to the domestic. In the end, all he wants to know about these Chicana protesters is whether they can cook and clean. As a result, after the fast, the three join him to set up house in his small apartment on Sixth Street. Acosta remains the revolutionary fighting the battles for Chicano nationalism and the three teenagers become Adelitas, cooking for their revolutionary warrior and providing physical solace.[8]

Throughout Acosta's books there is an incessant, anxious assertion of masculinity, misogyny, and homophobia. Yet, as a basis for identity, the idea of racial mixture asserts a melding of identities as necessary in the formation of new subjectivities. Thus Acosta's resolidification of repressive identity positions runs counter to the logic and critical intent of mestizo identity formation.

In Chicano cultural production, the mestizo body stands as a text, a site of ideological contestation. As we have seen, the racialized body is often strategically elided with culture, the body elided with political practice, the body elided with an affirmation of alterity and resistance. As Acosta's narratives reveal, the affirmation of mestizo bodies also can too easily subsume revolution, a revolution where long-rehearsed and repressive social scripts, unexamined, return. Mestizaje, on either a cultural or a racial level, does not guarantee contestation. Only a constantly critical and questioning deployment of mestizaje—a mestizaje on the margins, so to speak—can move processes of identification beyond established and disabling social scripts.

The limitations of Acosta's actions are not restricted to issues of gender. The mestizo and the mestiza body both become subsumed by his adherence to a nationalist discourse. In a rather intricate middle section of his book, Acosta recounts the trials of the Fernandez family, whose son, Robert, has been found dead in his Los Angeles County jail cell. The sheriffs claim his death is a suicide; the family claims Robert was murdered. The family contacts Acosta, who in turn persuades the county coroner to conduct an inquest into the death.

As the family's representative, Acosta is present at the autopsy of the exhumed body. To determine whether trauma had occurred before or after death, that portion of tissue where discoloration appears must be removed for microscopic examination. The body again serves as a signifier, here as a sign of police brutality and repressive state action. As the corpse has already begun to decompose, there are an extensive number of discolored sites that require removal. Acosta acts as supervisor:

> I cannot believe what is happening. I lean over the body and look at the ears. Can they get a notch from the left one?
>
> Slit-slit-slice blut! . . . into a jar. . . .
>
> "Would you please try the legs? . . . Those big splotches on the left."
>
> "How about the chin?"
>
> "Here, on the left side of the face."
>
> "What's this on the neck?"
>
> "Try this little spot here."
>
> "We're this far into it . . . Get a piece from the stomach there."
>
> Cut here. Slice there. Here. There. Cut, cut, cut! Slice slice slice! And into a jar. Soon we have a whole row of jars with little pieces of meat. (Ibid., 101–2)

This scene presents the mestizo body in disintegration. One narrative of Robert as a mestizo, as an outlaw, as a member of a caring family, gives way to another Robert as a series of specimens, as a murder victim, as a subject of oppression. The body as signifier shifts quite dramatically from one narrative to the other. Consequently, the narrator exclaims: *"There is no face!* . . . The face is hanging down the back of the head. The face is a mask. The mouth is where the brain . . . the nose is at the back of the neck. The hair is the ears. The brown nose is hanging where the neck" (103). The fragmented bodily remains that result from the inquest horrify Acosta. The elliptical narrative recounts Robert's loss of identity, the dismemberment of his body so complete that no body remains, just jars of specimens and separate parts hanging in macabre juxtaposition. The disjointed narrative combines with Robert's disaggregated body to tell a story of simultaneous destruction and creation.

This narrative section closes with Acosta addressing directly "the cut up brown body of that Chicano boy." He tells the corpse:

Forgive me, Robert, for the sake of the living brown. Forgive me and forgive me and forgive me. I am no worse off than you. For the rest of my born days, I will suffer the knowledge of your death and your second death and your ashes to my ashes, your dust to my dust . . . Goodbye, *ese*. Viva la Raza! (104)

Acosta imagines a communion with the dead boy where ash melds with ash, dust with dust. The individual body, though violently undone, forges a future political body of "the living brown." The mestizo body meets its destruction and simultaneous resurrection, a resurrection enacted in another form. This finally is the great Chicano nationalist dream: to create sociopolitical bodies out of overdetermined brown bodies, bodies already situated in so many disempowering positions of subalternity. There is no coming together of that inextricable contradiction suggested by the close of Acosta's text. The narrative imagines resurrection: the mortal finality of "Goodbye, *ese*" juxtaposed with the war cry "Viva la Raza!" But the resurrection is purely rhetorical. Acosta seeks to give voice again to the mestizo body—exhumed, deceased, disassembled. This voice can only be heard within the register of a Chicano nationalist discourse. Beyond death, however, despite Acosta's most fervent wish, nothing sounds but an airless, silent void.

## Difference and *Différance*

Even as he speaks for the dead, Acosta gives voice to a discourse of liberation that leads to a loss of identity and agency. His desire to move beyond oppression leads to a type of delusion, an impossible resurrection. Acosta's narrative gives voice to the mestizo body only through preestablished oppositional politics. The mestizo is therefore buried in history, the voice of a resistant but nevertheless contained revolutionary actor. Acosta is not alone in transforming the significance of the mestizo body to suit a particular discursive point. There are, for example, recent critics who employ mestizaje as a strategy of absolute transformation, as a marker of discursive dislocation, as a free-floating signifier. The French academic Jean-Luc Nancy, for one—while warning against biological or cultural essentialism when deploying the term "mestizo"—highlights the deterritorializing quality of mestizaje. Mestizaje for him represents the process of disunity in meaning:

> Like any proper name, *Chicano* does not appropriate any meaning: it exposes an event, a singular sense. As soon as such a name arises—cut—it exposes all of us to it, to the cut of sense that it is, that it makes, far beyond all signifying. "Chicano" breaks into my identity as a "gringo." It cuts into and re-composes it. It makes us all *mestizo*. (1994, 121)

The event of "Chicano" is the call for subjectivity in history, but it is not a transcendent signifier. Rather, the event of naming reveals the restless and endless quest for identity. Each identity, for Nancy, breaks into another, crosses the border of identity, and so we are all "mestizo." Mestizaje represents a means by which to undo—meaning, place, self— so that all of us as "mestizos" stand "on the very border of *meaning*" (ibid., 123). The signifying process is unsettled and transgressive.

A dilemma arises in thus representing the mestizo as a perpetually new subject. Taking up the issues Nancy raises in his essay, Norma Alarcón points out that this recasting of mestizaje as transgression, as a marker of signification's endless play, as an unfixed referent, makes the mestizo and mestiza a free-floating signifier. Nancy's view leads to "a reobjectification of the 'new subject,' a reification or a denial of the historical meaning posited by the differential signifier [mestizo/a]" (1994, 131). As a reified new subject, the mestizo ceases being subject to discourses that invest brown bodies with meaning but also can no longer be an agent in history.

Instead, the mestizo becomes pure signifier, endlessly subversive, free-floating, and detached from the historically bound practices that both form and delimit the mestiza body. Alarcón explains that "the very contingent currents through which the geopolitical subject-in-process is dislocated and forced into (im)migration will retain an irreducible difference that refuses to neatly correspond to the subject's account of herself and the theory we produce to account for her appearance" (ibid., 137). Ultimately, there is an irreducible difference in the signifying process of mestiza/o bodies. This difference lies not in the thing itself, but rather between the circuits of power affecting mestizo bodies and the self-meaning the mestiza names for herself.

It is a mistake to overemphasize the transformative possibilities, the fantasy of endless mutability, in notions of mestizaje. Mestizaje finds its very power in its evocation of historical and social conditions in which Chicanos and mestizas in the Americas live. More, it is those conditions *lived in the body* that make mestizaje such a powerful trope in understanding Chicano and Chicana culture and identity. Mestizaje functions within elaborate racial codes that delimit subjectivity and agency just as they open up the subject to identity. The construction of Chicano subjectivity moves through contested territory, dynamically shaping something familiar and yet something other.

Neither wholly bound by the repeated drone of prescriptive discourses nor asserting an absolute emancipation, the poetry of Lorna Dee Cervantes offers a different vision of mestizaje. In her work, mestizaje becomes a complicated cultural condition that both explores interstitiality and asserts historical connection. Her poetry does more, then, than attempt to move toward a borderless identity. Cervantes's poetic imagination envisions a self that asserts its presence in relation to others. Mestizaje becomes something more than a movement away or a movement toward, something other than an interstitial hanging between states of being in perpetual potentiality. Her poetry affirms something that already is, an identity that is other but not purely Other; that is, it asserts a position in which self and language are neither fully foreign nor yet wholly familiar.

Throughout her career, Cervantes has been concerned with the intersectionality between racial identity, gender empowerment, and linguistic expression. In her 1981 collection *Emplumada*, Cervantes's poem "Crow" articulates one aspect of this complex vision. The speaker identifies, in a moment of poetic flight, with a crow startled from a field by a rifle shot:

> She started and shot from the pine,
> then brilliantly settled in the west field
> and sunned herself purple.

I saw myself: twig and rasp, dry
in breath and ammonia smelling.
Women taught me to clean

and then build my own house.
Before men came they whispered,
Know good polished oak.

Learn hammer and Phillips.
Learn socket and rivet. I ran
over rocks and gravel they placed

by hand, leaving burly arguments
to fester the bedrooms. With my best jeans,
a twenty and a shepherd pup, I ran

flushed and shadowed by no one
alone I settled stiff in mouth
with the words women gave me. (1981, 19)

The poem asserts a subject self-sufficient and articulate, though am-
biguously so. The speaker identifies with both herself and other, here
represented by the crow. Simultaneously, she identifies with both the
feminized role of cleaning house and the masculinized role of constructing it. Not mute before worlds of exclusion (neither Spanish nor English,
neither male nor female), the poetic voice affirms a self premised on
the assertion of women as the givers of speech. Although the speaker
"settle[s] stiff in mouth," suggesting an ambiguous articulateness, the
speaker claims for herself the words that other women have given her.
This assertion brings us quite a distance from Acosta's representation
of women solely as sexual mates, food makers, and caregivers. Rather
than affirm the gendered roles ascribed to women, the poem presents
an affirmation of a hybrid identity within and without preestablished
discursive orders.

Here, the mestiza body is not a hybrid entity holding out the possibility of what is to come. That ambitious prophetic power cannot be claimed by bodies already so overwritten by historical discourses. Instead, the mestizo body offers a vision of cultural development very much unfolding in—and so constrained by—a contradictory and complicated historical present.

In her analysis of Cervantes's poetry, Ada Savin invokes Bakhtin's notion of dialogized discourse in order to explore the "whole field of bi- or interlingual (Chicano) literature" (1994, 215). In bilingual Chicano poetry, Savin asserts, "The alternate use of Spanish and English . . . is indicative of a process of identity search through a dialogization of the two cultures" (ibid., 217). Thus the multilingualism of Chicano literature "is necessarily of the existential kind; their poetry acts out the living contact between the cultures in contact and their respective languages" (ibid.). Because of this "contact" between the Mexican and American, Cervantes "is confronted day after day with an ambivalent reality which throws her identity into permanent question. The historico-political context is burdensome, the cultural conflict is painfully alive" (ibid., 218). The devaluation of the Mexican by the American and the rejection of one by the other create a sense of pained loss. The contact Savin asserts is neither productive like that found in Mary Pratt's "contact zones" nor innovative like the "bilanguaging" Walter Mignolo asserts can lead to new epistemologies. Rather, Savin suggests, the forms of contact traced in Cervantes's poetry can only mark an endlessly interstitial condition of estrangement from self and other. The equation of the mestizo body with a cultural mestizaje in Savin's model is premised on an essential lack: the mestizo is neither Mexican nor American, neither Spanish nor English, neither Indian nor European, neither foreign nor familiar.

It is important to underscore, however, that mestiza/o identity represents not a site of absence. Although it speaks of loss, the mestizo voice is not one of emptiness, but one of overdetermination. Too many discourses engage in a contested dialogue seeking to claim the significance, meaning, and function of the mestizo. Cervantes's poem "Refugee Ship" offers a literary example of this overdetermination:

Mama raised me without language.
I'm orphaned from my Spanish name.

The words are foreign, stumbling
on my tongue. I see in the mirror
my reflection: bronzed skin, black hair. (1981, 41)

The bronzed body, the dark hair should signal a connection to the mestizo name, the Spanish language. In her analysis of Cervantes's poetry, Savin suggests that the lack of linguistic ability marks an estrangement between the signifier (the mestiza body) and the signified (mestizo culture). Significantly, "Refugee Ship" is the only poem in the collection *Emplumada* that Cervantes has translated into Spanish. Thus, although she suggests that the poem marks a feeling of "overwhelming estrangement from one's essential identity markers; name, physical appearance, and language" (1994, 218), the two poems—one written in English, the other translated into Spanish—taken together suggest something else. Although not necessarily a manifestation of sociocultural wholeness and completion, the two poems do represent something more dynamic, more empowered, and more deliberate at work than an essential estrangement. The poems mark the body as a site where linguistic, familial, racial, and cultural vectors cross. These do not serve as essential identity markers. Instead, they form signs—sites of discourse—that charge the mestiza body with a number of meanings.

As the body is an overdetermined signifier, the cultural text too needs to be understood as a multidimensional system of signification. The double-voiced text does not only undermine, as Savin suggests, "the official authoritative discourse, whether mainstream American or Mexican" (ibid., 217). It does not simply hang suspended between two worlds to which the text does not belong and into which it cannot dissolve. The double-voiced text moves among those worlds. Chicana/o culture as a form of mestizaje does not mark a paradigmatic quest for self-definition: it enacts that self-definition in multiple ways.

## Daughters of History

The enactment of multiple subjectivities traced in Cervantes's poetry takes place within relational contexts. These contexts forge new meanings and means of expressing identity, making a critical mestizaje the site for developing voice. The movement to make the margin a productive site of speech and agency forms a central concern in Sandra Cisneros's story "Woman Hollering Creek" (1991). Echoing some of the thematics developed in Cervantes's poetry, Cisneros provides a galvanizing image of how an isolated individual can gain voice through the collective efforts of mestiza women working in common cause.

The central figure of the story is a young woman named Cleófilas, newly married and taken by her husband from her hometown in Mexico to Seguín, a small town in Texas several hours north of the border. Suffering from isolation in her new surroundings, separated from friends and family, Cleófilas's misery soon multiplies as her husband, Juan Pedro, begins to beat her regularly. He inevitably apologizes afterward and begs forgiveness, but he always repeats the same pattern of abuse. In part, the story explores the intersection between geopolitical landscapes and gender imbalance. It is because Juan Pedro takes her away from home, community, and culture in Mexico that he has the power to violently enforce his will upon her. As Mary Pat Brady notes, "Woman Hollering Creek" explores "how private violence is tacitly sanctioned by the arrangement of public space" (2002, 133).[9] Patriarchal order does not just manifest itself as an ideological condition, but it is made physically present through the very arrangement of the new and strange town.

Within the closely circumscribed world of violence she occupies, Cleófilas finds herself forced to assume the roles of both obedient wife and caring mother, not just for her son but for her husband as well. Cisneros likens Cleófilas to Juan Pedro's mother figure when, after beating her, Juan Pedro comes crying for forgiveness: "She could think of nothing to say, said nothing. Just stroked the dark curls of the man who wept and would weep like a child, his tears of repentance and shame, this time and each" (1991, 48). Cleófilas is called upon to play the comforting and forgiving mother for her husband, reinscribing the violence of male privilege through maternal love. This role leaves her, as the narrative is careful to explain, voiceless. She can think of nothing to say when called upon to play such a clearly circumscribed and familiar role. She thus remains voiceless.[10]

Although it seems that Cleófilas accepts this role with resignation, one moment arises when she is offered an opportunity to possibly subvert this role. Sitting by the side of the arroyo with her little son (Juan Pedrito), Cleófilas listens to the rushing water. She begins to wonder if it is La Llorona calling her, if "something as quiet as this drives a woman to the darkness under the trees" (1991, 51). In legend, La Llorona is the weeping woman who drowned her own children and now wails near bodies of water, luring unsuspecting children to their watery doom. At this moment we soon realize that Cleófilas, thinking of this violent script, might be giving way to the desire to kill the offspring bearing the name of her husband. She ultimately refuses to play the role that destructively betrays mother love. By refusing to play the proscribed role implied by the legend, Cleófilas opens new avenues of gendered subjectivity. The story, which in part examines the various impoverished roles offered women by their closely circumscribed social networks, moves toward the promise of voice and agency.

Isolated in a new town, Cleófilas is allowed little social interaction by her husband. What little interaction she does find is extremely limited, underscoring the idea of empty gender scripts allowed her. Her neighbors, Soledad and Dolores, display no interest in her situation beyond Soledad occasionally retelling the latest plot of the telenovela *María de Nadie*, a name suggesting an unidentified suffering woman. Surrounded by Soledad (solitude) and Dolores (pain), Cleófilas is surrounded as well by a town "of dust and despair" and emptiness: "nothing, nothing, nothing of interest. Nothing one could walk to, at any rate. Because the towns here are built so that you have to depend on your husbands. Or you stay home. Or you drive. If you're rich enough to own, allowed to drive, your own car" (ibid., 50–51). The economic and gendered constraints that bind her life are reinforced by the geography of the town whose social activity revolves around commodity exchange and not human interaction. The only interaction allowed Cleófilas is the care of her small son, Juan Pedrito. As a diminutive of the father's name, the son's name suggests that the pattern of violence Cleófilas endures is not just one that Juan Pedro repeats, but one that will be passed on through generations.

Where the violence visited on Cleófilas is continually enabled by her spatial isolation, it takes the intervention of women working in solidarity to break through the isolation and enable her to articulate her own sense of empowered subjectivity. When she becomes pregnant with her second child, Cleófilas insists on visiting the doctor, "Because she is going to make sure the baby is not turned around backward this time to split her down the center" (53). The nurse at the pediatrician's office, Graciela, alarmed by the bruises on Cleófilas's body, phones her friend Felice for help. The two arrange to get Cleófilas and Juan Pedrito on a bus bound back to her family in Mexico. When Felice agrees to escort the pregnant woman and her child to the Greyhound station, Graciela tells Felice, "When her kid's born she'll have to name her after us, right?" (55). As a counterpoint to Juan Pedrito's name, associated with patriarchal violence, the women intervene in order to reproduce the name of female solidarity.

These new names inscribe new identities for Cleófilas and her future family. As Ana María Carbonell notes, "The names of these supportive women, Graciela and Felice—roughly translated as Grace and Happiness—sharply contrast with those of [Cleófilas's uncaring neighbors] Soledad and Dolores. As these names suggest, Graciela and Felice replace the ideology of male-focused, romanticized suffering embraced by Cleófilas's two neighbors, with female autonomy and self-fulfillment. . . . Felice embodies a relational self whose own self-sufficiency, materialized in her pickup, benefits the broader female community" (1999, 68). Felice serves to embody women's collective action as she and Graciela work to free Cleófilas from domestic violence.

The end offers an image of new possibilities. Driving across La Gritona creek, Felice "opened her mouth and let out a yell as loud as any mariachi. Which startled not only Cleófilas, but Juan Pedrito as well" (1991, 55). This yell seems to represent for Cleófilas a new beginning. One might be very tempted to read the fact that it startled not just Cleófilas but also Juan Pedrito as a sign of how female empowerment can "startle" the named inheritor of patriarchal privilege. Symbolically, this may indeed be one of the narrative lines that can be traced. However, we need to separate this symbolic disruption from those that occur within the tight constraints that bound Cleófilas's life. As she is driven by Felice, Cleófilas realizes:

Felice was like no woman she'd ever met. Can you imagine, when we crossed the *arroyo* she just started yelling like a crazy, she would say later to her father and brothers. Just like that. Who would've thought?

Who would've? Pain or rage, perhaps, but not a hoot like the one Felice had just let go. Makes you want to holler like Tarzan, Felice had said.

Then Felice began laughing again, but it wasn't Felice laughing. It was gurgling out of her own throat, a long ribbon of laughter, like water. (Ibid., 56)

This represents the turning point, one most critics of the story read as the moment when Cleófilas finds her own sense of voice and power. Significantly, the passage equates water with laughter, transforming the Llorona myth by equating water not with drowning but with rebirth, just as La Llorona's cry is transformed into a long ribbon of laughter.

Besides driving a truck and hollering with the gusto of a mariachi, Felice represents a new gender identity for Cleófilas, one that may empower her to forge new social relations based on a personal agency and voice. It is the bodily image of Felice as a woman challenging gender roles that opens new relational vistas for Cleófilas. Sonia Saldívar-Hull has made just this point: "Felice, a politically active Chicana who defies heterosexual and lesbian labels but who flaunts her feminist politics, hints at the possibility that Cleófilas can cross over to her compañeras in Mexico with 'hollering' narratives, new legends that have the power to change the subject of the old Llorona laments and other ultimately misogynist plots" (2000, 123). That Felice challenges clearly scripted gender roles is tremendously significant in reshaping Cleófilas's sense of the possible and permissible. After all, it is this difference that she notes when retelling the story to her father and brothers.

Jacqueline Doyle also reads in Cleófilas's return to Mexico a highly optimistic future: "Back home with her children, father, and brothers, Cleófilas overcomes the 'tradition of silence' and claims her right to speak in tongues" (1996, 64). Although one is left with a sense of hope at the transformations that have taken place in Cleófilas's life—she has fled her abusive husband and feels laughter flowing up through her—hers must be read finally as an attenuated hope. We might recall the opening of the story where she can only "dream of returning to the chores that never ended, six good-for-nothing brothers, and one old man's complaints" (1991, 43). This is not a world molded by female company, and hardly a promising community for personal empowerment. If her past at home is any indication, Cleófilas's return to Mexico will undoubtedly be difficult.

Although her sense of fulfillment may not necessarily be complete, as readers we do take a certain narrative pleasure in reading about her body's ability to express joy: the gurgling laughter that fills the last lines of the story. But this expression is not the same as her gaining voice. That project remains, by the end of the story, rather ambiguous. The greatest sense of hope the story offers may not lie in how Cleófilas's life changes through her geographic relocation, but in another kind of change. The unborn child Cleófilas carries may wind up bearing the names of the women who worked in common cause to help her. This potential naming offers a contrapuntal moment to the patriarchal naming of Juan Pedrito.

What the story comes to represent, then, is Cleófilas's flight away from scripts ensuring that women serve as either victim or victimizer. This does not mean that she has as yet realized a new empowering gender role. The old static scripts are replaced by a dynamic, fluid script-under-construction leading toward—though not fully assuring—empowerment.

Narratively, a transformation takes place at the level of cultural iconography. Cisneros's text, according to Carbonell, "transculturates depictions of La Llorona that portray her as a wailing, suffering victim by reconstructing her as a hollering, resourceful figure" (1999, 67). Along a similar vein, Tey Diana Rebolledo argues that the transformative powers of the story lie narratively in its rewriting of the Llorona myth. Cisneros, she argues, "has used the underlying symbolism of La Llorona to turn the image into a source of strength for the Chicana. In this short story, Cisneros underpins the narrative with the myth of a woman heard crying at night. . . . This hollering is no longer the rage or anguish of women suffering. It is the pure shout of triumph, of the celebration of life" (1995, 80). Jean Wyatt argues along the same lines, though she moves the argument into what might be considered an essentializing position:

> To the Mexican woman whose sexual and maternal identity is imbricated with her culture's images of women, the Chicana's bicultural—and cross-gender—flexibility opens a new range of female possibilities. Not only does the *llorar* of the stream give way to a resounding *grito*, not only does Cleófilas see beyond the whimpering lamentation of the long-suffering woman to the possibility of a woman who shouts out triumphantly 'a yell as loud as any mariachi' (p. 55), but the example of Felice's loud self-assertion apparently enables Cleófilas to regain her own voice. She shapes her experience into the story she will tell her father and brothers. (1995, 258)

Wyatt's argument suggests that Mexican culture exists as fluidity's Other, oppressive in its iconographic incarceration of women's bodies and identities. Thus she concludes: "Accepting the ideals of womanhood as they are defined by Mexican culture does not provide a stage for ongoing development, as the example of Cleófilas demonstrates: identifying with La Llorona commits her to the long-suffering endurance of oppression, her powers of self-expression limited to a wail" (ibid., 266). Wyatt reads both Mexican culture and the Llorona story as static objects eternally reinscribing the same disempowering gender scripts. Culture does not work in such a static and predictable manner. As Saldívar-Hull points out in her analysis of the story (2000, 120ff.), there are many variants to the story of La Llorona and La Malinche, and thus the notion of a unitary and unceasingly oppressive "Mexican culture" proves to be something of a straw man in Wyatt's argument.

Ultimately, the point is the revision of cultural scripts enacted through the communal action of women working to create power through voice. Early in the story Cleófilas meditates on the name of the arroyo: La Gritona. She finds the name odd, unsure whether the hollering was the result of anger or pain. Her thinking reveals the failed double role with which she can voice her own subjectivity: as angry victimizer killing her offspring or pained victim enduring abuse. The townspeople offer no better insight for her on the meaning of the creek's name, shrugging: "Pues, allá de los indios, quién sabe" (Well, it's an Indian thing, who knows) (1991, 46). The townspeople associate the unknowability of the creek's name with the inscrutability of the Indian.

As the expression of new potentiality comes to her—the "long ribbon of laughter, like water" that gurgles from her throat (ibid., 56)—she begins a process that may ultimately create new significance for herself and her life. She makes the unknowability of the Indian name into something new, something that expresses not so much a new language as a new potential. As James Phelan observes: "Cisneros invites us to thematize voice through her choice of title and through her frequent reliance upon the voices of characters to carry the story. . . . The ending makes it clear that Cisneros is as concerned with 'the voice of the body' as with the voice of the intellect" (1998, 228). The voice of the mestiza body in this instance makes the unknowable new, takes a lost Indian past and recrafts it into an expression of hope. This hope lies in the possibility that there may be new beginnings, new meanings, and a new mestiza voice. But the story does not signal yet the formation of that voice.

## The Mestiza Voice

"Woman Hollering Creek" serves to remind us of the long process by which voice is enacted. The story does not, I argue, serve as an instance in which the main character successfully finds a voice to make new meanings. In this I stand slightly at odds with those readings of the story that see Cleófilas assert a new identity, an assertion resulting directly from the transgressive role Felice plays in Cleófilas's flight. Saldívar-Hull offers a particularly lucid articulation of this position: "Cleófilas becomes a *producer* of meaning rather than merely a consumer of dominant ideology—transforming herself from the *object* of dominant discourse to the *agent* of an alternative vision. As Felice, a Chicana whose sexual identity is pointedly ambiguous, drives Cleófilas to the bus that will take her back to Mexico, Cleófilas observes a different picture of how to be a woman" (2000, 121–22). What Cleófilas's alternative vision offers, I suggest, remains rather unclear by the end of the story.

Rather than read the story as a culmination of identity, I see a nascent transformation in Cleófilas that enables her to find a voice that does not yet speak a language, but that does express a bodily liberation. The issue of voice in the story is more modulated than the coming into agency of the main character.[11] The story instead reminds us that the infinite remolding of the mestiza body—the recasting of the mestiza voice—is perforce delimited. History traces the ways in which discourses about race, ethnicity, sexuality, and gender bring together language and power. Both circumscribe the social and physical worlds in which historical subjects move.

As the mestiza is given voice, as meaning is ascribed to notions of mestizaje, one can trace numerous modulations in the significance of the term. Meaning moves from the racial to the cultural, from the body to the text. In this circulation of significance, patterns emerge that reveal limitations in the way mestizaje has been employed. It can be situated within a pluralist vision of participatory politics, within an androcentric ethnic-nationalist discourse, within a radically disengaged project of poststructural liberation. Each position charges the mestiza body with a different significance. And although each can offer a tenuous and attenuated voice to the mestiza, each also does not necessarily ensure agency. As with Cleófilas, we can see that the attainment of voice—though an important step in empowerment—is not the end point in gaining agency. Chicana/o culture helps thematize this insight.

The mestizo body, transformed and transmogrified, can still speak. Mestizo bodies signify precisely as they are bound in and bounded by the social and historical conditions in which they act. They serve as signifier, but not as fully free-floating, not as endlessly regressive, not as fully transgressive.

The face of the mestiza is a mask, one that appears simultaneously real and unreal. The body of the mestizo is one created and dissolved, one that changes function and significance as it moves through different systems of exchange. The voice of the mestizo speaks an Other language, a language in creation, a language suspended between English and Spanish. But the voice of the mestiza also sounds the depths of cultural transformation, tests the limits of social configurations, articulates the formation of culture in transition. It changes register and pitch depending on where and why it speaks, whom and which systems of power it addresses. The voice of the mestiza sounds that which, finally, speaks about a longing for agency arising out of a colonial legacy of silence.

PART II

# Fashioning Mestizaje

# CHAPTER 3

# Popular Music and
# Postmodern Mestizaje

We live in revolutionary times. The powder keg that exploded in Los
Angeles in 1992 after the acquittal of the police officers who brutalized
Rodney King only made more visible the perpetual powder keg of race
and class polarization created by twenty years of neoconservative economics and politics. This apocalypse on the installment plan hurts people
of all ages, but it has exacted particularly high costs from young people,
leaving them with little hope for a better future. . . . young people who
have been demonized by cultural representations logically address the
terrain of culture as a crucial site for creative confrontation.

—George Lipsitz, "We Know What Time It Is"

In terms of thinking about the mestizo body, agency, and voice, it is
at once ironic and oddly appropriate that Puerto Rican pop star Ricky
Martin inducted Chicano rocker Ritchie Valens into the Rock and Roll
Hall of Fame on March 19, 2001. Martin's career stretches from his early
days as a member of the boy band Menudo, through his stint as a Mexican
and U.S. soap-opera actor, to his ascendancy finally as an internation-
ally recognized solo musical star. At the dawn of the new millennium,
he became an icon for Latino music's ostensible fin de siècle crossover
into the mainstream. By contrast, Valens's career as a singer/songwriter
lasted merely eight months. He died along with Buddy Holly and the Big
Bopper in a plane crash on February 3, 1959. However, Valens left behind
three chart-topping hits and a lasting cultural impact that overshadows
the brevity of his recording life.

The juxtaposition of these two figures is not accidental. That Ricky
Martin served to induct Valens into the Hall of Fame forty years after
Valens's death was undoubtedly meant to appear as a symbolic gesture

of inclusion. Martin, as a Puertoriqueño serving to induct Valens, a Chicano, would affirm the idea that there truly is a comprehensive "Latino" identity. It also would situate Valens in a narrative of progress regarding Latino cultural presence in the United States. He thus would become part of a long struggle by Latino musical artists to "cross over" and win acceptance by a larger audience.

This narrative subsumes both the Chicano and the Puerto Rican under a unitary Latino identity. The cultural elision erases the historical specificity and sense of agency that Valens, in the Chicano cultural imagination, represents. Ricky Martin produces music that represents at best a kind of bland pop commodity that does not undertake the same kind of dislocation and semiotic reformation that Valens's does.[1] Valens's innovation—one could even view it as a type of cultural intervention—highlights the sense of dislocation and cultural mixture characteristic of Chicano music. Chicano music serves to embody the type of decentering and doubling implicit in an identity born of mixed-race consciousness.[2]

From mid-1958 to early 1959, the seventeen-year-old Valens recorded a number of hit records despite being a musical neophyte; he knew little more than four or five chords on his guitar. His producer, Bob Keane, owner of Del-Fi records, played an interesting role in the development of Valens's career. On the one hand, he persuaded Ritchie to change his name—Richard Valenzuela sounded too ethnic for the general market. On the other, he convinced him to record a version of the Mexican folk song "La Bamba." Keane had heard Ritchie strumming the tune and thought it would make a good Latin-rock song: the term "crossover" had not yet been introduced into the cultural lexicon. At first Ritchie demurred, afraid of violating his cultural heritage, but he was at last convinced to record the piece as a rock-and-roll number. Because he could not speak Spanish, Ritchie had his aunt write out the lyrics for him. She ended up writing out only one verse. Where the original *huapango* is composed of numerous verses, some often improvised on the spot as a part of each performance, Ritchie repeated the same verse over and over in a half-mumbling, stumbling Spanish.[3]

In Valens's version of "La Bamba," recorded and released in late 1958, Bob Keanes mixed the song so that the woodblock clacking out a cha-cha beat comes to the fore. Keanes obviously wanted to foreground the "Latin" element of the song, signaling its ethnicity by sonically highlighting the quite popular dance rhythm. There is no mistaking, however, that the beat is grounded in the rock-and-roll genre of the period, one whose rhythms are echoed in such standards as the Isley Brothers' "Twist and Shout." Valens's version of "La Bamba" creates an aesthetic dislocation that forges new semiotic significance, placing traditional Mexican music in a novel commercial and cultural context. Valens's song serves also to highlight the idea of a local literacy in contrast to global consumption. At one level, his illiteracy in Spanish is represented in his stumbling repetition of "La Bamba." Yet this type of illiteracy resonates with the experience of the Spanish language shared by many Chicanos and Chicanas. The anxiety over a lack of proficiency in the native tongue is one that marks a Chicano condition, especially in the 1950s when the stigma of being *pochado* or "ruined" was a hallmark of a conflicted Chicano identity.[4]

There is thus a semiotic richness to the manner in which Chicano music is consumed and produced. It is significant that music is a site where a Chicano and Latino presence is most evident on the U.S. cultural landscape. The media has proclaimed a new Latino musical boom, touting the successful marketing crossover of such artists as Martin, Jennifer Lopez, and Marc Anthony as the apotheosis of a new consumerist multiculturalism. Rather than embrace such a hollow notion of U.S. multiculturalism, it is imperative that a critical mestizaje contend with Latino and Chicano musical modes that both invoke and create a multidimensional cultural history. The media celebrations of a Latino musical explosion supposedly serve to signal the final arrival of U.S. Latinos as influential agents on the historical stage. In actuality, this view erases a continuing cultural legacy, one that calls up Chicanos and other Latinos as agents in a complex historical, cultural, and social landscape.

Chicano popular music reveals the contours of a critical mestizaje. In the following discussion, I employ the term "Chicano music" to indicate music that thematically—in terms of both lyrics and music—situates itself within a context of Chicano cultural production. The music forms a kind of hybrid creation, one that acknowledges both African American and Latino art forms and that evokes a cultural as well as, at times, histori-cal and political connection to Chicano and Latino social communities. Whereas the preceding chapter explored the problem with voice and its relation to mestizo agency, in this part of my discussion I want to focus on the empowering uses of mestizaje (even as it is overdetermined) in a cultural context. As mestizaje carries with it the ideological impli-cations of its colonial history, and as it serves to locate the body in a doubled position as both subject and agent, mestizaje becomes a means by which a history of cultural and political connection can be forged.

Chicano musical artists bring together a variety of styles and sto-ries in order to situate themselves within a broad and often global history of struggle related to racial discrimination and a demand for civil rights. Given the dominant role that African American artists have played in shaping the music of the United States, the development of Chicano mu-sical expression represents an important recognition of the African pres-ence within Chicano mestizaje. Although the racial history of mestizaje within a Mexican and U.S. context has, of course, always included people of African descent, the deployment of African American musical forms as part and parcel of Chicano expressive culture represents a progres-sive acknowledgment of the relational condition of Chicano/a culture. At one level, this deployment marks the recognition of a shared history and a shared struggle between Chicanos and African Americans.

## From Caló to *Culo*

In *The Black Atlantic*, Paul Gilroy notes that one problem in particular arises when analyzing contemporary forms of black expressive culture: "How are we to think critically about artistic products and aesthetic codes which, though they may be traceable back to one distinct location, have been changed whether by the passage of time or by their displacement, relocation, or dissemination through networks of communication and cultural exchange?" (1993, 80). This question resonates when consider-ing the significance of music produced by Chicano composers and musi-cians creating within and rejecting many features of U.S. popular music.

Contemporary Chicano music represents an incongruity between its desire to demarcate an expressive cultural identity and its incorporation of numerous musical influences. It responds and corresponds to influential musical movements of North and Latin America, yet it also seeks to articulate a distinct Chicano cultural sound. It evokes a sense of connection to a specific, largely Southwest geography while simultaneously recasting aesthetic and semiotic codes. Thus, in 1978 a group called Los Lobos del Este de Los Angeles (The Wolves of East Los Angeles) released their independent debut album and self-consciously titled it *Just Another Band from East L.A.* In 1992 Kid Frost christened his second album *East Side Story.* In 1996 Delinquent Habits performed their rap single "Tres Delinquentes" on MTV and gave a shout out to Norwalk, their working-class neighborhood in Los Angeles. In each instance, the musicians sought to affirm their sense of identity located within geographic areas largely composed of Latino populations.

This emphasis on specificity of place and identity represents a kind of locational principle. At one level the emphasis on community and locality underscores the ideas of connection, identity, home, and place. There is a situatedness, a fixity, at work. Simultaneously, the musical style these musicians employ highlights a formal hybridity. They produce a style of displacement, one that emphasizes mixture through the synthesis of various musical forms: rap, soul, heavy metal, ska, hip-hop, reggae, salsa, *banda, cumbia,* rock and roll, and punk. The hybridity of the music becomes not just a means of blending various cultural influences and styles, but rather a way to highlight the relational quality of Chicano/a identity.

Rap and hip-hop use sampling, mixing, toasting, wordplay, punning, and personal affirmation—indeed, creation—of self. These are manifestations of a formal and thematic mestizaje. As Tricia Rose shows in "A Style Nobody Can Deal With," hip-hop manifests properties of "flow, layering and rupture [that] simultaneously reflect and contest the social roles open to urban inner city youth at the end of the twentieth century" (1994, 72). Rap and hip-hop as postmodern art forms evoke a simultaneous placement and displacement.[5] Yet rather than simply appropriate rap, hip-hop, and rock and roll as modes of expression, Chicano music transforms these genres, synthesizing and hybridizing them in order to express a sense of mixture on both a thematic and a technical level.

As we have seen, the titles of albums by Chicano artists often reflect an interest in geographic placement. Similarly, the lyrics of Chicano rap music often highlight a concern with the naming and placing of self through linguistic mixture. Given the political battles waged over the uses and "purity" of language, it should be no surprise that Chicano popular music highlights the significance of languages—such as English, Spanish, caló, and street slang.[6] On his 1990 song "La Raza" from *Hispanic Causing Panic*, Kid Frost, one of the first nationally recognized Chicano rappers, busts lyrics that rhyme and pun cross-lingually:

> The form that I'm speaking is known as caló,
> ¿Y sabes qué, loco? Yo soy muy malo [And you know what, dude? I'm
>     a badass].
> Tú no sabes nada [you know nothing], your brain is hollow,
> Been hit in the head too many times with a palo [stick].
> Still you try to act cool, but you should know,
> You think you're so cool that I'm a call you a culo [asshole].

In a sense, this is a creative manifesto, announcing the foundation for Frost's work. He uses caló to mark linguistically both his Chicano identity and his position of power in relation to an imagined addressee (where Frost claims he is a badass, he calls the auditor an asshole). The punning and dissing—characteristic of the wordplay of African American rap—in Frost's polyglossic Chicano rhyming works only for those auditors able to make the linguistic leaps between Spanish, English, and caló. This musical use of code-switching has been a facet of popular Chicano culture since even before the famous count-off that opens "Wooly Bully" by Sam the Sham and the Pharaohs ("One, two—Uno, dos, tres, cuatro"). Where Sam the Sham briefly code-switches to express play and celebration, Kid Frost switches between languages in order to establish a sense of imagined community between himself and his audience.

This switching represents one strategic use for the polyglossia characteristic of Chicano linguistic expression.[7] Although the use of multilingual expression is not unique to Kid Frost, his work combines polyglossia and wordplay in order to affirm a particular Chicano racial and cultural identity. His work thus helps to establish one dominant chord struck in contemporary Chicano music: linguistic mixture calls up and addresses a particular audience in order to foster a sense of renewed community.

Language is not the only element that enacts a process of inclusion and exclusion. As evidenced by Kid Frost's "La Raza," a heterosexual, masculinist, and peculiarly nationalist conjoining of the personal and the political is key to the citizenship his cultural work imagines. The song affirms a strictly male self who forms a locus for the cultural and racial characteristics with which the rapper's imagined audience presumably would identify:

> It's in my blood to be an Aztec warrior
> Go to any extreme, we hold no barrier.
> Chicano, and I'm brown and proud.
> *Guantes, chingazos. Simón, ese,* let's get down [Gloves, blows. Yes, dude, let's get down]
> Right now, in the dirt
> What's the matter? You 'fraid you're gonna get hurt?
> I'm with my homeboys, my *camaradas* [comrades].
> Kicking back con mi llaga, y pa' mi no digas nada [Kicking back with my weed, and don't even talk to me].
> Yo soy chingón, ese [I'm the boss, dude].
> Like Al Capone, ese.
> Can throw a throw so don't ever try to sweat me.
> Some of you don't know what's happening ¿Qué pasa?
> It's not for you anyway
> 'Cause this is for the raza.

*Raza* is a term used widely to signal Mexican, Chicano, or even a broader Latino identity, particularly one that derives from a mestizo heritage. Formally and thematically, the song brings together images of warriors and mobsters—iconic bad boys—in a violently masculinized affirmation of Chicano identity as part of a larger Latino/Mexicano community. The song is for "the raza," for a community whose cultural repertoire would allow it to comprehend the linguistic shifts and puns and rhymes. This construction of community highlights the mestizo qualities of a post-revolutionary Mexican nationalist discourse that has in so many ways shaped images of Chicano racial and cultural identities. The emphasis on an indigenous heritage envisioned in masculinist terms, on a racial identity as "brown and proud," on a polyglossic form of expression all make mestizaje a dominant key in this form of Chicano rap. Musically as well, the song asserts a type of mestizaje in its fade-out, referencing both the marimba used in *música veracruzana* and the Latin jazz work of musicians such as Willie Bobo. On numerous semantic levels, the work of Kid Frost positions mestizaje as a central concern in social, cultural, and racial formations.[8]

While it celebrates mestizaje, the meaning of Frost's song oscillates between two poles: a static notion of a nationalist/masculinist mestizaje on one end and a critical, transformative becoming of the Chicana/o community on the other. As with much of Chicano/a culture, these two polarities of being and becoming form the horizons of Chicano music. They fruitfully and problematically employ notions of mestizaje as a trope of relational identity.[9] Other forms of self-identification, other types of cultural creation, other means of social struggle are possible.

At the same time, as a historical and social fact, mestizaje is one of the unifying factors that invaders, migrants, and immigrants from Mexico have shared across time: all are born from a history of violent encounters. From the earliest explorers of what is now the U.S. Southwest to the African and indigenous peoples enslaved both in Mexico and in the United States to the latest migrant workers braving the militarized U.S.–Mexico border, a mestizo heritage forged by often repressive deployments of power ingrains in the mestizo/a racial and cultural subject an identity intimate with uneven legacies of colonial and imperial pasts.

## Poverty and Purity

It is striking, then, that the history of Chicano and Mexican American music would be viewed through a critical prism that diminishes the role of cultural hybridity. Within some Chicano musical criticism, cultural mestizaje at times has been viewed as a type of assimilation. Manuel Peña, for example, has argued that Chicano music oscillates between poles of "authenticity" and "assimilation." In his 1985 book *The Texas-Mexican Conjunto*, Peña attempts to draw distinctions between *conjunto* music as a resistant cultural product of the working class and *orquesta* music as an example of assimilationist desires expressed by the middle class. Thus *conjunto* music (composed of accordion with guitar and vocal) is more "organic" to the working class and working poor of Mexican descent, while *orquesta* music (more orchestrated, elaborate, and akin to American swing bands) represents a type of cultural disloyalty—an act of betrayal or *malinchismo*. This disloyalty stems from the contradictory position of an emergent Chicano middle class that does not identify with the working class but that, in turn, is not accepted by a xenophobic American society.

Peña argues that the music created by Mexicans in Texas reflects the complexities of their experiences as they try to adapt to difficult life conditions in the United States:

> These conditions, often uncompromising, have forced Texas-Mexicans to yield to the stronger power, but not without resistance, not without a determined effort to counter American cultural hegemony by striving to maintain some of their antecedent symbols—or creating new ones as they reinterpreted newly introduced American cultural elements into more familiar symbolic structures. As a countercultural symbol forged by proletarian artists, *conjunto* falls under the former category; as a symbol of the middle class's doubly contradictory position vis-à-vis the working class and a formidable ethnic boundary, *orquesta* falls under the latter category. (1985, 13–14)

The *orquesta*, with its transculturation of dominant Euro-American musical styles, becomes a mark of cultural distinction by members of an aspiring Chicano middle class. This group recognizes its exclusion from dominant society and yet rejects identifying with the Chicano/Mexicano working class. The mestizaje implied in the incorporation of American swing music by Mexican musicians represents not the creation of a new, critical, empowered identity, Peña argues, but one of betrayal. *Orquesta* music represents a turn away from "authentic" working-class origins and an economically poorer but culturally purer Chicano/Mexicano population.

The paradox of Peña's argument lies in the fact that Mexican music itself emerges from the very cultural melding he views with suspicion in relation to the *orquesta*. The *son jarocho*, for instance, originated in Veracruz and developed during the seventeenth and eighteenth centuries as, Steven Loza explains, "a stylistic amalgam of influences derived from the Spanish colonizers of Mexico, from Africans taken to New Spain as slaves, and from the indigenous population of the southeastern region of Mexico" (1992, 179). Musical forms per se cannot be easily ascribed to any particular ideological position.

The mixing of styles as a process of transculturation makes Chicano music a more complex and conflicted field of expression than Peña's study would suggest. George Lipsitz finds ingenious and evocative strategies in Chicano music that create for communities not an ideological positioning but a historical consciousness. In terms of contemporary music, the reality of commercialization and mass distribution of consumer culture does not simply wipe out local forms of knowledge and resistance. Rather, the commodification of music can enable moments of critical consciousness. Contemporary musicians can "use the powers of electronic mass media to transcend time and space, connecting themselves to the pasts of others, pasts that bear moral and political lessons. Instead of serving as an instrument of division, commercial culture in these instances serves as a way for bridging barriers of time, class, race, region, ethnicity, gender, and even nationality. This 'return of the repressed' within the media creates one of its conditions of possibility" (1991a, 261). Musical production contests dominant power as subcultural groups resignify form in order to voice historical memory and subjectivity.

In ways that range from Los Lobos' use of the *son jarocho* to the sampling of El Chicano's "Viva Tirado" (1970) on Kid Frost's "La Raza" (1990), historical memory serves to identify ethnic and political subjectivities. The critical mestizaje of musical form represents the reclamation of historical connection and an acknowledgment of identity as already always relational. Steven Loza notes, for instance, "Los Lobos' conscious adoption of and stylistic adaptation to Mexican musical genres represented an affirmation of their ethnic origin and identity. The form of nationalism that evolved among mestizos in Mexico during the nineteenth century is not substantially different from the political spirit and awareness among twentieth-century Chicanos, mestizos of a particular sort themselves" (1992, 186). The connections between contemporary musical production and historical moments of ethnic formation or political struggle evoke a cultural memory even within the potentially unsettling fun house of postmodern mass culture.

Although oftentimes ignored by mainstream history, cultural memory serves to evoke a historically conscious counternarrative. Kid Frost's use of the popular El Chicano's "Viva Tirado" evokes the Chicano movement, that moment of great political and social activism among Chicano populations in the late 1960s and early 1970s. From the affirmation of Brown Power to the Blowouts (high school protests in East Los Angeles), this period represented a high-water mark in the struggle by Americans of Mexican descent for civil rights and political engagement. The musical evocation of the group El Chicano serves both to index and to evoke this period of subaltern resistance.

The transformation of musical forms through mass cultural distribution is one means by which Chicano musicians formulate a critical mestizaje, one that highlights a hybridization of form as well as identity. But this identity is not some passively formed mosaic. Rather, it serves to foreground an identity forged from political struggle and unequal access to power and resources. The music reveals that aesthetic choices have social causes and consequences. Understanding these choices is part of a cultural literacy forged from a Chicano consciousness aware of its own asymmetrical relation to power.

George Lipsitz articulates this position admirably. He argues that the "buried" narratives of Chicano music—"narratives about group identity, oppositional subcultures, and a desire for unity—amount to more than a 'political unconscious.' As Chicano musicians demonstrate in their comments about their work, their music reflects a quite conscious cultural politics that seeks inclusion in the American mainstream by transforming it" (1991b, 159). This quest for inclusion does not signal a desire for acceptance through assimilation. Rather, the dynamic construction of new musical formations—via the reinterpretation and re-presentation of traditional music or the incorporation of popular, even commercial forms—serves to deterritorialize culture.[10] A critical mestizaje of musical forms stands as an active and impassioned assertion of a subcultural self into a larger national culture. This transculturation represents an attempt to shift the form and semiotics of American culture.

The use of traditional or established musical styles stands as one of the incongruities that Chicano music manifests. How does one comprehend the complex insertion of premodern forms within postmodern music as, for example, that composed and performed by Los Lobos? In his study of subcultural music, Peter Manuel concludes that "the interdependence of postmodern and more traditional discursive realms can be seen to illustrate how subcultures communicate, compete, conflict and contrast with other cultures in the process of indigenising and re-signifying transnational cultural forms. Postmodernism is at once an underlying condition and an aesthetic vehicle for this struggle" (1995, 238). Chicano music as a manifestation of postmodernism melds multiple musical forms in a process of resignification.

Los Lobos, for example, gained huge national exposure through their 1987 sound track to *La Bamba*, Luis Valdez's biographical movie about Ritchie Valens. Rather than capitalize on the success of this album with another collection of popular rock songs, the following year the group released *La Pistola y el Corazón*, a collection of traditional songs and original compositions echoing premodern Mexican folk music. Their decision was an attempt to root the band in Mexican and Chicano cultures as a statement refuting the hubbub of commercialism, fame, and celebrity they found in the wake of the film's popularity. Rather than reassert, as they had on their previous albums, the same type of musical mestizaje—an appealing and seamless combination of rhythm and blues, rock and roll, country western, and Mexican musical forms—Los Lobos invoked an earlier moment of cultural melding. This reexamination and redefinition of cultural mestizaje underscored on *La Pistola y el Corazón* seeks historically and culturally bounded ethnic, national, and linguistic identifications. Although the album moves away from a hypermelding of divergent styles, it does reference various Mexican musical forms, at once asserting a type of cultural affirmation and an implicit critique of a consumerist and avaricious global mass culture. *La Pistola* is the group's reaction to the easy commodification of Chicano/Mexicano identity.

## Hip-Hop, Hypermasculinity, and the Lyrical Flood

Although this type of oppositional cultural stance represents one response to the mass marketing of Chicano music, another is evinced by groups such as Cypress Hill that plunge headlong into the aural experimentation, quotation, and sampling characteristic of hip-hop as a postmodern phenomenon. Their music, generally speaking, lacks the same type of cultural or social critique articulated by such artists as Los Lobos or Kid Frost. Cypress Hill's 1993 album *Black Sunday*, for example, does occasionally drop lexical signals of Chicanismo such as "let's kick it, ese," or "who you trying to get crazy with, ese? Don't you know I'm loco?" However, with song titles such as "I Wanna Get High," "Insane in the Brain," "Legalize It," and "Hits from the Bong," the general thematic thrust of Cypress Hill's work is amply clear.

Nevertheless, Cypress Hill reflects the cultural expression of a new mestizo identity. The group represents a local sense of identity among Chicanos, Latinos, and others in the southeast suburbs of Los Angeles. These are often new immigrants who identify with mestizaje of a different kind: interethnic alliances based on a shared and developing culture rather than on racial or national affiliation. In part, this explains why the complex ethnic makeup of Cypress Hill (Italian, Cuban, Mexican, and black) might make them appealing. Their sense of self-identification and racial/ethnic mixing resonates with the increasingly complex composition of inter- and multiethnic Los Angeles.

Musically, their work is characterized by a heavy hip-hop beat, clever sampling from a variety of sources ranging from De La Soul to Gene Chandler's "Duke of Earl," and a whiny rap voice attesting to the finer uses of cannabis. The beats are compelling and mesmerizing, and the sophisticated use of samples to create intricate rhythms distinguishes Cypress Hill as a master hip-hop combo. Moreover, their celebration of ganja smoke over gun smoke is widely viewed as a statement of peace and unity over violence and interethnic combat. Although on a formal level their reliance on postmodern pastiche does not situate them within the same context as, for example, Los Lobos, they represent another form of critical mestizaje, one that mirrors the complex face of developing communities and changing social dynamics.

A similar complexity is reflected in the work of the musical cooperative Latin Alliance, an experimental hip-hop group. Latin Alliance brought together Latino rap artists from both the East and West Coasts in order to create a multicultural, multiracial alliance to—in the words of the liner notes for their self-titled 1991 album—"uplift the minds of our Raza." In part this uplift manifests a sense of Latino identity that is truly multiracial and configures mestizaje as Native American and African as well as European. Thus it configures Latino identity as a relational one by drawing upon a broad constellation of racial, national, and cultural communities. While evoking cultural distinction, the group acknowledges and deploys the overdetermined mestizaje inherent in Chicano and U.S. Latino culture.

For example, the opening track of their album *Latin Alliance*, "Lowrider (On the Boulevard)," samples the 1975 hit "Lowrider" by War. The song was a widely popular hit in the mid-1970s, especially among those youth who took to cruising in lavishly modified automobiles as a form of social interaction. Slipped into Latin Alliance's mix is a brief sample of "Evil Ways" by Carlos Santana, another Chicano musician whose synthesis of Latino rhythms with rock guitar virtuosity has proven inspirational for numerous artists. These musical samples suggest a celebration of cultural difference and affirm those elements of distinction by weaving and reweaving familiar melodies and rhythms in the hip-hop styling of the early 1990s. This mestizaje on a musical level affirms the racial and linguistic mixture that characterizes Chicano and other Latino cultures in the United States.

The sonic interaction is one of play and celebration as Kid Frost, ALT, and Mellow Man Ace take turns rapping about the joys of cruising along the boulevard: "Kicking back and yo I'm soaring like an eagle / Frost in a Jeep and Ralph ends in a Regal / We're looking at the fine ladies bumping the fresh tapes / Seeing the sparks from my car when the frame scrapes." By reveling in heterosexual courtship, flirtation, car culture—backed by some quintessential mid-1970s Chicano music—Latin Alliance sonically reconfigures a space of familiarity and celebration, asserting a recognition and affirmation of lived daily practices within the Chicano/Latino community.

This sonic reconfiguration, however, significantly asserts the primacy of the male gaze, affirms only a hypermasculinized and predatory perspective. It is significant to note that much of the Chicano music scene is dominated by male figures, male voices, male perspectives. Perhaps this is why the issues of power that run along axes of gender and sexuality do not come under critical scrutiny in much of the music. As with the lyrics in "Lowrider (On the Boulevard)," the scene often evoked by Chicano hip-hop is viewed from the privileged perspective of the masculinized Latino eye. In granting to the male viewer the agency both to move enjoyably through an urban landscape and to form community with other male Latinos, the songs occlude a female perspective. While the song's sampling evokes music linked to the formation of a newly politicized and socially active Chicano community, the lyrics write a problematic and predictable script. They manifest a hypermasculine gaze privileging male control and heterosexual identifications.[11]

When it comes to power in relation to national and economic—as opposed to gender—relations, a number of Latin Alliance's productions produce a strong counternarrative. For example, "Runnin'" addresses the dilemma of undocumented immigrants maneuvering through the militarized Mexico–U.S. border zone. Over an energized beat, the song samples actual radio communication between border-patrol agents as they track down Latinos crossing into U.S. territory. The tape is chilling in its clearly militarized tones. A mechanized voice calls for assistance in apprehending suspects: "Hello, zero-niner, I'm in chopper one, I need help. I need assistance, I need assistance right now. I got about twenty heading toward the border right about now." In juxtaposition to these heated calls for help, the coldly officious tone of the Immigration and Naturalization Service (INS) answering machine ("To find out how to report illegal aliens, or employers of illegal aliens, dial 6 now") forms a counterpoint. Adding a third element to the mix, Kid Frost's voice forges a vestigial countermemory:

Let's go back into history.
It's not much of a mystery.
The Indians run for the mountains and hills
As the white man hunts and kills.
Murder in the first degree today
But way back when it was okay.
What they teach in school is the dumbest,
And don't talk no shit about Christopher Columbus.

The melding of these voices highlights the contested position of the mestizo within contemporary society. The official governmental discourse about undocumented migrants, the discourse of a militarized police state, and the countermemory linking today's violence against mestizos with historical genocide all combine to signal how the mestizo body is incessantly inscribed with meaning. Certainly, the mestizo does not solely represent a free-floating agent of deterritorialization, nor do the mobile and multiple registers of mestizaje represent a kind of assured stability. Rather, mestizaje becomes at once both a source of repression and a locus of reclamation and resistance.

The sense of affirmation and resistance evident in the mix of Latin Alliance parallels how mestizaje is thematized as a racial reality and a source of personal pride. On "What Is an American?" ALT raps over samples from "Heartbeat" by War and "On Your Face" by Earth Wind and Fire, affirming the nexus of racial and cultural mestizaje that has led to Latino culture:

Two, now it's three flowing together,
It's Hispanic and French blood,
Create a lyrical flood.
Latin Alliance band together to speak out
For those who are afraid, you should stand up and shriek out:
"I'm proud!"

The mixing of French, Spanish, and indigenous blood becomes the locus for pride in mestizaje as well as the font for the "lyrical flood" that ALT's rap best represents. Blood as an index of racial and cultural identity coalesces through the lyrics in an affirmation of a hybrid self. The lyrical flood that rushes forth becomes a wellspring of pride and a call for alliance politics. The meditation on personal identity inflected by cultural, racial, and political power produces an affirmative and assertive consciousness. ALT raps:

> Call me a wetback then get back,
> Better yet open your mind and set back.
> And just think about it,
> Homeboy, what are you dumb?
> If you're not Indian then where did your family come from?

The rapper calls for a rejection of pejorative names and their link to discriminatory behavior. The lyrics directly challenge the listener to consider the indigenous ancestry of his or her own Latino identity. As with Kid Frost, the lyrics call up a community identity based on common descent and common cause. In this case, the rapper calls on his audience to consider dominant and pejorative constructions of racial and ethnic identity.

The song calls for reclaiming racial pride and rejecting a disempowered sense of identity. The call for an affirming self-identity sets up the song's didactic lesson:

> 'Cause I feel freedom is golden,
> No border patrollin'
> The land that you stand on is stolen.
> Word up, yo, I'm saying it loud
> Every Hispanic in the crowd stay proud.

The evocation of stolen land refers both to the European invasion of indigenous lands and U.S. imperial expansion. In rejecting the militarization of the border and the military invasion of Native lands, the rap offers both a well-worn critique common to Chicano critical discourses and a reason to take pride in the right of "every Hispanic in the crowd" to claim a place in U.S. society. The racial and cultural mestizaje that helps demarcate *latinidad* works to dissolve and transgress national boundaries. Racial mixture becomes a locus for the transformation of cultural and national borders, serving as a central trope in rethinking ideas of place and the nature of belonging.

## A Premillennial Funk

As the work of both Latin Alliance and Cypress Hill illustrates, the issues of racial and cultural identification become more complex in the increasingly inmixed world that a multiethnic, multiracial location such as Los Angeles represents.[12] For this reason, three Los Angeles bands that released albums in mid-1996—Delinquent Habits, Rage Against the Machine, and Los Lobos—offer illuminating examples of how notions and strategies of mestizaje resonated through Chicano music at the end of the millennium.

In their four releases—*Delinquent Habits* (1996), *Here Come the Horns* (1998), *Merry Go Round* (2001), and *Freedom Band* (2003)—the multiracial rap group Delinquent Habits makes it a point to highlight the hybrid nature of their cultural and racial identities. The group, composed of rappers Ives, Kemo the Blaxican, and deejay O. G. Style, employs code-switching and bilingualism as both their linguistic and personal identities are brought to the fore. In the single "Tres Delinquentes" from their first CD, executive-produced by Cypress Hill's Sea Dog, the rappers trade off busting rhymes, interweaving Spanish and caló, English and street slang:

¿Qué hondas muchacho? Hay vienes, te miro.
Si me traes bronca me aloco de atiro.
Me paro, te tombo, no es tu rumbo.
Y con el lingo tal vez te confundo.

[What's up, dude? You're coming, I see you.
If you bring trouble I get mad crazy.
I stand up, I hit you, this isn't your neighborhood.
And with my lingo maybe I confuse you.]

> Shifts the attack with the five foot ten
> The blaxican once again with the cocktail pin
> As I emerge from the depths of the realm my son
> I got the black gat, fat track, coke and rum.

The linguistic mestizaje of the rap serves to distinguish and establish a linguistically initiated audience. Thematically, the rhymes do little more than assert the supremacy of the rapper over an imagined adversary. However, there is an interesting elision between the linguistic and racial mestizaje addressed in the song:

> Otra vez ya lo ves en the crew somos tres [Once again in the crew we
>     are three]
> One blaxican on the squad you don't test
> Sitting hard like an Aztec, swift like a Zulu
> That's what it's like when the pump shot through you.

The multiracial background of the "blaxican" Kemo is thematized in the rhymes and romanticized through the iconic images of the hard Aztec and the swift Zulu. The rap represents an acknowledgment of the complicated interracial and multiracial relationships that have helped develop the diverse societies and cultures of the Americas (and again hold up a masculinized identity as an ideal subjectivity). In these passages the song addresses the ways mestizo cultures and societies come to terms with the cultural significance of multiple racial identities.

Although the song offers a thematic engagement with a different aspect of contemporary racial and cultural mestizaje, formally "Tres Delinquentes" employs predictable sampling techniques that reflect the blank parody of postmodern pastiche.[13] Drawing on "The Lonely Bull" recorded by Herb Alpert & the Tijuana Brass, Delinquent Habits invokes a simulacrum of Latino music, a shadow of mariachi music, a sanitized version of pleasant melodies with a slight tinge of ethnic flavor. Despite Herb Alpert's popularity at one moment, he has not enjoyed the kind of iconic stature and cultural identification as, say, War, Earth Wind and Fire, or Carlos Santana.[14]

The musical simulacrum finds its correlative in the video produced for the promotion of "Tres Delinquentes." To the trumpeting of "The Lonely Bull," the video opens by panning a set that evokes the atmosphere of an over-the-top Sergio Leone spaghetti western. Absurdly, the trio strolls through the dusty streets of a seemingly abandoned town while mustachioed *bandidos* and menacing soldiers look on. The video references clichéd images of desperate Mexican bandits chomping on cigarillos and dusty revolutionary soldiers crossed by bandoliers and clutching wood-handled rifles. It makes the song part of a cultural fun house involving endless quotation and dissociated references. The video's images do not form a dialogue with the song's lyrics but, rather, evoke stereotyped images of Mexicans created through cheaply produced mass-appeal films. In short, the visual and musical production represents typically uncritical postmodern play. Although Delinquent Habit's lyrics thematize multivalent racial identities as integral to contemporary U.S. social experience, their musical and visual representations engender an affirmative and uncritical cultural mestizaje. The cultural product, at least at this early point in their career, affirms a process of commodification and racial fetish rather than asserting a historical and cultural context for its discussion of multiracial, multiethnic self-identification.[15]

By contrast, Rage Against the Machine (though now disbanded) offers a particularly critical and politically conscious form of musical mestizaje. Lead singer Zack de la Rocha uses his lyrics to assert his Chicano identity and identify with numerous Third World struggles.[16] The sound created by the band on its four albums—*Rage Against the Machine* (1993), *Evil Empire* (1996), *The Battle of Los Angeles* (1999), and *Renegade* (2000)—is a cross between rap and speed metal. This rap metal sound, pioneered by Rage, represents a hybrid musical form that grew to be extremely popular and influential in the 1990s. The music creates a driving sonic beat over which de la Rocha spits anti-imperialist and anticapitalist rants about resistance to repressive authority.[17]

Exhibiting an intense mixing of musical, cultural, and political influences, Rage Against the Machine, unlike many hip-hop bands, does not use samples, keyboards, or synthesizers in creating the sonic bombardment that roils behind de la Rocha's defiant lyrics. Tom Morello creates complex scratching and wailing sounds via effects on his guitar, a fact that harks back to the stylings of rock-and-roll guitar heroes such as Jimi Hendrix, Eric Clapton, and Jimmy Page. The influence of rock as performance melds with the influence of hip-hop and its emphasis on heavy aural experimentation.

Against the funk bass and sonic distortion of electric guitar, de la Rocha articulates a sharp political critique against continued economic and cultural imperial power of the U.S. government. "People of the Sun" on *Evil Empire* provides an excellent example:

> Since 1516 minds attacked and overseen
> Now crawl amidst the ruins of this empty dream
> With their borders and boots on top of us
> Pulling knobs on the floor of their toxic metropolis.
> So how you gonna get what you need to get?
> The gut eaters, blood drenched get offensive like Tet.
> When the fifth sun sets, get back, reclaim
> The spirit of Cuauhtémoc alive and untamed.
> Face the funk now blasting out ya speaker, one to one Maya, Mexica.
> That vulture came to try and steal your name, but now you found a gun.
> This is for the people of the sun,
> It's coming back around again,
> This is for the people of the sun.

As with other Chicano music, the lyrics formulate a type of counter-memory. They construe a particularly resistant history meant to critique and reflect on contemporary ills perceived through a historical prism. In many ways, this strategy reflects the kind of historical reconstruction undertaken by so-called nationalist Chicano poetry of the 1960s and 1970s. The rhetoric of rebellion, the critique of colonial dispossession, the claims for indigenous rights, the invocation of pre-Cortesian imagery, and the convergence of Third World struggles come together in the lyrics that are set against a barrage of funk bass lines and industrial guitar wailing.

The imagery of the "knobs on the floor of their toxic metropolis" draws upon the familiar Chicano trope that envisions industrialized capitalism as the source for a mechanistic and sterile U.S. society. Against the consuming and violent order of "borders and boots," a new spiritual world is born out of the setting of the "fifth sun." The allusion to the fifth sun references the Mexica belief that ours is the fifth time the gods have created the world. Just as with the previous four, it is destined to be destroyed in a cataclysmic event. Again, the evocation of Aztec apocalyptic destruction and spiritual rebirth is a common referent in Chicano cultural discourse.

Many of the band's critics note the discrepancy between such radical political commentary and the role the band plays as a part of the contemporary culture industry; which is to say, its critics suggest that the band may claim a voice, but it does not manifest agency, against the economic forces that surround it.[18] Guitarist Tom Morello—a Harvard graduate with a political science major—does not avoid the contradictions inherent in the way Rage circulates its music. Speaking on behalf of the band, he argues that, "given the injustices perpetrated by our economic system, we have no choice but to talk about them. . . . For the time being, just letting people know that confrontation is okay is a worthwhile exercise. That's something we do every night and on every record sold" (Smith 1993, 10). Through mass marketing, Rage Against the Machine could disseminate a political message encouraging action and involvement to audiences it might not otherwise reach. The efficacy of such a strategy for political involvement remains ambiguous. Nevertheless, such negotiations through the belly of the transnational corporate beast may be a way politically conscious artists can articulate a complicitous critique of the systems in which they find themselves.[19] Such negotiation may reveal some of the contestatory strategies artists involved with corporate marketing can employ to make counterdiscourse possible in a postmodern cultural context.

It would be too tedious to recount the ways in which discussions about postmodernism and politics have played themselves out. As is well known, either postmodernism is the death of political action through the co-optation of all resistant impulses and actions, or it enables a more effective, decentered, and insidious form of political activism. Rather than perform such well-rehearsed debates, what the study of contemporary Chicano music explores is the way critical consciousness articulates itself through specific cultural forms. As Philip Bohlman notes, "The arguments for resistance, post-colonial discourse, and subaltern voices are already in the musics that surround us, and we ignore them only by not listening to them" (1993, 435). Chicano music forms a space in contemporary culture where a critical dialogue about the nature and shape of American consciousness continues to develop. It creates this space by deploying notions of racial and cultural mestizaje—a mestizaje that already represents an overdetermined trope within the production of Chicano/a culture. Rather than simply replay all-too-common moves in relation to mestizaje, Chicano musicians redeploy it on both a formal and thematic level in order to question the role of cultural and personal identity.

The incessant sonic assault employed by Rage emblematizes the urgency of this interrogation. The convergence of rap, hip-hop, speed metal, political commentary, and industrial noise driven by a heavy bass beat represents a form of aural mestizaje different than that offered by more conventional forms of Chicano rap. The contradictions inherent in the production and distribution of the music created by Rage indicate the ways Chicano music moves into new cultural, social, and creative territory.

The move beyond established boundaries evident in Rage's music is undertaken with equal delight and equal innovation by that standard-bearer of mestizo music, Los Lobos. The band began its recording career with the 1978 independent release of acoustic Mexican music, *Just Another Band from East L.A.* Its first three albums—*. . . And a Time to Dance* (1983), *How Will the Wolf Survive?* (1984), and *By the Light of the Moon* (1987)—blend rhythm and blues, rock and roll, country and western, as well as *rancheras, norteños,* and *conjunto* music in an adventurous and very accessible musical style. The 1987 sound track *La Bamba,* the quite distinct *La Pistola y el Corazón* (1988), and the more sonically innovative *The Neighborhood* (1990) and *Kiko* (1992) indicate the ways the band fuses diverse musical influences and styles to create a compelling and critically acclaimed musical art.

Stylistically, a significant shift occurred in 1994 as the main songwriting team, guitarist David Hidalgo and percussionist Louie Pérez, undertook a side project. Working with Los Lobos' producers Mitchell Froom and Tchad Blake, they created a musically experimental group under the name Latin Playboys. Colored as much by mariachi music as by avant-garde jazz (Louie Pérez warmly embraces the improvisational work of Roland Kirk and John Coltrane), their albums—*Latin Playboys* (1994) and *Dose* (1999)—move among a wide variety of musical references. The songs range from the Puerto Rican *plena* heard in the rhythm of "Same Brown Earth" to the bolero stylings of "Manifold de Amor." The move toward greater experimentation with and a dislocation of influences shifts away from a reliance on sources specifically marked as ethnic or Third World. Rather than mining familiar sources for an affirmation of identity, this move reflects a greater challenge to the substance of mestizaje. As Louie Pérez explained on the release of the Latin Playboy's first album, "We don't even know what our own Chicano fans will think about it, because it really stretches the definition of what Chicanos should do" (García 1994, H27).

Over dissonant horns, clanging bells, an inverted Afro-Latin rhythm, and an indigenous drumbeat, David Hidalgo sings on "Same Brown Earth": "When woman was a rock / On distant mountaintop / When woman was like that / Reflecting like the moon." On the one hand, the sense of mysticism and pre-Cortesian imagery connects the song to a well-established repertoire of Chicano cultural iconography. On the other hand, the musical references are surprising and the experimentation with electronic distortion, squawking guitar, and clanging and banging percussion presents a challenging aural experience. These songs challenge some notions of what Chicano music should be, and it is clear where the band members stand in this regard. Louie Pérez views the move as a logical progression in a culture that is based so profoundly on notions of mestizaje: "Chicanos are like antennas. . . . We have all this information. We pick up all these different stations, and it blurs into one thing, and that's the Chicano experience" (ibid.). This blurring represents an evolving sense of cultural hybridity as a hallmark of Chicano culture.

In 1996 Hidalgo and Pérez returned to Los Lobos to release *Colossal Head*, an album that reflects the experimentalism of the Latin Playboys. The song "Marisela" calls on the *plena* to provide a driving rhythm over which César Rosas sings a paean to Puerto Rico ("Allí en la isla del encanto / Orgulloso yo les canto / Con sus sierras y sus santos / Y un placer a mí me ha dado [There in the land of enchantment / Proud I sing to you / With its mountains and its saints / And a pleasure it has given me]").[20] A mid-tempo jam absurdly called "Buddy Ebsen Loves the Night Time" swings through a traditional three-chord blues progression and allows David Hidalgo to repeat and improvise on a distorted guitar riff. The album as a whole weaves together sonic distortion, stuttering guitars, funk rhythms, references to traditional African American, Latin American, and Latino musical traditions, as well as the odd, accidental, or improvisational moments such as coughs, gurgling PVC tubes, police sirens, and random street noise.

Analogously, the song lyrics often emphasize the comic, the absurd, and the surreal. On the loose and bluesy "Manny's Bones," for example, David Hidalgo sings:

Manny's dead and didn't leave me nothing.
Went off to heaven, left his bed undone.
Gone away, he didn't leave us sad.
The dogs are all wondering where their daddy went, oh my.

"Don't go leave me here by myself.
Won't hear me calling when you all done left.
Guess I didn't make it out this time.
But I'll be waiting on the other side, bye-bye."

Way down in Manny's bones
The dry old river and a dusty soul
We'll take him to the fishing hole
And let the water take him to his home.

The use of blank and near rhymes creates a sense of unease juxtaposed against the relatively structured musical framework of honky-tonk pianos and honking baritone saxophones. The lyrics allude to traditional blues songs about death and mourning but shift the content enough to highlight the incommensurable. Mestizaje here represents less an affirmation of an established historical or racial identity and becomes instead the site of transformation, a borderlands with an emphasis on the what may yet be, not the what already is at hand.

Throughout *Colossal Head* there is a mixture of the familiar with the defamiliarizing. This thematization of unease is struck in the first cut, "Revolution." The song is a meditation on the failed revolutionary practices that Rage Against the Machine so staunchly affirms. The song proves finally to be a touching questioning of youthful illusion:

Where did it go?
Can't say that I know
Those times of revolution.
The burning burning burning
All so cool and gone
What was just was.

We try my brother
To hold on to our faith
But was it late for revolution
Too tired, too tired sister
To hold my fist so high
Now that it's gone.

Where the questioning of revolutionary change takes place on a thematic level, on a musical and cultural level there is an insistence on change, on transformation, on affirming revolution as a turn, not an overthrow. Los Lobos help to make that turn by inviting their auditors into a space that reexamines terms of mestizaje on a political and (most potently) a cultural level. If Chicano music is characterized by its deployment of mestizaje as an affirming and resistant strategy, as a way of giving meaning to Chicano racial identity, then Los Lobos amplify this strategy as their songs engage on a sonic and discursive level with what mestizaje— what meaning itself—means.

### The New Lyrical Drive-by

As a coda to this chapter, I would like to underscore that the fluidity of musical—indeed, all cultural creation—prohibits closure to the term "Chicano music." The ground beneath one's feet shifts with every step. To view music as a semiotic system informed by racial discourse leads one into the treacherous terrain of identity and identification. A group such as the Los Angeles rap group Aztlan Underground highlights these difficulties. It melds indigenous instrumentation, rap rhythms and images ("This is a lyrical drive-by, / so hit the ground, / don't make a sound / and watch the truth fly. / I got the rage, / I got the rage, / I got the rage / to pump the twelve-gauge"), statements recorded by the Zapatista Sub-comandante Marcos ("Ser Zapatista es buscar una nueva forma de vida y una nueva forma de relacionarse [To be Zapatista is to look for a new way of living and relating]"), and Nahuatl incantations ("Intonan / Intotah / Tlatecuhtli / Tonatiuh / For our mother / our father / the earth / and the sun"). The numerous political and musical references suggest a movement through national, transnational, and international spaces. Tellingly, disparate identity formations associated with these locales are all brought together in hopes of achieving a revolutionary, critical position.

Likewise, the group Ozomatli reveals a concern for transnational issues both political and cultural. A multiracial group living in Los Angeles, its songs move among and mix North American hip-hop, Central American *cumbia*, Puerto Rican salsa, Dominican merengue, Spanish flamenco, Argentine tango, and Mexican mariachi. The group's song "Como Ves," from its self-titled first album, borrows South African guitar riffs, Brazilian samba beats (complete with *surdo* drums and whistles), and lyrics that declare transnational connectivity:

> Como ves, como ves
> La historia no es como crees.
> Como ves, como ves
> Cuba y África, soy hermano
> con todo mi corazón.
> Cuba y África, soy hermano
> y veo su dolor.
> Quiero besar su espíritu
> y su alma.

> As you see, as you see
> history is not what you believe.
> As you see, as you see

Cuba and Africa, I am your brother
with all my heart.
Cuba and Africa, I am your brother
and I see your pain.
I want to kiss your spirit
and your soul.

The group invokes a Third World alliance, suggesting a new cultural and political geography. Drawing together the locations of an African diasporic experience, the song revels in the emotional and political connections between culturally consonant but geographically disparate sites. The group's work responds to transnational globalism by highlighting the political and cultural relations forged from diasporic conditions. Its lyrics evoke connectivity and relation in the face of a dominant history that seeks to erase these cultural and political connections.

The face of Chicano music continues to undergo a profound transformation as the Latino population in the United States—and in traditionally Chicano communities—comes to be more and more diverse in terms of national origin and identification. The continued flows and fluxes of transnational movements signal an ever-shifting musical landscape. With the growing success of Rock en Español, the increased exchange of musical commodities across national and cultural borders, the proliferation and diversification of music and music video programming in all countries and continents, the term "Chicano music" seems somewhat antiquated. At the 1999 Cinco de Mayo festivities in Los Angeles, for example, the live entertainment was composed of bands that mixed, matched, and melded numerous musical influences: Tejano, *cumbia*, *ranchera*, *norteño*, *banda*, merengue, and salsa. A programming director for a Latino radio station in Los Angeles—where Spanish-language radio has a greater market share than its English-language counterparts—commented on the diverse lineup: "There's a demand for different kinds of music. There's a lot of crossover in styles now that you didn't have before" (Valdes-Rodriguez 1999, F1). This crossover, this mestizaje, may very well mark the end to one phase of Chicano musical development.

Or perhaps this increased mixture signals the bright note that

Chicano music has always sought to strike, a note that resounds with the ideals of inclusion, transformation, critique, and affirmation. It would be impossible to characterize inclusively the broad spectrum of Chicano musical expression. Equally, it is impossible to miss the vitality and urgency infusing that expression. In part, this vitality arises from the racialized imaginary of Chicano and Mexican populations. Although its production is dominated by male actors, there emerges in the music the recognition that a broad conceptualization of mestizaje can be both a liberating process and one inscribed by tremendous political, social, and cultural conflict. The music highlights a double movement connecting culture to a troubled history and affirming its liberatory inspiration. This marks one node of possibility made evident by a critical mestizaje.

# CHAPTER 4

# Land and Race in Chicano Public Art

The elision of racial imagery with images of the land often highlights is-sues of mestizaje, identity, and (dis)placement in Chicana/o culture. The present chapter focuses on the role land and place play in Chicana public art as part of the visual articulation of mestizo/a subjectivity.[1] Through an examination of Chicano poster art in California, some of the contours shaping the complex relationship between identity and geography come into focus. While referencing a sense of displacement and dislocation as part of identification, the art also calls up images of land that evoke a mes-tizo subjectivity engaged in the revision of political, social, and economic struggle. The art envisions both a present displacement and an antici-pated re-placement of the mestiza body. In this respect, the relationship between land and mestizo/a selves proves to be an elemental aspect of Chicano culture.

In many ways, land lies at the heart of the Chicano movement. The United Farm Workers (UFW) campaign, beginning in the 1960s, to unionize the fields fostered political and social changes for Chicanas and Chicanos, changes felt to this day. Although the roots for these changes run through the entire history of Mexicans in the United States, contem-porary Chicano consciousness traces its development through the farm workers' struggle as it helped give form and voice to the fight against long-felt injustices. The continued exploitation of cheap Mexican migrant labor met up with labor struggles and civil rights movements arising in the

1950s and 1960s. As a rejuvenated jolt of ethnic and racial consciousness raced across the nation, Chicano activists found fertile soil in which to nurture a new sense of Chicano/a social, political, and cultural identity. Part of this process involved communities of Mexican descent activating against the persistent discrimination and prejudices long a part of the American landscape.

## The Ruptured Territory of Public Art

For Chicano communities, this American landscape is marked by the legacy of U.S. imperial adventures during the nineteenth century. Although marginalized by mainstream historical accounts, the term "America" used to refer to the United States and the word "American" to refer to its citizens are vestiges of these nineteenth-century (mis)adventures. A historical memory of them is not lost on communities weaned on tales of Anglo-American invasion and exploitation. The land to the north of Mexico represents not an alien, but a misappropriated, territory in the Mexican national imaginary.

It is not surprising, then, that the appropriation of Mexican territory by an imperial United States has served to mark the birth of Chicano (more properly, at that point, "Mexican American") culture. The year 1848 represents Mexican national rupture, when the land was divided and a new historical subject—the Mexican American—was born into a landscape of dispossession. Indeed, there is an inextricable connection between land and the Chicano body. As was discussed in chapter 1, the mestizo body became racialized as the imperial project of manifest destiny came to fruition in the latter half of the nineteenth century. The (dis)possession of land and the racial (dis)identification of the mestizo form an integral nexus in the formation of Chicano subjectivity. The moment the United States came to possess Mexican lands was the moment people of Mexican descent began to undergo an ideological realignment of identity.

Whereas 1848 marks the geopolitical inception of what would become Chicano identity, it has been observed that "the more contemporary date of 1965 is significant as a *symbolic spiritual rebirth* or resurgence. That year the Teatro Campesino joined the social struggle of La Causa with César Chávez. Literature and social reality converged in an inseparable entity" (Lomelí 1984, 105). This convergence of the social and aesthetic (along with the historical and political) led to numerous explosions of literary, musical, and visual artistic production that came to form the body of what is now Chicano culture.

The year 1965 also marked the moment when the idea of a politicized Chicano consciousness broke out into the open. Héctor Calderón notes that as a result of the UFW strike of the lettuce fields in Delano, California, many students "rallied and joined forces with farm workers on the picket lines. This turned out to be a decisive moment, for it was the youth, high school, and university students who were to give these regional events the sense of a broad social movement" (1990, 218). Much of the art examined in this chapter either emerged directly as a result of this fertile social tumult or in some manner reflect (or reflect upon) its spirit of political resistance and construction of historical memory.

One might say, then, that Chicano consciousness was born on September 16, 1965: that day a vote was taken by the NFWA (National Farm Workers Association, later the UFW) led by César Chávez to join the Filipino grape pickers' strike.[2] This moment of ethnic and political coalition represented a coming together in common cause, a recognition of a shared struggle—intimately linked to land and labor—that ignited what came to be known as the Chicano movement.

As one of its first acts, the group undertook a 250-mile pilgrimage to Sacramento during which "El Plan de Delano" was issued as a call to action and an explanation of the farmworkers' cause. In part, the plan reads: "Our sweat and our blood have fallen on this land to make other men rich. This pilgrimage is a witness to the suffering we have seen for generations" ("Plan de Delano" 1973, 197). The force, energy, and earnestness that compelled the farmworkers to march to Sacramento seem to explode in the images and colors of the first Chicano poster artists who took up visual expression to foster community activism and political intervention. Activism and intervention prove a strong catalyst for the artistic production evident in much Chicano public art, and lie at the heart of much poster art. This art is propelled by the sociopolitical explosion (and all its echoes and repercussions) sparked by one simple labor vote in the dusty fields of Delano.

The year 1965, then, represented an opportunity to address and redress the decades of rancor, injustice, and discontent evoked by 1848. As Rafael Jesús González explains:

> It would appear that 1965 was the year in which Chicanismo . . . was born. This was the year of two extremely important events for the Chicano Movement. During 1965, U.S. intervention in Vietnam unmasked itself as an atrocious war in which the Chicano saw reflections of the United States invasion of Mexico. Also in that year, the workers in the vineyards of Delano declared themselves on strike under the leadership of César Chávez and the banner of Our Lady of Guadalupe. These two historical events were sufficiently strong enough to congeal the political and cultural disquiet and hopes of the people of Mexican descent into a movement with a sense of its uniqueness—it called itself Chicano. (1977, 132)

González's analysis helps make clear how the idea of historical memory—most significantly, a memory of invasion and colonization—informs Chicana/o cultural and ethnic identity. These historical and political connections make present in Chicana cultural expression a recollection of the past, a memory kept alive in order to understand the inequity and struggle of a people historically made, by both popular perception and public policy, into a permanent underclass. Chicano public art often seeks to serve as the articulation and representation of historical memory.

For example, images of Mexican national heroes such as Pancho Villa (Figure 1) and Emiliano Zapata (Figure 2) appear again and again as icons imbricated in a historical memory meant to evoke national pride, cultural distinction, political resistance, and a sense of shared community. Similarly, heroes of the Mexican Revolution appear in order to foster a sense of historical connection and recollection of resistance to unjust persecution (Figure 3). Of course, these images offer a double valence. On the one hand, they evoke a Mexican national identity, and thus suggest that there can exist such a thing as a Chicano national character. On the other hand, they invoke the dream of liberation, the hope for a process of empowerment in which land across the Americas can be returned to those who claim rightful ownership: the indigenous, the farmworker, the campesino, the people.

Figure 1. *Viva Villa* (Long Live Villa) by Manuel Cruz (1977) illustrates the use of Mexican national iconography, here as part of a calendar series.

Tere Romo discusses the changing iconography found in Chicano poster art as it undertakes a variety of projects. Initially, she notes, the art began by "visually articulating the Chicano movement's political stance, [although] it also had as a central goal the formation and affirmation of a Chicano cultural identity. In visualizing this new identity, artists became

Figure 2. *Rifa* (1972) by Leonard Castellanos depicts a powerful and somewhat roman-ticized image of Emiliano Zapata. *Rifa* is slang indicating a sense of power or supremacy.

part of a cultural reclamation process to reintroduce Mexican art and history, revitalize popular artistic expressions, and support community cultural activities" (2001, 100).[3] Thus the formation of Chicano public art played a dynamic role in the social formation of Chicano public life.

At the same time, Chicano poster art has followed its own aes-thetic development. The art not only reveals a desire to create a his-

Figure 3. Rodolfo "Rudy" O. Cuellar, *Celebración de independencia de 1810* (Celebration of the 1810 Independence) (1978). Four of the heroes from the struggle for Mexican independence from Spain appear juxtaposed against a hemispheric map of North, Central, and South America to announce a celebration on Sunday, September 17. Note that the raffling of a 1965 Chevy Impala is used as a main draw to the event. Used by permission of the artist.

torical memory and foster a political consciousness, but also works at developing an aesthetic sensibility that seeks to delineate new identities and possibilities. There has been a tension in the development of art and culture identified as Chicano. This tension turns on debates about the social function of art and the individual interest in aesthetics and expression. Within discussions of art's function—particularly in relation to early considerations of Chicano identity—it was often thought that the more an artist manifested interest in aesthetic questions, the more she separated herself from the social, historical, and political concerns that have so strongly informed Chicano/a consciousness.[4] This is, of course, a false opposition between aesthetics and politics, one that could lead to a critical impoverishment in our understanding of Chicano art. The significance of the poster in this art is the manner in which it foregrounds the intersection of Chicano public life with aesthetic creation. The poster has played a role as both an aesthetic object and a sociopolitical tool by which to transform the reality of Chicano/a communities. By its very nature a hybrid cultural formation, poster art decisively links the aesthetic to the political.

The divorce of the aesthetic from material and social considerations has led to a devaluation of Chicano art as worth less than mainstream, putatively apolitical art.[5] Chicano art—in particular public art, and especially poster art—foregrounds how art emerges from a complex interplay of sociopolitical forces. Thus the art makes clear how its production is dependent on social and political networks and dynamics, manifesting a simultaneous interest in aesthetic and material interventions.

A closer examination of poster art offers interesting insight into debates over the public function of art. When considering the poster as aesthetic expression, it is clear that although projects of cultural and personal affirmation partly drove its production, the art does not simply reiterate well-worn patterns of self-identification. Poster art challenges itself on formal and thematic levels as it reflects the varying needs of personal expression, community building, social identity, and aesthetic experimentation. As producers and critics of Chicano public art wrestle with the demands made by these various forces, they intervene in a reworking of the relationship between self, society, and aesthetics.

In large measure, this is because the poster as a public form of visual art conveys a desire for social and community connection. Chon Noriega writes: "The poster exists somewhere between the unique art object and the mass media. It lends the formal qualities of both in order to reach an audience neither cares about: urban exiles in search of community. As such, the poster's message is inherently complicated, making the poster ideally suited to the Chicano experience" (2001b, 23). Chicano poster art engages the very public discourses of cultural identity, political activism, and social purpose. It addresses and forges a community out of exiles, representing complex systems of meaning and forming an inherently hybrid artistic expression. It also forges a sense of aesthetic immediacy. The production of the poster is often generated by the immediacy of a pressing sociopolitical event: a protest, a celebration, a fund-raiser, a community meeting.

During and after the zenith of the Chicano movement, Karen Mary Davalos notes, artists chose public art forms as a preferred method of aesthetic expression. She addresses how public art challenges established distinctions about the function of art: "Though artists experimented with a range of forms, during the height of the Movimiento, many chose media—such as the mural, poster, flyer, and leaflet—that allowed them to publicly proclaim a Chicano position on local politics while rejecting notions of 'high' or 'fine' art" (2001, 67). As an aesthetic form, the poster stands somewhere between the public monumentality of a mural and the evanescent immediacy of the leaflet. Unlike a flyer or a leaflet, the poster often suggests a certain aesthetic permanency. Unlike the mural, it reflects an immediacy in both form and, more centrally, content. As a form of public expression, it seeks to forge a sense of Chicano/a community and identity. And it marks a peculiarly significant break with modernism and the aesthetic of the avant-garde.[6] Andreas Huyssen's comments about postmodernism and its break with critical distinctions of "fine" and "popular" art seem appropriate here: "it is precisely the recent self-assertion of minority cultures and their emergence into public consciousness which has undermined the modernist belief that high and low culture have to be categorically kept apart; such rigorous segregation simply does not make much sense *within* a given minority culture which has always existed outside in the shadow of the dominant culture" (1984, 23). Artistic forms created by communities of color challenge the manner in which high art is often understood as for and by dominant culture.

In this sense, the poster—rejecting elitist notions of high against popular art—engages the very pressing issues of art's relationship to its society and political environment. The Chicano poster is premised on a connection between the aesthetic and the evocation of community. As well, it asserts a connection between the mixed-race body and the conflicted history that has produced its contemporary geographies. The breakdown between high and low is undertaken in the service of community formation and the articulation of identity. This process redefines the contours and significance of those geographies. The coalescence of land and body is part of a new visioning of identity and subjectivity that drives much Chicano art.[7]

Both Noriega and Davalos address the nature of Chicano public art as a hybrid artistic expression breaking down boundaries between the fine and the popular in addition to producing connections between the self and the community. It locates subjectivities in history as they attempt to define public space according to new racial and ethnic configurations. In this way, land becomes a central concern as a site of public space. Land in all its different significances returns again and again in the works of Chicano/a public art: land as national border, land as militarized frontier, land as political front line, land as the guarantor of citizenship. Land becomes a fictional figment that at once separates the "Us" of the U.S. from the dark Other and yet encompasses both Us and Other. The work of the poster is to reenvision this fictional figment, making of it something not exclusive but encompassing. It seeks to reenvision land not as the grounds for exclusion but as the basis on which to forge connection and community. The thematic and strategic concerns of Chicano public art are to redefine the significance of land and, in the process, transform the public spaces mestizo bodies occupy.

*E.L.A. apoya a César Chávez* by Armando Cabrera (Figure 4) provides an excellent example of this reconfiguration. This poster stands out because it is a historical expression of progressive labor policies and a cultural representation of two very different but conjoined geographies. The poster employs stark, monochromatic red and black—colors representative of the UFW. This evocation of the UFW fosters a sense of

Figure 4. *E.L.A. apoya a César Chávez* (East L.A. supports César Chávez) (1972) by Armando E. Cabrera reflects the often political nature of poster art. Although it misspells Chávez's first name, the poster is clearly meant to serve as an organizing tool for the UFW. Used by permission of the artist.

Chicano community—here indexed by East L.A.—within a landscape of alienated farm labor and the struggle for unionization. The bottom half of the poster thus asserts a pro-labor, antibusiness proclamation: "Abajo los Republicanos" (Down with the Republicans). This marks a reaction to Republican politicians who worked against the unionization efforts of the UFW in the interest of large agribusiness concerns. In a bit of obvious symbolism, the stolid eagle of the UFW consumes the (racially significant) white elephant of the Republican Party. In its beak, the eagle carries the elephant by the tail as if it were a dead rat.

Graffiti lettering that might be scrawled along a barrio wall spatially dominates the poster. *Placas* mark identity and territory, forming—for those who can decipher their meanings—a simultaneous public broadcast and self-advertisement.[8] Visually, the poster draws together two disputed geographies, urban and rural, barrio and field: sites where contemporary Chicano social and political activism took root in the mid-1960s. The poster recasts two quite distinct physical localities in order to forge something new: a political consciousness that envisions land in its relation to community in transformative and empowering ways. The poster seeks to generate support for the work of the UFW and César Chávez as part of a geographic realignment affirming Calderón's observation that regional events granted a sense of broad social change during the Chicano movement.

## Prison House of Landscapes

As we have seen, poster art can intervene in articulating the significance of land as it envisions a geopolitical transformation. At the same time, the art makes clear the ways land is employed within systems of power. Echoing the doubleness of critical mestizaje, Chicano poster art makes manifest the doubleness of land's significance within the Chicano cultural imaginary. Chicano art grew out of the doubled experiences of mestizaje, a national "outsider" claiming a right to articulate an identity within (in order to transform) the nation. This double valence is evident in the sense of outrage and defiance that sets the tone for much of the politically inflected visual arts. For example, in Yolanda López's *Who's the Illegal Alien, Pilgrim?* (Figure 5), the pose of the angry Aztec warrior

Figure 5. *Who's the Illegal Alien, Pilgrim?* (1978) by Yolanda López uses irony to mirror James Montgomery Flagg's rendering of Uncle Sam. Used by permission of the artist.

serves to question the idea of legitimacy and land rights in the so-called New World. The Aztec figure mimics James Montgomery Flagg's iconic poster of Uncle Sam pointing a finger above the words "I Want You for the U.S. Army." Both posters share a sense of militancy and urgency and present a challenge to the viewer's sense of citizenship. Of course, in each poster citizenship works at cross-purposes. Flagg's poster challenges the (clearly male) viewer to prove his patriotism and right to citizenship.[9] López's lithograph points the finger in the other direction, so to speak, aggressively reminding the viewer that it was the European as invader/immigrant who unlawfully occupied the Americas. The whole issue of citizenship and belonging is thereby turned around. Visually, the stylized headdress of the warrior echoes the black wings found on the UFW eagle. More significantly, the warrior crushes a copy of an immigration reform act, one of many such acts passed in response to continued movement into the United States by Mexican nationals.

The defiance of López's poster is a response to the idea of dislocation and displacement in relation to the land Chicanos occupy. A tortured sense of a dislocated self—a self at once called up and rejected—can be seen in Malaquias Montoya's *The Immigrant's Dream: The American Response* (Figure 6). The poster advertises a conference on immigration and refugee advocacy, situating itself clearly in the interstices between aesthetic object and political engagement. The colorless grays playing off the muted red, white, and blue of Old Glory represent the notion of the American Dream as a now faded, sullied, and discredited ideology. The dreary colors underscore the image of bondage and the strong suggestion of violence represented by the undocumented immigrant mummified in the American flag. Is it a return address label stamped "undocumented" or a coroner's tag that hangs from the neck? For many would-be immigrants whose status as political refugee runs counter to official U.S. policy, death is more than an abstract threat. Montoya's poster makes this threat seem all the more real through the surreal, nightmarish quality conveyed by this silkscreen. The images underscore the vexed relation that bodies bear to land when caught in the constraints of national ideology and immigration policy.

In a similar vein, Yreina Cervántez conveys the plight of the undocumented immigrant in *¡Alerta!* (Figure 7). The poster is cast in bright red, framing the literal flight of a man dressed in work boots, jeans, a bright yellow shirt, and a red cap. He runs across a field of clouds toward a bright yellow spot evocative of the sun. He is led by what appears to be an eagle as red roses fall after him, suggesting perhaps sacrifice, passion,

Figure 6. *The Immigrant's Dream: The American Response* (1983) by Malaquias Montoya portrays the nightmarish status of undocumented aliens. Used by permission of the artist.

Figure 7. ¡*Alerta!* (Beware!) (1987) by Yreina Cervántez conveys the sense of despera-
tion and danger involved in unofficial border crossing. Used by permission of the artist.

or hope. Behind him trail a couple of men, also running, and below him
a woman turns in mid-flight as if checking on her pursuers. A barbed
wire loops below, encircling two other running figures. The images of
flight give the poster a sense of urgency. This urgency is underscored by

the phrase at the base of the frame. The word *Alertan* (They alert), slightly askew, is printed in bold, next to which reads *Alertan a Indocumentados* (They alert undocumenteds). The phrases and the title of the poster create an ambiguous meaning. The title is imperative: "Beware!" The expectation is that one be alert to the fleeing of undocumented workers into the United States. But the phrases at the bottom of the poster suggest something else, that unnamed people warn undocumented immigrants—of what? The danger they will find in the United States? The encroaching INS? The exploitation and repression they may find in this new country? The ambiguity is slightly unsettling, just as the images of fleeing figures, barbed wire, eagles in flight, and roses provide an unsettling juxtaposition. Interestingly, the ground on which these immigrants run is absent. Instead, the only landscape is the central one, a representation of sky and clouds across which the main figure races. Even while evoking the panic and jarring uncertainty of the immigrant's run to the border, the poster seems to offer a vision of utopian possibility, transcendence, and, perhaps, safety.

All three posters, by López, Montoya, and Cervántez, share critical characteristics. They evoke a sense of personal identity intercut by political and social inequities. They also call up an image of land (and its absence) in presenting the contested experience of individual subjectivity wrestling with national, economic, and political power. These posters reflect a sensibility and awareness that personhood and self-identity are not created fully by free will. Individual identity is delimited by the geographic, cultural, political, and social landscapes through which it moves. Land thus represents both possibility and limitation.

### The Short Circuits of Power

The cultural and social forces that influence the creation of Chicano poster art help make it a unique expression concerned with the regional, specific, and local, and yet also connected with transnational and global movements. Chicana and Chicano artists have overtly or covertly understood their work to be part of a globalized and interconnected world. Seen in this light, Chicano culture—like other subnational cultures—provides a potentially telling and informative system of knowledge in the postmodern world. As an identity forged out of globalizing currents,

Chicano identity negotiates global forces through a regional specificity of expression and culture.

The stratification of wealth, the accumulation of resources by a few, and the struggle by the vast population of the world for improvement and survival have been a persistent concern for many politicians, intellectuals, artists, and others. Chicano culture plays a particularly relevant role in this debate because it is born out of the conditions that have formed modernity and postmodernity. Chicano culture has been forged in the fires of industrial and postindustrial America. As an integral part of the labor force driving North American production, Chicanos know all too intimately the reality of an identity that does not have a center and that cannot claim a homeland. Chicano culture recognizes the violence that can result from the pursuit of certain so-called master narratives—a belief in endless technological development, faith in perpetual progress, the inevitability of capitalist expansion, and the truth of manifest destiny. This is not to say that Chicanos have been responsible for the formation of postmodern culture, but Chicanos have lived and survived the social inequities made plain by the critical light of postmodernism.

As Chicano public art illustrates, the relation between art and politics, between aesthetics and social struggle, is complex. It is, in many ways, central to understanding the expression of Chicano consciousness and culture. For better or worse, land forms a site where the dynamics of this relationship have often taken place. Whether understood as a homeland, as a borderlands, or as a postmodern battleground, land links Chicano culture with a concern over self, power, and place. Chicano culture and consciousness often strongly emphasize the connection between international, Third World, and domestic struggles of Chicanos/as and other communities of color. These groups all find common cause as they identify themselves as disempowered, minority, or underrepresented constituencies in the social and political theaters of U.S. power.[10]

From this perspective, an interest in land serves not just to help mark a Chicano national territory, but to form a connection to a more extensive geography, one whose smoldering revolutionary fervor is reflected in Otoño Luján's *Break It!* (Figure 8). The "It" refers to the militarized U.S.–Mexico border signified by the barbed-wire fence in the

Figure 8. By evoking a barbed-wire fence, *Break It!* (1993) by Otoño Luján speaks to the need for a demilitarization of the border. Used by permission of the artist.

background. The fiery reds, browns, and oranges stand in stark contrast to the white jagged borders highlighting the broken fence. The clenched fists of the rifle-toting man and woman, the sharp knives clutched in their hands, and the crossed bandoliers across their chests match the militancy of the imperative title. The bandoliers evoke images of the Mexican Revolution, whose figures of male and female resistance—the *soldado* and his *adelita*—are recast here as urban guerrillas. What subtlety the poster lacks is offset by its political message, which suggests that the struggle to reform, resist, or repeal U.S. immigration policies represents a kind of revolutionary action. The poster thus reflects a fervor fueling the desire to tear down barriers to immigration. These smoldering emotions have been stoked by the vexed uses to which national borders have often been put, drawn and erased for the benefit of military and business interests.

The central imagery of Luján's poster plays a key role in Malaquias Montoya's *Argentina . . . One Year of Military Dictatorship* (Figure 9). Whereas the barbed wire represents the U.S.–Mexico border in *Break It!*, in

Figure 9. *Argentina . . . One Year of Military Dictatorship* (1977) by Malaquias Montoya reflects the internationalist concerns that characterize much Chicano poster art. Used by permission of the artist.

Montoya's poster the loop of wire evokes the horrific Argentinean military prisons where thousands of people considered dangerous to the dictatorial state were "disappeared": kidnapped, tortured, and murdered. The occasion of the poster is a protest in Berkeley on behalf of *los desaparecidos* and others suffering military repression half a world away. As with Luján's work, the message is meant to be direct and forceful. The bleeding flower conveys the brutality of the military junta. The barbed wire symbolizes state repression and violence. Taken together, the imagery in the posters by Luján and Montoya helps one to understand in more global terms how the misuse of military power is a repressive act, whether that power is wielded in the name of immigration control or in the service of oppressive social order. In both cases, the use of violence defends national and political interests at the cost of human life, freedom, and dignity. These artistic works reveal an understanding of geographic space that encompasses all of the Americas, connecting the suffering of oppressed people from San Ysidro to Buenos Aires.

Land turns into an extended metaphor for the suffering of the poor, the helpless, and the powerless who struggle to better their plight by either fighting or fleeing. These representations highlight the significance of land not simply within a national context. They map quite a different geography. This new geography traces the interconnection between land and self, each a necessary circuit in the circulation of various forms of power. Self-identification and place are inflected—in some ways determined—by economic power, national interest, and racial construction. Yet so too does the body serve as a site where numerous other borders cross.

Violence against the mestizo body becomes a central concern of much public art. Gilbert "Magu" Luján's *Hermanos, Stop Gang War* (Figure 10) provides a prime example. One man with a long braid of hair and a bandana tied around his forehead stabs another as the bloody culmination to a knife fight. The poster pulsates with a sense of motion, underscored by the succession of black lines characteristic of comic-book art from which Magu draws inspiration. Emblazoned below the combatants is the command "Hermanos, Stop Gang War." The imperative clearly appeals to a sense of brotherhood based on common Chicano identity, the need to

Figure 10. *Hermanos, Stop Gang War* (1977) by Gilbert "Magu" Luján employs violent imagery to convey a message of peace. Used by permission of the artist.

stop brown-on-brown violence graphically displayed. The spilled blood is, of course, evocative of violence, yet the blood also indexes a racial identification. Thus the appeal to a racial brotherhood suggests the logic for formation of a new sense of community and racial unification.

Although the representation of violence is graphic and bloody, the medium is highly stylized. The comic-book flatness of the rendering creates some distance between the observer and the violent action depicted. The poster, employing the stylized world of comic-book violence, at once evokes and distances the bloodletting that is gutting the community's power. This distancing foregrounds the aesthetic representation, in part because the piece is meant to be part of a ritualized commemoration. The lithograph is part of a calendar series, a long tradition in both Mexican and Chicano culture. The year-end creation and circulation of calendars—from stores, businesses, and community groups—is part of a yearly expression of community building. In this case, the plea for an end to violence is based on the very idea of community and brotherhood that the calendar is meant to foster. The poster suggests that bodies in action forge or disrupt community bonds, thus creating new cartographies by which to understand one's ever-evolving geography. Luján's work envisions this evolving geography as one that might increasingly prevent the type of violence that hobbles community and ethnic bonds.

The rejection of violence on an artistic level is matched by a reclamation of that which has been violated, a sense of union through shared identity. The calendar becomes a means to engender belonging, to identify a neighborhood as a community. Alfredo de Batuc's *Seven Views of City Hall* (Figure 11) also invokes the notion of community in its playful reconfiguration of the Los Angeles City Hall. Here the building assumes the same spatial position as the Virgin Mary does in traditional paintings of the Virgen de Guadalupe. On the one hand, this conflation claims the city and its iconic landmarks as part of an ethnic identity. After all, no icon has proved more durable for Mexican national and Chicana cultural identity than has the Virgin. On the other hand, de Batuc's artwork parodies the local political machine—indexed by the multiple figures of city hall—representative of governmental power that has historically failed to represent Chicana community concerns. The imagery evokes a sense of placement and displacement within new and problematic spatial relations.

By echoing the luminous halo that surrounds the Virgen de Guadalupe, de Batuc displays city hall as either a glowing abstract Madonna

Figure 11. Suggestive of both the Virgen de Guadalupe and a floating phallus, *Seven Views of City Hall* (1987) by Alfredo de Batuc represents an ethnicized and sexualized portrayal of the seat of political power in Los Angeles. Used by permission of the artist.

or as a floating phallus. The object of reverence and worship can suggest both political power and homosexual desire, suggesting new configurations of community in terms of sexual as well as racial/ethnic identities. The image of city hall becomes part of an altered and reconfigured geography in which the seat of city government becomes the basis for de Batuc's aesthetic play. The piece evokes signs of alienation and geographic dislocation. City hall as a symbol of state power becomes incorporated into the aesthetic text as a transformed symbol of desire and belonging, troping on the idea of home, land, power, and religious/ethnic identification.

Ester Hernández also references the Virgen de Guadalupe in a less playful and wholly more controversial way. *La Ofrenda* (The offering) (1988) has evoked controversy through its use of revered religious iconography to recognize lesbian love. This furor has superseded a measured discussion of the many levels of sanctity, holiness, and giving that the work evokes.[11] The tattooed back of the butch lover forms a human altar before which a fleshy rose is placed. The evocation of vaginal images underscores the sense of both erotic and holy delight suggested by the poster. The idea of *ofrenda* points to both the traditional religious offering of flowers made to the Virgin during a Mexican wedding mass and the offering of love and passion symbolized by the voluptuous pink flower. Although the figure of the Virgin is placed within a scenario of quite explicit homosexual desire, there is no overt irreverence. Indeed, the lithograph serves to venerate the feminine power of the Virgin. Hernández thus draws together an icon of Mexican identity and a reference to the Nahuatl earth goddess Coatlalopeuh in the mixture of Indian and Spanish religious culture and a celebration of lesbian desire, love, and commitment.

This mixture of images suggests the kind of borderlands aesthetic in the writing of Gloria Anzaldúa discussed in chapter 1. Anzaldúa's mestiza conceptualizations of the self and the borderlands highlight how power circulates in relation to politics, sexuality, religion, race, and national and class identity. At its most promising, the crossroads of the borderlands forms a site where one looks not to the past for a sense of wholeness or completion but to the present as a constantly negotiated and troubling terrain. In Hernández's work, the body of the butch lover aggregates all the images—of both submerged and sexualized pre-Cortesian goddess and revered religious Catholic icon—which in its present configuration has fostered such furor and outrage.

## A New World Border

The perception and reconfiguration of land becomes part of the aesthetic repertoire of Chicano culture, one example being the borderlands as an interstitial site where multiple circuits of power and their discourses meet. *La Ofrenda* offers a visual representation of this intersection. In this respect, Hernández's lithograph *Sun Mad* (Figure 12) offers a similar representation, though in a very different key. In this poster, Hernández conceives of land as a site intimately connected to the bodies who work and inhabit it. This explains the sense of outrage—though registered in a parodic tone—evinced by this recasting of the Sun Maid raisins logo. The poster highlights the dangerous poisons used in the fields to which the pickers are daily exposed (the poster duly notes: "Unnaturally Grown with Insecticides, Miticides, Herbicides, Fungicides"). *La Ofrenda* evokes the iconic figure of the Virgin in a sexually subversive way, threatening stable notions of Chicana identity and subjectivity. In *Sun Mad*, Hernández is working very much within an established framework of Chicana discourse by championing the cause of the farmworkers whose health is crippled as a result of their daily exposure to pesticides. Yet both posters emerge from the same creative and critical impulse. This energy is drawn from the insights honed by feminist and queer theorists regarding the interconnection between power and the body. The notion that social power is played out through the human body—that the personal is political—has greatly influenced the direction that Chicana/o cultural and critical work has taken. Just as the need for labor in the United States fostered the development of a Chicano consciousness, Chicano identity has often been expressed in terms of personal and cultural development at the nexus of various systems of economic, political, and cultural exchange.

Figure 12. *Sun Mad* (1982) by Ester Hernández attacks the dangers pesticides pose to workers in the grape fields. Used by permission of the artist. Copyright 1982 Ester Hernández.

This awareness informs Mark Vallen's *New World Odor* (Figure 13). The title puns on the phrase President George Herbert Walker Bush used in the early 1990s to characterize the sociopolitical configuration of the world after the fall of the Soviet Union. The poster suggests that this

Figure 13. *New World Odor* (1991) by Mark Vallen conveys a concern with the United States' power in a post–Cold War world. Used by permission of the artist.

new world order means nothing but the same carnage under a different regime. The pile of skulls tumbling toward the viewer presents a macabre, perhaps slightly mocking vision of what awaits us in a world dominated by capital and commerce. The gothic lettering and the sepia tones reference the poster art of the Third Reich, suggesting that the fall of communism has ensured the triumph of fascistic forces. The critique here is part of that strain in Chicano public art concerned with repression at a local level in the service of global and international political solidarity.

Ricardo Duffy's *The New Order* (Figure 14) offers a similar vision, echoing Vallen's concern with the social and political world at the end of the last century. The new order here is located at the international border between Mexico and the United States. In the foreground sits a portrait of a white-wigged, pale-faced George Washington smoking a cigarette. The figure can serve as a metonym for the United States, mapped in red, white, and blue at the bottom of the frame, and at the same time for the U.S. currency. Pinned to Washington's right chest are the initials "INS" for the Immigration and Naturalization Service. Above the initials, a skeleton adorned as a Native with tomahawk and feather headband and the word "Chicano" etched on his skull seems to collapse and become disarticulated. Pinned to Washington's left chest is a red Maltese cross—suggestive again of a militarized Germany—above

Figure 14. *The New Order* (1995) by Duffy Ricardo suggests the commercialized interests that compose the geopolitical borderlands of the United States. Used by permission of the artist.

which hovers a smiling skeleton, rising perhaps in triumph. The skeleton's skull is echoed in the intermediate background. Buried skulls and crossbones fill the ground. Across this macabre landscape an INS truck, followed by a cowboy on horseback, is out on patrol.

Inscribed among the skulls is the phrase "Prop. 187," a reference to the proposition (later found largely unconstitutional) passed by California voters in 1994 denying undocumented immigrants access to health care and education. The skulls could represent the potential victims of the proposition as well as those many thousands who have died trying to cross the militarized border into the United States. At the far left is a freeway sign found in the southern stretch of California's Highway 5. It shows the black silhouettes of a man, woman, and small child holding a doll running in a line across the sign, warning drivers about the possibility of fleeing immigrants who may cross unexpectedly in front of their cars. The image of a woman wrapped in a rebozo can be seen faintly traced in blue across the sign, adding a human face to the coldly efficient iconography of the freeway sign. The far background of the poster represents the rugged red terrain of the high deserts of the Southwest. Across the top and bottom of the poster is part of the advertising campaign used to sell cigarettes: "Come to Marlboro Country." Only the last two words are visible, superimposed by the word "monstrous," suggesting that in the new world order any sense of invitation has been withdrawn. All that remains is an image of the border as a contested terrain marked by death and overrun by economic and military concerns.

The many elements of the poster present the United States as a land of commercial exploitation and consumerism, the new world odor. The invitation to "Come to Marlboro Country" seems not meant for those undocumented workers forced by necessity into an exploitative process of economic exchange. The invitation proves utterly bankrupt, as is made clear by the allusion to the anti-immigrant Proposition 187. Commerce and capital run the new order the poster invokes as part of a transnational system of exchange whose extralegal forms—the immigration of undocumented workers—is aggressively controlled. The poster highlights the dynamic and complicated processes at work within an international setting. The poster suggests a geopolitical order by which the move-ment between Mexico and the United States is subject to surveillance. Chicano/a identity represents a complex crossroads where economic, per-sonal, political, familial, social, and national concerns converge.

At the same time, the desire to name a new sense of self evident in these posters resonates with the more liberatory and creative forces associated with mestizaje. The geography of the borderlands incessantly places the subject in relation to matrices of meaning, identity, and power. Chicana/o cultural practices translate this new space into signifying sys-tems that highlight multivalent tactics of survival and opposition at work within the borderlands. Chicano poster art highlights these processes of opposition. Various evocations of land within Chicana graphic arts re-veal how identities of the self and of the nation conjoin and conflict in a naked struggle for power. Land connects metonymically to an extensive political and economic geography always under contestation.

## Revisiting Aztlán

The geopolitical contestation these posters evoke centers on issues of possession and belonging. Chicano poster art helps to trace how a sub-national culture responds to the alienation and geographic dislocation caused both by persistent prejudice, an elision of national and racial identity, and by a history of exploitative national public policy. One re-sponse is to insist on something stable, a solid foundation on which to base collective identity and political agency. One strong vein of Chicano thought has ascribed this stability to land. In this regard, Mary Pat Brady discusses the appeal of Aztlán, which lies

> in the stability land seems to lend; land in this formulation is understood not as shifting, not as under production, but rather as pre-given, natural, as beyond or prior to the cultural. Despite its reliance on an opaque con-cept of space, the proclamation of Aztlán successfully called attention to the naturalizing work of the geopolitical narrative of the United States. It claimed the moral authority of history in an effort to disrupt the con-struction of nationalist norms. . . . Aztlán offers a counteraesthetics by calling attention to the ideologies of nation building. (2002, 146)

The idea of Aztlán as an alternative geopolitical frame ties history to land, envisioning a unity beyond ideological constructs such as the nation. In this respect, Chicano/a art helps to envision Aztlán and transform it into a dynamic cartography of belonging. The significance of Aztlán as an alternate geography in Chicano/a cultural discourse therefore cannot be overstated. The concern with land is part and parcel of the way in which Chicano culture comes to terms with the past and the present in hopes of a better, more just, and less violent future. The very contradictions of Aztlán help in understanding the difficulties involved in conceiving of such a future.

"Aztlán" names the mythic homeland of the Aztecs before their migration to the high valley of central Mexico. "Aztlán" names, according to legend, the Mexican place of origin—the land of seven caves (Chicomostoc), the place of the Twisted Hill (Colhuacán), the place of whiteness (Aztlán)—from which the Mexica migrated southward toward the Mexican plateau in AD 820 (Nash 1978, 351). The ideas embodied in Aztlán draw together geography, culture, history, myth, genetics, migration, tradition, heritage, unity, and authenticity. It crystallizes in one term a history of dispossession endured by Mexicans, Mexican Americans, and Chicanos alike. Or, as Rodolfo Acuña puts it in his characteristically blunt manner, Aztlán not only reaffirmed the Indian heritage of Chicanos but also "the fact that Chicanos were indigenous to the Southwest; therefore, if the Anglo-Americans did not like it there, they could go back to from where they came" (1972, 229).

The idea of Aztlán was most widely introduced to Chicano thought with "El Plan Espiritual de Aztlán," drafted in March 1969 for the Chicano Youth Conference held in Denver, Colorado. The Plan declares:

> Brotherhood unites us and love for our brothers makes us a people whose time has come and who struggle against the foreigner "Gabacho," who exploits our riches and destroys our culture. . . . Before the world, before all of North America, before all our brothers in the Bronze Continent, We are a Nation, We are a Union of free pueblos, We are Aztlán. (1973, 403)

As a mythic homeland, Aztlán grants a prior claim to the land Chicanos occupy. As a concept, Aztlán both grants legitimacy and makes overt the indigenous roots of Chicanismo. By referring to Aztlán, Chicano artists signal that the United States is neither a wholly sovereign nation-state nor an end point of migration, but rather a part of a more extensive political, economic, historic, and cultural landscape, one that predates the arrival of European civilization. However, as Rosa Linda Fregoso and Angie Chabram have noted, "By recuperating the mythic pre-Columbian past and reformulating this as the basis of our shared identity, Chicano academic intellectuals of the post-colonial condition failed to see that cultural identities have histories, that they undergo constant transformation and that far from being etched in the past, cultural identities are constantly being constructed" (1990, 206). Not simply a reification of identity, this recuperation envisioned a highly androcentric notion of Chicano identity as a "brotherhood." The critiques of an essentialized Chicano identity have been numerous and incisive.[12]

Nonetheless, the evocation of a historical consciousness served to link body to land and seemed to assert the notion of indigenous connectivity as the baseline for mestizaje. Under this logic, the somatic manifestation of "Indianness" becomes the marker of one's identity. This explains the emphasis in the famous "Plan Espiritual de Aztlán" on race: "We Declare the independence of our Mestizo Nation. We are a Bronze People with a Bronze Culture" (1973, 403). Within an essential nationalist discourse, Chicanismo is measured by the color of the skin and the details of physiognomy. Clearly, this position can easily translate into other nonracialized areas: the test of ethnic identity can be tied to one's linguistic skills—fluency with code-switching, bilingualism, slang—one's clothes, taste in music, economic condition, place of domicile, nationality, and so on. Chicano/a ethnic identity becomes essentialized, premised on meeting quite specific physical or social conditions.

In its most utopian configurations, Aztlán came to embody ideas of place and endurance in the Chicano imaginary. Teresa McKenna notes that during the 1960s and early 1970s, "Aztlán symbolized an ideal state of unification of past and present of a nation divided by war. Aztlán became the idyll that was lost but could be regained. It was a symbol of hope and an image of natural wholeness from which society had become estranged. It became a political rallying point and generated an intense literary activity" (1997, 16). This idealization of land and origin led, especially in the most fervid nationalist conceptualizations of Aztlán, to a racialized essentialism that correlated racial identity with an inherent claim to land and location. As a cultural icon, Aztlán served as a countercultural signifier reclaiming the U.S. Southwest as indigenous land, as Mexica land, as a homeland. It is these tropes of land as connection to pre-Cortesian life that Gloria Anzaldúa evokes in her subversion of a masculinist Chicano nationalism. In company with Cherríe Moraga, Ana Castillo, Sandra Cisneros, and many other Chicana writers, Anzaldúa—as discussed in chapter 1—reshapes the rhetoric of indigenism in order to stake a claim for a more inclusive articulation of Chicano/a identity and to assert a quest for spiritual transformation to counter the dominance of Western technology in the service of capital expansion.

The discursive process that established Chicano indigenous ancestry valorized a (racial, spiritual, ancestral) relation to land that was home prior to both the Spanish invasion in 1521 and Anglo-American dispossession in 1848. Although the somatic presence of many Chicanos manifests this indigenous link, the relevance of pre-European connections to the Americas is not simply traced by a line of genetic encryption. The significance of indigenous ancestry is constructed and reconstructed, the crystallization of historical and personal memories interjected into contemporary social and political situations.

As a myth, the idea of Aztlán comes down through hearsay. It was a story conveyed to Fray Bernardino de Sahagún years after the fall of Tenochtitlán on August 13, 1521. The myth was written down by Sahagún's native informants, themselves converted and Christianized members of what was once the Aztec princely class. As Daniel Cooper Alarcón explains, the story of Aztlán thus becomes a palimpsest, a foundational legend recounted by Christianized informants, written in Nahuatl in 1555 for a Spanish friar who lost the original account, reconstructed it in Spanish, and completed a Nahuatl revision in 1585. Alarcón suggests that Aztlán offers a dynamic model that highlights the complicated processes by which Mexicans and those identified with Mexican culture have come to occupy space within the national borders of the United States:

a palimpsest is a site where a text has been erased (often incompletely) in order to accommodate a new one, and it is this unique structure of competing yet interwoven narratives that changes the way we think of cultural identity and its representation, as well as enabling an examination of history, cultural identity, ethnicity, literature, and politics *in relationship to each other*, providing a new vantage point on the relationship of the United States and Mexico at a time when these two nations are more intimately linked than ever. (1997, xvi)

This intimate link provides—from a certain perspective—an unwanted proximity. The media often represent the border as a dangerous and illicit erogenous zone. The border becomes America's back door through which illicit alien bodies thrust themselves, greasy, wet, invading, and polluting the purity of the national body. In the face of such discourses, Alarcón suggests that the idea of Aztlán as palimpsest highlights the fluid, conflicted, and overdetermined site that is evoked when one calls oneself "Chicano." Aztlán as palimpsest, as a text that is overwritten with the remnants of past textualities still present, offers a trope, a discursive and cultural model by which to understand the dynamic condition enacted by the name "mestizo."

Aztlán as an affirmation of an indigenous nationalism becomes a palimpsest of the Mexican Revolution and also of the institutionalization of "revolutionary consciousness" enacted by the patriarchal structures of the Mexican Partido Revolucionario Institucional (PRI). Aztlán invariably stands as a conflicted counterdiscursive trope, an icon evoking nationhood, a performative enunciation, a postcolonial naming and unnaming, a calling up from history.[13]

The usefulness and resiliency of Aztlán has not been its ability to name a Chicano homeland or nation; rather, its strength has always been its plasticity. Aztlán is more myth than place, an idea rendered well by Victor Ochoa's *Border Mezz-teez-o* (Figure 15). The poster plays with verbal and visual puns, contrasting phrases such as "La Frontera" with "The Border," "Aztlán" with "Acquired," "Rodillas" (knees) with "Rodino." This last pairing is a metonymic connection, the knees suggesting submission and Rodino the name of the congressman who sponsored immigration reform in the 1980s. The visual references to the dollar bill, the U.S. Constitution, the Janus face of the border—one side its indigenous profile and the other its Spanish conquistador whose mouth guard

Figure 15. *Border Mezz-teez-o* (1993) by Victor Ochoa offers a satirical view of border-land identity. Used by permission of the artist.

is inscribed "English only"—all serve to convey the conflicted sense of history that land makes present. These playful, painful, and ironic turns are characteristic of Chicano aesthetics, aesthetics sometimes character-ized as *rasquache*. *Rasquachismo* represents a type of reverential kitsch, a complex irony at once satiric and compassionate.[14]

Within this framework, artists often evoke Aztlán in order to con-sider an ironic remapping of the United States, one that both recognizes and inverts the notion of margin and center. On the one hand, Aztlán challenges secured boundaries, confirmed norms, and social facts such as nation, citizenry, and home. On the other, it reshapes its own rigidly de-fined codes. Aztlán questions notions of loyalty, citizenship, nationhood, and belonging. In *Chicano Poetics*, Alfred Arteaga argues: "Aztlán aims at the homeland, at the nation as people, as state. It offers an interwoven history and myth of presence. It provides the principle of definition in the present and defines an idealized state in the future. As such it functions as the national myth" (1997, 14). Aztlán becomes a highly problematic and ironized national myth when actually employed in Chicano expressive culture. The interwoven myth, the utopian hope of some vaguely articulated nation-state that characterizes the most ardent expressions of Chicano nationalist thought, can become a means to articulate a sense of self always in the process of becoming and transforming.

In her essay "Queer Aztlán," Cherríe Moraga seeks to articulate the nature of this transformation. She reconfigures the significance of land and the complicated relationship between space and subject in a Chicana context. Her essay relocates Chicano nationalist concerns associated with Aztlán by simultaneously expanding and contracting its metaphorical qualities, reconnecting the idea of Aztlán to numerous forms of social struggle. Thus Aztlán as a metaphor for land stands as an overdetermined signifier: "For immigrant and native alike, land is . . . the factories where we work, the water our children drink, and the housing projects where we live. For women, lesbians, and gay men, land is that physical mass called our bodies. Throughout las Américas, all these 'lands' remain under occupation by an Anglo-centric, patriarchal, imperialist United States" (1993, 173). The site of conflict becomes enmeshed in a broader context. Her work highlights the interconnection between localities of work and environment, nation and family, land and body. She asserts that the idea of Aztlán allows one to forge solidarity with a number of national and international social struggles for justice. Aztlán comes to represent on a symbolic level another type of reclamation, one enacted, for example, by the queering of iconic figures such as the Virgen de Guadalupe undertaken by de Batuc and Hernández. Moraga isolates Aztlán as a symbolic site where microlocalities—work and environment, family and self—emerge as sites of anti-imperial struggle.

It is not surprising, then, that references to land and place return again and again as motifs in Chicano thought. Whether it is one's sense of place as a farmworker or homemaker, student activist or U.S. soldier, immigrant or migrant worker, undocumented resident or third-generation American, one's connection to land and place influences the way that Chicano identity explodes across the cultural landscape. Chicano public art is part and parcel of that explosion: fragments of a Chicano and Chicana identity coming into being. The images found in poster art name and represent a Chicano and Chicana self that lives as a highly complex citizen-subject. Chicanos are called upon to be good "American" citizens; or working diligently at menial jobs in the expectation that the opportunity for advancement will eventually open before them; or as any number of other roles available within social and economic structures that ensure the perpetuation of a Latino underclass. As part of these structures, Chicanos are made to feel like outsiders, as if living in the United States represents an invasion of sorts, a temporary condition that a combination of national policy and cultural politics will somehow cure.

Whether explicitly drawing on images of land or not, Chicano public art helps illuminate and illustrate the way in which people can conceive of themselves as both belonging and not belonging at the same time. Implicit in this attitude is a form of mestizaje, an incorporation of the self and the Other. In relation to land, the thematic representation of mestizaje offers an insight into simultaneous feelings of alienation and home. Land becomes, in these visual texts, something both familiar and strange. Chicano public art offers a vision in which mestizo and mestiza bodies, made to feel as strangers in their own land, can believe—with humor and dignity and faith—in the possibility of a better world. The next chapter discusses the manner in which mestizaje on the level of the sexual makes mestizas and mestizos strangers in their own bodies. They are made to feel aliens within a Chicano context that values border crossing on a geographic and cultural level. However, this crossing becomes suspect when it comes to issues of sexuality and gender division.

# PART III

# Challenging Mestizaje

# CHAPTER 5

# The Transgressive Body
# and Sexual Mestizaje

For speculation socializes me and reassures others as to my good inten-
tions in both meanings and morals; but, in regard to my dreamed body,
sets forth to them only that which the physician's speculum reveals: a
de-eroticized surface which I concede to him in the wink of an eye by
which I make him believe he is not an *other*, but has only to look at me
as I myself would do if I were he—complicity of the barrier operating on
the hither side of the retina, snare which captures him rather than me.

—Julia Kristeva, "Ellipsis on Dread and the Specular Seduction" (1980)

One element implicit in mestizaje and the racialized body only lightly
touched on thus far is the biology of reproduction. This chapter treats
narratives that raise the specter of violence in relation to sexuality and
gender. In the fictional works of Gil Cuadros and Emma Pérez, the embodiment of a mestizo/a identity is manifested through sexual longing
and physical desire. Gender—its perception, its models, and its forms—
becomes a central problematic for individual characters required to
neatly align their sense of self within socially sanctioned configurations
of identity. The mestizo/a body becomes both text and agent, at once
read within and acting upon forms of repressive social order. The body
moves through social networks with the goal of achieving a kind of liberatory position that cannot yet be openly expressed.[1]

At the same time, these narratives convey the sense of constraint
the queer mestizo and mestiza find in daily social interaction and activity. Both Cuadros's 1994 collection of short stories and poetry, *City
of God*, and Pérez's 1996 novella, *Gulf Dreams*, measure the length as
well as the depth of repression regarding homosexuality within mestizo
spaces. These little-discussed works prove significant not only because

they register the means by which sexually transgressive bodies are disciplined, but because they foreground the aesthetic and imaginative as realms that may move the mestiza/o body beyond restrictive measures.

Although he saw his work anthologized and published in small magazines, Gil Cuadros enjoyed a much too brief career as a poet and writer. Yet his career was not without some acclaim: he won the 1991 Brody Literature Fellowship and one of the first PEN Center USA/West grants to writers with HIV.[2] His poems and short stories were collected in *City of God*, published by City Lights Books two years before his death in 1996. Emma Pérez, though known primarily for her scholarly work, which I have referenced in this discussion, is also a writer of highly polished and self-reflexive prose. The small Third Woman Press under the directorship of Norma Alarcón published *Gulf Dreams* in 1996, Pérez's only published work of fiction. The book is, as of this date, out of print. Although her writing career is nascent, Pérez's academic career—at the University of Texas, El Paso, and more recently the University of Colorado at Boulder—has been exemplary. Although both Cuadros and Pérez have a limited publication history with their fiction, their work is illustrative of the vexed intersection of race and queer sexuality.

### The Familial Roots of Queer Desire

Evoking Saint Augustine's apocalyptic title, Gil Cuadros's stories in *City of God* center on the city of Los Angeles, which serves—as José Monteagudo notes in his review of the book—as "an un-godly city torn by its own 'viruses,' race and class divisions that affect the book's protagonist as much as his own sexual orientation or HIV status" (1995, 34). Throughout the short stories that compose the collection, the bodies of the characters are not just bound and shaped by the cityscape through which they pass, but in effect they merge with the city. The body invaded and eventually ravaged by HIV forms a correlative for Los Angeles as it is rent by the ruptures between different communities organized around singular ethnic or racial or sexual identities. The characters thus struggle not just with their illnesses but also with their search for a sense of place and belonging when the social conditions they encounter preclude a home for the queer mestizo body. It is against this backdrop of the city and body in turmoil that Cuadros's stories trace the development and destruction of the transgressive mixed-race body, locating its central conflicts within the social and familial contradictions that give birth to mestizo homosexuality.

The nine stories in *City of God* delineate what might be thought of as a single life lived by a variety of different characters.[3] The stories trace a development of mestizo sexuality told through the experiences of various characters at different ages and phases of their lives. All the characters experience a sense of their sexual selves as alien to accepted modes of sexual identity and are, therefore, in some manner transgressive. This issue of transgression is crystallized most clearly and concretely through the AIDS-related illnesses a number of the characters endure.

Thematically the stories break into three groups of three. The first cluster of stories—"Indulgences," "Reynaldo," and "Chivalry"—deal with issues of origins, taking into account the way childhood experiences determine sexual and gender identification. These stories are set in the Central Valley of California, a locale that represents a kind of rural site of origin, and each story deals with the return of its main character seeking to reconnect with his relatives. The rural background of the family forms a touchstone from whence this new sexual mestizo departs.[4] The evocation of a familial past creates a sense of cultural difference, one in which religious faith and belief in the family establish a framework of supposed normativity against which homosexuality represents the aberrant.

The middle three stories—"My Aztlan: White Place," "Unprotected," and "Holy"—deal with processes of identification and the manner in which a (homo)sexual self is established even in the face of familial and social opposition.[5] A graphic sexual content that reveals the difficult interconnection between sexualized and racialized bodies characterizes these stories. They foreground the conflicts individuals undergo in locating an appropriate relationship between their ethnic and sexual selves. Each story deals with the way the queer mestizo body becomes a marker—of desire, of exclusion, of rejection, of exoticism, and, ultimately, of hope.

The final three stories—"Baptism," "Letting Go," and "Sight"— highlight processes of self-transformation in the face of physical danger and disease. In these stories the body undergoes a process of dissolution. As illness ravages the physical body and homophobia leads to a social and familial rejection of the queer mestizo, the characters undergo a metamorphosis. This transformation promises that the suffering experienced by the individual body is part of a spiritualizing process. However, whether this change is merely a hopeful wish or the embodiment of a genuine passing remains ambiguous. Only through the textualization of the stories does the vision of a productive transformation of the queer mestizo into a spiritual power become embodied. Thus the stories illustrate how the narrative text becomes the only site in which a reconfiguration of the mestizo body can take place. The aesthetic realm becomes the privileged space of transformative power, the body that finally undergoes a profound mestizaje.

All nine stories (as well as the poems I do not consider in this present discussion) share a concern with the formulation of identity, the significance of materiality, and the role love plays as a power involved in both transformation and violation. What is traced through these stories is the development and transformation of a new mestizo subject, one forced to accommodate an ethnic identity and experience with an alienating but crucial sexual identity.

However, this accommodation takes place primarily within the realm of the imaginative. Where the changes these stories trace highlight the value of aesthetic expression, they also mark a particular social disempowerment. Empowering transformations can take place only within the space of the imaginative. Cuadros's stories mark a particularly impoverished position for its queer mestizo bodies. Nowhere do the stories consider the possibility of new communities that include or are composed of a queer mestizaje. Thus the stories, though promising in terms of a spiritual and aesthetic reconfiguration of queer and diseased bodies, fail to take into account the changes that occur within the social realm, which by the early 1990s included queer communities of color forging power in coalition.

The story "Reynaldo" is thematically representative of the first group of origin stories. It deals with issues of family judgment and homelessness and is composed of three different narratives. The first is set in late summer around 1970 and deals with an adolescent boy named Reynaldo about to attend a new school. Reynaldo is anxious about how he will fit in with the other children and whether the teachers will be as kind as "his own Mr. Lloyd or Mr. Palmer" (1994, 15). This anxiety vexes the boy as summer comes to a close and he is brought to visit his grandmother. During this visit, his father hopes to engage the boy in highly gendered activities such as fishing, playing catch, and barbecuing, activities meant both to bond father and son and to initiate the boy into the activities of manhood.

Interspersed with this third-person narration is a contemporary first-person narrative written as a journal by an adult Reynaldo, now infected with HIV. He has been sent by his family to take care of the elderly grandmother dying of cancer: "They say since I have experience with medical situations, I know what to do" (16). The reasoning reveals both the family's callous attitude about Reynaldo's illness and a profound deferral of responsibility about the grandmother's care. Compounded with these elements, it quickly becomes clear that the family—particularly his mother—strongly denies both Reynaldo's HIV status and the truth about his sexuality.

These two narratives alternate, the one set in the present and focusing on the adult Reynaldo's physical decay with its attendant suffering and pain, and the second set in his boyhood in a pastoral world of strawberry fields and apricot orchards. It is this world where the young Reynaldo knows "as sure as the sun and the moon" that upon their arrival from Los Angeles, his grandmother will greet his family with food and "a big hug and kiss. . . . her tiny hands tickling his side, her nose rubbing his ear" (18). The image of family origin in this story suggests a realm of affection, love, and acceptance that—emblematized by the dying grandmother—is irrevocably lost in the present moment of the story.

At one point, as the adult Reynaldo idly passes time sifting through the attic, he finds an old, mildewed diary filled with postcards addressed to Reynaldo's long-dead grandfather, Jesus. These postcards create a third narrative told in epistolary form and set in the 1920s. Taken together, the postcards reveal a story of love and betrayal between Jesus and his friend, also named—not coincidentally—Reynaldo. Jesus and his friend Reynaldo had grown up together and remained fast friends through early adulthood. The postcards recollect the plans they had made to save money and travel the world together on a grand adventure. Yet the present-day Reynaldo realizes that their friendship had been strained. He reads the apology Reynaldo wrote to Jesus, for "spitting venomous words that were sure to hurt. The accusations about her [Jesus's girlfriend] were really uncalled for on my part, I'm sure she's a handsome woman" (19). The nature of the two men's relationship is never overtly revealed, yet the sense of jealousy and desire certainly suggests an amorous, if not sexual, intimacy.

It soon becomes clear that the plans the two friends had made to travel the world are disrupted as Jesus decides to remain in California and pursue his courtship with the as yet unnamed woman. Toward the end of August 1923 Reynaldo leaves for his travels alone. He writes Jesus frequently only to learn in November that Jesus is to marry. Reynaldo writes: "I hope this changes nothing between us. Do I still have a room in your home?" (34). The three narratives alternate in the story, moving between the epistolary account of lost love, the boyhood summer Reynaldo spends in his grandmother's home, and the narrative present in which the adult Reynaldo struggles physically and emotionally with his own illness while standing vigil over his dying grandmother.

Soon the story takes a fantastical turn, as the young Reynaldo encounters a ghost in his grandmother's attic. The ghost is his grandfather's friend, Reynaldo, who recounts the story of his relationship with Jesus, their separation, his travels, and the marriage of Jesus to a woman named Rosario, who would become the grandmother Reynaldo loves as a boy and cares for as an adult. The boy sees such an expression of sorrow on the face of the ghost that he wishes "the ghost were solid like he, that he could put his arms around the ghost's neck and squeeze, to let the ghost know he would always be his friend" (32). As a sign of friendship, the ghost unwraps a silk scarf from around his neck and presents it to the boy, promising him that as long as he is fair and accepting of people there will always be people who will love him in return. The scarf later takes on a symbolic quality as only those who are kind to Reynaldo can ever see it. It indexes a special bond both between Reynaldo and the ghostly friend/lover of his grandfather as well as between Reynaldo and other boys and men in his life.

This moment of ghostly apparition, though gothic in its evocation of diaphanous presences, proves central to the thematic concerns that the three narratives develop. Most of Cuadros's stories deal not with romantic notions of ghosts and mildewed postcards, but with very realistic and often graphic depictions of sexuality, desire, and disease. Yet "Reynaldo" is typical of his stories in that it addresses the impossibility of the character's finding real contact with a loving family and supportive community. The mestizo body remains bereft of an emotional home.

As the narrative past unfolds in the story, Reynaldo's present is marred by the death of his grandmother and his own recurring AIDS illness. Although he wishes for his family's support, he recalls that not one member attended the funeral of his last lover and that his mother tells her friends that her son has inoperable cancer: "It makes it easier for her, she says" (33). Such betrayals parallel those endured by the Reynaldo of the 1920s. The ghostly echo of betrayal does not simply involve the present Reynaldo's feelings of family abandonment because of his illness and sexual identity. The very nature of his illness is a betrayal by his own body: his immune system fails him and he falls ill. His physical body turns against itself. Thus the body and the social collapse one into each other. Only feelings of abandonment, suffering, and pain remain. Against this stark reality, the ghostly world of his grandfather's lover alone offers a flickering sense of solace.

By the end of the story, all three narratives resolve into one. The young Reynaldo does start a new school where he makes new friends (all boys) every time he wears the ghost's silk scarf. Although he suspects that no one can see the scarf, the two male teachers who befriend him mention it on the first morning of school; one calls it "diaphanous." Thus the ghost's words prove prophetic and Reynaldo as a boy does find acceptance. This narrative concludes with him finding a tin can full of gold coins with a note: "For you and your good friend" (35)—signed simply with the initials RJ for Reynaldo Jesus, his grandfather's friend/lover. The boyhood adventure narrative comes to a satisfying and optimistic conclusion, yet this satisfaction is based entirely on Reynaldo's ephemeral belief in a ghostly presence. The gossamer dream of this third-person romantic narrative (replete with long-lost epistles, ghostly figures, and gold treasure) finds a parallel in the last journal entry by the adult Reynaldo. As he leaves the hospital following a bout of pneumonia and meningitis, he writes:

> I know I will get better at home. I am filled with love for myself. Healing will begin. I draw hearts with colored markers, then branches leading away. In the center I write "I am loved," and on each branch I give an example: because I am a creation of God, because I have a loving family, because I've created loving relationships, and so on. It doesn't matter if it's not true, as long as I believe it is. (Ibid.)

As an adult, Reynaldo's imaginative reach allows him to assert a positive force in order to counteract the devastating effects of both his illness and his family's rejection. He indulges in an imagined resolution, one that affirms the possibility of love and support represented by his drawing of interconnected colored hearts. The reality of this faith in love—like his faith in ghosts as a boy—does not matter so long as he believes it true. Such wishful hoping seems more wistful than real.

Yet the story offers the possibility that love may indeed yet be manifested in the material world, not just in the realm of the imagination. The epistolary narrative closes the story. The adult Reynaldo finds an old letter written by his grandmother dated July 22, 1962, addressed to Reynaldo, the long-absent friend of her husband. In the letter, Rosario tells Reynaldo of Jesus's death from cancer. She admits that she was once jealous of Reynaldo, but now with her husband's death she no longer feels anything but acceptance. She informs Reynaldo that there will always be a room for him in her house. Moreover, she wishes to keep "Jesus's memory alive, and you along with him, so we've named our grandson Reynaldo, after you" (36). The three narratives come together in a neat resolution, nestled together in this forging of familial and loving connections.

On the one hand, this sense of connectivity is manifested through the aesthetic of the story, the interweaving of three distinct narratives that cross generational and emotional gaps in order to allow for a sense of home and place. On the other, this connection is premised on fantasies, daydreams, and wishfulness. The story envisions the possibility for ways of giving and accepting love beyond the bounds of the socially acceptable. The three narratives together trace a world in which the kind of homosexual love and desire the contemporary Reynaldo seeks has a place within his family's history and becomes possible in his childhood experiences at school. In a sense, these narratives offer a vision of an alternate family history, in which acceptance of same-sex love is interwoven within the family genealogy. Thus the narrator/protagonist Reynaldo paints parallel portraits of the desire for acceptance and loving relationships whose significance, like any good ghost story, "doesn't matter if it's not true," as long as someone believes it is.

The story foregrounds the narrative concerns that all of Cuadros's stories share. "Reynaldo" balances an interest in the realist details of illness and suffering with a fantastical and otherworldly tale of spirits beyond the grave.[6] While exploring the possibility of this spiritual element, Cuadros grounds his narratives in concrete and conflicted social and cultural experiences. The movement into the fantastical and out of the "real" leads to a very specific time and reality in which the conflicted and conflictual racial and sexual identities of the queer mestizo form the primary focus.

## A House of Cards

Where the initial stories in *City of God* treat the origins and complications of queer Chicano desire, the middle cluster establishes the troubling reality of mestizo homosexuality. These middle stories all situate the sexual and mestizo body in a social and cultural milieu where the expression of forbidden sexual desire runs counter to regimes of social control. Most significantly, this social control is made manifest through the family, the apparatus by which relations of production are reproduced.[7] The body in these stories gets situated within a very specific system of control and reproduction. It becomes the site of an ideological and biological process of reproduction, one that seeks to regiment ideas of family, sexuality, and race.

The story in *City of God* that best represents this regimentation of mestizo sexuality is "My Aztlan: White Place." This story stands as a thematic and technical tour de force. In "My Aztlan" and the stories that follow, the main character is a young adult male living with AIDS. "My Aztlan" opens with the narrator longing for his childhood home in East Los Angeles while driving in a drunken stupor after a night of cruising West Hollywood bars. The story thus opens with an image of geographic and emotional dislocation, a dislocation central to the concerns of the story. He thinks of the kind of men to whom he is attracted—blond, blue-eyed "West Hollywood bar types"—who "twist my gold chain with a wedding ring on it. Their fingers are pale compared to my darker skin. They run them down my neck, under my lapel. They ask where I'm from, disappointed at my answers, as if *they* are the natives" (1994, 53). The narrative highlights the coloring of skin as a signifier of identity, a signifier the narrator turns on its head by indicating that he, not the white men who flirt with him, are the natives. The term "native" takes on a double resonance: either a native of Los Angeles or of indigenous ancestry. Clearly, the men want the dark narrator to be the Latin American Other, the immigrant whom they can consume as an exotic object of desire. They are disappointed when the narrator is not exotic enough.

The gold ring the narrator wears on his neck is from his lover (a white man older than him) who has recently died of AIDS. Thus the story opens by evoking a number of different types of desire: for the narrator's childhood home, for his lost lover, for the white men in West Hollywood's gay bars. In every case, these desires are racialized. His childhood home represents a site of ethnic longing. The narrator is desirable precisely because of his dark skin. The other men are desirable because of their light skin color. As a mestizo and a Chicano, the narrator's subjectivity serves to foster confusion centered on the complex idea of origin. Each actor in this play of desire believes that he and not the other is the native.

Thus the title of the story proves highly ironic. Aztlán, as discussed in the preceding chapter, means "the place of whiteness" and is the mythical homeland of the ancient Mexica people. At one level, the title asserts the narrator's sense of belonging and an original claim to the city in which he lives. At the same time, the narrator's race makes him exotic, an object of desire, alien to the gay white world he inhabits. The name "Aztlán" evokes within the context of these stories not just a racial/cultural homeland but also the drug AZT that the narrator takes to combat his illness. Thus the AZT in Aztlán signifies a sense of hope, of rebirth, of a new homeland. We soon learn, however, that the narrator feels alienated from his home and family precisely because of his homosexuality and his illness, which his family believes represent a double curse they must endure. The story raises the question: where, given these conditions, is home for the narrator?

His physical childhood home is buried beneath the black expanse of the San Bernardino Freeway, demolished and covered over in the expansion of the Los Angeles freeway system. This destruction symbolizes the fact that his home has long been buried to him. Covered by concrete and asphalt, any sense of family connection and childhood innocence is inaccessible, part of an impenetrable and hardened past. In large part, this inaccessibility is the result of his family's rejection of him because of his sexuality. The narrator ruminates on his mother and her denial of his illness: "She doesn't want to think about the white man who infected me. 'He might as well have shot you,' she said once. My mother let me know that she turns in her sleep, sick at the thought of his dick up my ass or in my mouth. A milky white fluid floats in my body's space, breaks into the secret bonding of her sex, my father's sex, and the marriage of their cells" (54). The homosexual intimacy with his white lover breaks the family bonds between husband and wife, mother and son. The suggestion of a nurturing breast providing the "milky white fluid" of mother's milk and motherhood is replaced by the lover's dick in the narrator's mouth. Thus semen replaces breast milk, and the image of heterosexual reproduction is disrupted. With their son's sexuality and illness, there will be no further biological reproduction, no affirmation of heterosexual coupling, no marriage on a social or physical level. His sexuality and illness meld to disrupt the mother's view of familial reproduction and perpetuation, his queer body rending the carefully woven heteronormative social fabric that his mother imagines represents reality.

This sense of reality—of social stability premised on the sanctity of marriage and family—proves ultimately an illusion. Drunk and lonely, the narrator drives to the location where his house used to be. Looking out at the freeway, knowing that the old house lies buried, the narrator thinks: "Hidden under a modern city, this is my Aztlan, a glimpse of my ancient home, my family" (55). This sense of ancient home, he knows, is a phantasm. He recalls the real dynamics of his family, the conflicted relationship with his parents, the fighting and physical abuse he endured. The image of homeland collapses beneath the flood of harsh memories:

> Mom, why did you burn my hands with the iron and say it was an accident? tattoo my arms with the car's cigarette lighter? make me wish your wish, that I was never born? . . . My father would get this drunk, call me out of my bed to hold me. . . . His brown mechanic's hand would slip under my shirt, rub my stomach. He'd press his finger in the hole, my umbilical cord's scar till I screamed, writhing and laughing. My mother hated my father like this. (55–56)

For the narrator, his family represents a source of pain and love, of hatred and desire emblematized by the image of his father pressing his hard workingman's finger into his son's belly button. The birth scar physically marks his biological connection to the family and becomes the site of a symbolically ambiguous sexualized violation, eliciting screams and laughter. The family stands as a place of origin where images of a normative heterosexuality and family bonding get undone. The ambiguity and irony of the story's title manifest themselves in the complicated and contradictory conditions of home and place marked by sexual anxiety, economic necessity, and racialized identity.

The flight from his family provides the narrator little sense of escape from the contradictory forces that shape his subjectivity. Leaving home, he takes up with a white lover who is older, one who "made it easy to leave my folks behind. I became white, too, uncolored by age in his over-forty crowd" (56). The narrative suggests that the narrator's youth made his race less of an issue among the more mature acquaintances who became his social group. The narrator is "whitened" by virtue of his youth, accepted into the company of these middle-aged gay men.

Moreover, the narrator never raises controversial subjects linked to ethnicity, class, or race: "For our sake, I kept Sleepy Lagoon, Indian massacres, and insecticides taboo subjects to avoid arguments and misunderstandings. My lover played no part in these atrocities. I believed that the color of our skin didn't matter, there was only he and I in this affair. He offered his life and I ate greedily. Like a disease-ridden blanket, revenge was on my parents to be gay and not speak Spanish" (ibid.). For the narrator, his deracination results from a desire to flee his family's rejection. Yet his new condition is no less problematic. The violent historical events he enumerates trace a kind of repressive context by which he understands his own racial history and identity in relation to his white lover. His description suggests a kind of colonization, not of land but of his body (evoking Cherríe Moraga's notion of a "Queer Aztlán"), a colonization in which he partakes "greedily." Embraced by whiteness, he views his own sexual and ethnic condition—to be gay and not speak Spanish—as a family betrayal emblematized by the disease-ridden blanket white missionaries offered as "gifts" to the indigenous people, part of a genocidal conquest. The narrator finds his life circumscribed and permeated by a violence that centers on his sexualized and racialized body.

The narrator believes he escapes the violence of his family by retreating into the infantilizing comfort of his lover's white world. This makes more poignant the last words of his lover before dying: "'When are you going to grow up?'" (57); for it is his lover who has brought him into a world that accepts him for his youth, where his race ceases to be an identity and becomes instead a marker of the innocent and exotic. Of his lover's friends, he states:

> They all treated me as a son, this little Mexican boy. . . . they would let me rest, small, unintimidated, in the folds of their leather, they would rub my nose in their heat. They said stuff like, "Hot latin, brown-skinned, warm, exotic, dark, dark, dark," buried under their bodies' weight, dirt and

asphalt, moist skin, muscle and blood. My face collides with their chests, their hearts are at my eardrums, their fire cracks louder than guns. (58)

The deracinated world into which he enters does not save him from the same sense of suffocation and violence that he finds in thinking about his family home. Indeed, his family home and his own body are buried beneath the weight of dirt and asphalt—the manifestation of "progress" that offers little movement forward. The narrative makes clear the impossible position in which the narrator has been placed. Forced to choose between an ethnic self that ensures a conflicted family belonging or a sexual identity that places him in a conflicted social relation, he searches for a sense of place and belonging. This emotional connection he finds in a landscape where home can only lie in the impossible reaches of Aztlán.

We might think here of Emma Pérez's essay "Sexuality and Discourse" and its theorization of the Lacanian symbolic order in relation to the experience of Chicano/a colonization. She argues that "Mestizos/as master the conqueror's language as the language of survival, but it never belongs to the conquered completely. For people whose language has been swindled twice, first the Native tongue, then the appropriated tongue, we are forced to stumble over colonizer language. As an adult, the Chicano male is perceived as the powerless son of the white Oedipal father who makes laws in his language" (1991, 168).[8] At one level, Cuadros's story represents the mestizo anxiety of full subjectivity and mature self-identity in relation to a dominant racial order. The narrator of "My Aztlan" internalizes that anxiety and imagines its resolution in the final images of the story when he finally sees that he "comes home."

After his drunken tour of the Los Angeles freeways that have buried his childhood home, the narrator returns to the home he had shared with his lover. In pain, cramping and throwing up, he takes a shower and attempts to soothe himself by masturbating to the remembered passion and heat of his encounters with the older white men:

My belief, when my skin has been oiled up, is that I won't be in so much pain afterwards. There is no punishment. I will come home. I can feel my body becoming tar, limbs divide, north and south. My house smells of earth and it rumbles from the traffic above. White clay sifts through the ceiling. My bones shine in the dark. (58)

The two homes—one he shared with his infantilizing lover, the other with his abusive family, both equally conflicted—converge at the end of the story. Through the act of pleasing his mestizo body, bringing together his racial and his sexual selves, the narrator is able to imagine himself coming home. His body becomes the very material of the city, making Los Angeles the impossible homeland where he can and cannot live; for, although he "comes" home through his masturbation, it is a homecoming that returns him to his origin and to a grave. The return is at once a birth and a death as he imagines a conflation of self with place and an ambiguous reunion of his racial and sexual body with the physical home of his family and his city. The story closes with this image of an ambivalent geography in which the racial and sexual universes the narrator occupies collapse.

## Spirits of Apocalypse

The final three stories set to resolve the ambivalence between place, self, and belonging that the preceding stories examine. From these last stories emerges a vision in which the queer mestizo body becomes a locus of transformation. The sexualized body, passing through disease, moves toward a heightened spirituality—though very much at the expense of transformative social agency.

The final few stories thus focus on the body in transition from the physical and social toward the spiritual and transcendent. For example, the last story—"Sight"—makes manifest the transition to a spiritual vision born of physical suffering and decay.[9] "Sight" opens with an apocalyptic sense of destruction worthy of an Augustinian *City of God*. The narrator, suffering from distorted vision as a result of AIDS, thinks at first: "it must be the fires and winds" raising "clouds of black smoke billowing off the mountains." These visions of fiery destruction are, the narrator decides, "signs, clues written in some ancient script, and I want to know what it all means" (1994, 95). His doctor tells him that his distorted vision is caused by illness and that he should begin taking medication in order to prevent a complete loss of sight.

The narrator refuses, reveling instead in this newfound vision. The disease leads his body to open a new optic, to be able to decipher the physical world around him as it is imbued with meaning, though he is not sure precisely how to decode these new visions. Sitting in the doctor's office, he notices that "everything, everyone in her office has a glow around their bodies" that he can read and understand (96). He perceives with a great acuity their feelings, their thoughts, their relations with others owing to the halos he senses surrounding his fellow patients. This diaphanous light, evocative of Reynaldo's scarf in the earlier story, suggests contact and interconnective relations that, under normal circumstances, prove impossible.

Leaving the doctor's office, the narrator drives home using not just sight but his other senses to guide him: "the scent of jacarandas and freshly cut, large-leaf philodendrons, the feel of bumps on the road, the dampness along my arm that means I've come into my underground parking space" (96–97). In the apartment house, he sees the colors of other people spewing from their bodies, reading these as signs of their emotional and physical health. These colors turn into signs not just of their condition but also of their connection to the narrator, himself wasting away because of his illness. In the elevator he sees an old woman whom he recognizes:

> Her hair is white, I know, but I see tumors instead, the stench of black rotted fruit, dappling her brain. Her heart is erratic and I feel as if it is my own and that I am the one who falls soon. I want to touch her. I sense the elevator aching to lift us up. She is saying something to herself, I hear her say the word "God" with the warm buzz of bees and wooden lutes in her mouth. I feel my palm near her shoulder and her body begins to change, slippery as mercury. Now I can see an amber light emanating from her stomach, her head. She is unsure of why she feels better, but she takes it like a gift of inestimable worth. (97–98)

The pair is lifted up, both by the elevator and by the truncated prayer the woman utters: "God." The sense of spiritual yearning both she and the narrator feel is matched by the "gift" the narrator offers the old woman with his laying on of hands. This gesture makes her feel better, though she is unsure why. A sense of spiritual awakening leads to the narrator's realization, as he lies alone in the dark, that it "used to make me sick, the thought of my family, but now I see it as a legacy I will not understand till much later" (98). The vexed relationship with his family becomes less a source of sickness than an awareness of a complex legacy. That legacy is one whose meaning is deferred—"a legacy I will not understand till much later"—but one he is sure to perceive with clarity at some point. Unlike the earlier stories, the thought of his family here does not evoke feelings of anxiety and dread. Rather, family has finally become a site of potential inheritance.

For the narrator, this realization is pushed aside as he senses a man—"white, bright as if a hundred candles were burning inside him"—watching him lying in bed. This man calls over "more of his people to the window" when he sees that the narrator is ready to die (ibid.). The spiritual rebirth of the narrator at his death is couched in images of the Catholic Mass: "At first I pretend not to know what he offers, can taste meat in my mouth, blood on my lips. There is no judgment on whatever I do; he is just there for me" (ibid.). Evocative of the resolution in "My Aztlan," the narrator's arrival into the City of God is characterized not by judgment but by simple acceptance. The Eucharist the narrator tastes is at once the sacrifice of God to the world and the embodiment of the narrator's sacrifice of his body. His new vision and sense of spiritual awakening come at the price of his own mestizo body.

This insight and sense of peace leads him to want to communicate with a number of people: with his roommate about what medications will keep him alive, with his ex-lover to explain that the narrator understands why he left him, with his mother to express his knowledge of from where her anger comes. He is certain that "if I could just touch a certain spot on her body, near her breastbone, it would all be released, she would always be warm after that" (98–99). The end is nigh, however, and the thin veil of life unravels as he "lets the angels consume me, each one biting into my body, until nothing is left, nothing but a small glow and even that begins to perish" (99). The final consumption of the body and spirit is complete. The result is that nothing remains but the collection of stories and poems Cuadros's readers hold in their hands. In this way, Cuadros as author makes clear the loss of his own physical life, a loss attenuated somewhat by the persistence of the aesthetic object the reader is able yet to consume.

Of course, neither the spiritual insights of the narrator nor the making of his transformation into narrative permits a transcendence of death and decay. The tension between the physical and spiritual worlds remains at the heart of *City of God*.[10] The specificity of those worlds is highly significant, however, as they shape and contain the movement of sexualized mestizo bodies. The spiritual healing that occurs at the end of "Sight" is made necessary by the physical and emotional rejection the characters throughout *City of God* suffer as a result of their cultural and racial context. Their families represent their connection to an ethnic identity marked by racial distinction. Yet their families' inability to accept their sexual identity is what makes healing necessary. Through an acceptance of their racial and ethnic legacy embodied by family in tandem with an embrace of their own sexual selves, healing is felt.

That healing, however, is not premised on a transformation of social spaces or dynamics. What transformation is possible in the stories of Cuadros offers a highly mediated sense of empowerment. The stories, in effect, represent an ever-shrinking world of human connection where, ultimately, the characters withdraw further into their own physical suffering and spiritual enlightenment. The narrator in "Sight" realizes that he could, were he able to touch his mother, comfort her; this realization comes just as the angels finally consume him body and soul. Thus transcendence as a means of human connectivity proves impossible.

In Cuadros's stories, the double marking of the mestizo body by race and illness serves to make it a site of textual interpretation but a failed source of social agency. As readers, we are invited to interpret the significance of the characters' illness as a sign of loss, as a judgment, and as a form of spiritual transformation. At the same time, the characters cannot call themselves into being in terms of relating their queer mestizo selves to other social actors and agents. Although the stories in *City of God* help to make present the tensions and contradictions involved in the articulation of a newly sexualized mestizaje, they also fail to convey the very necessary social transformation that could ultimately make queer mestizos find a sense of place and home within a newly configured social landscape. They trace a journey through physical transformation, one in which the dynamic qualities of mestizaje manifest themselves in a newfound hope for spiritual rebirth, but one that leaves very little room for a reconfiguration of effective social relations.

## Cartographies of Desire

Through an affirmation of aesthetic imagination, the characters in Cuadros's stories suggest the necessity for new relational conditions surrounding queer mestizo identities. At the same time, the stories signal the failure of these new conditions to be realized within such social configurations as class, ethnicity, citizenship, sexuality, HIV status, race, and gender. The mestizo body moves through new sociosexual geographies in search of a social belonging that seems always just out of reach. The queer mestizo seeks to embody racial and sexual identities in a cohesive sense of subjectivity that makes of the body and its desires a healthy wholeness. The illness that wracks the characters represents dissolution at a physical level that resonates with the disrupted social terrain the characters must negotiate. This physical dissolution serves finally to transform the body from a site of physical desire to one simultaneously of spiritual awareness and social dissociation. The body becomes a productive site of meaning even as it is ceaselessly overwritten by carefully scripted discourses of repressive identity and social alienation.

In Emma Pérez's 1996 novella *Gulf Dreams*, the main character also undergoes a process of bodily transformation, one that leads to an understanding of the body as both sign and site of new relational meanings. The book traces the way the unnamed narrator becomes aware that her body produces desire, recognition, and identity, forms of knowledge that conflict with those meaning systems produced by her social networks. Her body makes meaning at odds with the way her society understands her body. As a young woman who desires women, as a Chicana who aspires to knowledge, as a child of working-class parents who seeks a way out of economic impoverishment, the narrator tries to stand outside the social positions she is expected to occupy.

*Gulf Dreams* focuses on the transition from childhood through adolescence to young adulthood of a young Chicana—unnamed throughout the narrative—coming to terms with the certainty of her desire for another woman, also unnamed. Although she understands the social strictures against such a desire, she knows all too well the power of her desire and the manner in which it shapes her identity and behavior. She falls in love with a young woman who, despite her evident attraction to the narrator, denies her lesbian desire and succumbs to social convention by dating boys and feigning heterosexual behavior. Ultimately, this object of the narrator's desire marries a young Chicano, Pelón, who is involved in university politics and who eventually becomes a lawyer. As the narrative develops—a narrative highly evocative of a dream state and highly impressionistic—Pelón becomes jealous of the obvious attraction between his wife and the unnamed narrator. Eventually, he defends a group of men accused of raping a Chicana named Ermila. It is ultimately revealed that the main defendant, Chencho, happens to have been the same character who sexually violated the narrator when she was a little girl. Thus issues of desire, power, sexuality, and sexual violation are repeated themes that help tie the nonlinear narrative together.

In part, the narrative is so impressionistic because of its concern with the emotional turmoil and development of the narrator. The focus is on the ways she has had to come to terms with the disjuncture between her desires and social constraints. As the narrator becomes aware of her sexuality, she also realizes that the networks of social, economic, and cultural exchange prevent her from fully realizing a sense of place and belonging. The emotional turmoil she feels—growing up in a repressive small costal town in Texas that she eventually leaves—is matched by a physical destruction and violence enacted by herself and others upon her queer Chicana body. Evoking Anzaldúa's Coatlicue state and Sandoval's Barthean "punctum," the narrative follows the development of a forbidden but transformative love. The novella suggests that this love is ever evasive as a result of external and internal pressures forbidding woman-to-woman erotic love. It is a love that undoes solid social constructs, but a love that is also solidly challenged by the constraints of family, community, and peers.

Social meaning is inscribed on the body even as the body seeks to create new meanings. These new meanings are often evoked via a focus on the spiritual and mystical, embodied by both lesbian sexuality and individual psychosexual development. The title of the novella, *Gulf Dreams*, suggests the spiritual and psychological dimensions traced in the narrative. At one level, the dreams represent a hope by the narrator to form a cohesive identity in which her body's desires can be acted upon and accepted within the social networks that so constrain her racial and sexual being. The geographic gulf here is the actual Gulf of Mexico on which sits the rural town of the narrator's childhood, El Pueblo. This site forms the social geography on which she seeks to map a space for her incipient lesbian love. This desire proves, ultimately, impossible as her would-be lover succumbs to social convention and rejects her own lesbian desires. The social formations that define her town's geography are too pervasive to allow a new cartography of desire.

At another level, the dreams function as the psychologized desires of the narrator in their inexpressibility and incapacity to find fulfillment. The gulf as a fissure between dream and reality is the space between the knowledge of the body and the social geography that delimits how the mestiza body express itself. The book's epigraph, from Georges Bataille's *Story of the Eye*, serves to index the failure to bridge this gulf: "Thus it was that our sexual dream kept changing into a nightmare." The novella recounts a descent from dream to nightmare. Language and the ability to tell stories thus become primary concerns of the narrative. Indeed, a central tension in the book lies in the question whether language can, even tenuously, help fend off the inevitability of sexual dreams turned to nightmares. In the end, it is the re-creation of the narrator's desire through the telling of her story that creates a narrative of desire articulated even as it describes the impossibility of its fulfillment.

Language becomes the focus of Pérez's narrative, language as a locus for the creation and dissolution of meaning. The disrupted and surreal quality of the narrative suggests that this is a language in dissolution, a language seeking the expression of subjectivity at the limits of its ideological constraints. The evocation of desire in the narrative is told as a story of its own failure. In this regard, one might read Pérez's text alongside Julia Kristeva's discussion of linguistic expression in *Revolution in Poetic Language*. Kristeva addresses how language is a point of explosion between the subject and her ideological limits. The body's desires are expressed through a formal linguistic shattering that constitutes changes in the status of the subject: her relation to the body, to others, and to objects. In the artistic expression of language, Kristeva observes, "this shattering can display the productive basis of subjective and ideological signifying formations—a foundation that primitive societies call 'sacred' and modernity has rejected as 'schizophrenia'" (1984, 15). Poetic language is a disruptive language opening up the possibilities of new, potentially ecstatic expression. Yet, as Kristeva points out, in a modern context, this expressiveness might be construed as entirely meaningless beyond the sign of some psychological dis-ease.[11]

The opening of Pérez's novella suggests the skittishness of language and both its impossibility of expression and its shattering, a shattering that grasps for new formations of meaning. The use of repetition and doubling lends the narrative a sense of the meditative and dreamlike qualities that characterize the book. The narrator meditates on the germinal moment when she first casts eyes on the object of her nascent desire:

I met her in the summer of restless dreams. It was a time when infatuation emerges erotic and pure in a young girl's dreams. She was a small girl, a young woman. Her eyes revealed secrets, mysteries I yearned to know long after that summer ended.

My eldest sister introduced us. The young woman, the sister of my sister's best friend, became my friend. At our first meeting we went to the park. We walked, then stood under a tree for hours exchanging glances that bordered on awkward embarrassment. I remember we avoided the clarity of the afternoon. In a few moments, after her eyes sunk tenderly into mine, she caressed a part of me I never knew existed.

At fifteen, I hadn't known love. I don't know if I fell in love that day. I know I felt her deeply and reassuringly. Without a touch, her passion traced the outline of my face. I wanted to brush her cheek lightly with my hand, but I, too frightened, spoke in riddles, euphemistic yearnings: the sun so hot, the trees so full, the earth pressed beneath me. (1996, 11)

What is literal and what is metaphorical becomes nearly impossible to tell, indeed, very much like a dream remembered as reality. Through repetition, the narrative underscores a meditative state, the "restless dreams" that are the "young girl's dreams." The narrator describes her object of desire as a "small girl, a young woman," offering a jarring juxtaposition of girl/woman suggesting both innocence and desire. The narrator confesses that the girl "caressed a part of me I never knew existed," but only later notes that the girl's passion traced the outline of her face "without a touch." The narrative thus doubles back upon itself, at once evoking and then undercutting meaning. The final line of this passage suggests how language fails to convey adequately the certainties her body feels. The narrator wants to reach out and lightly touch the young girl, but instead relies on hackneyed euphemisms to express her feelings: the hot sun, the full trees, the pressing earth.

The narrative makes clear how disruptive this inexpressible desire becomes. Her sexual longing threatens to undo the social connections central to the world of female community that the narrator is expected to occupy. The certainties that the narrator's body conveys to her prove dangerous as they disrupt the homosocial bonds on which domestic femininity is founded. Eve Sedgwick has famously described the pattern underlying patriarchal control as the "diacritical opposition between the 'homosocial' and the 'homosexual'" (1985, 2). Within the logic of Pérez's narrative, the maintenance of a strict separation between female homosociability and homosexuality is central to the preservation of male control over female bodies. Hence, after first meeting, the narrator spends weeks dreaming about the passion she feels for the absent object of her desire before she again sees the young woman. Accompanied by her sister, the narrator visits the young woman's house:

No one knew why I had come. To see my new friend, they thought. To link families with four sisters who would be friends longer than their lifetimes through children who would bond them at baptismal rites. Comadres. We would become intimate friends sharing coffee, gossip and heartaches. We would endure the female life-cycle—adolescence, marriage, menopause, death, and even divorce, before or after menopause, before or after death. I had not come for that. I had come for her kiss. (1996, 13)

The narrator recognizes that the bond forged between women is expected to revolve around heterosexual coupling and reproduction. The privileged location afforded divorce in this description of the female life cycle underscores the centrality male figures play in this homosocial vision of expected fulfillment. Narratively, the narrator's bald declamation disrupts the stability of this vision: "I had come for her kiss." The frank homosexual desire she expresses narratively threatens to unsettle an unspoken homosocial friendship. The narrator's declaration thus unsettles the strictures that encompass the life of women in her social world.[12]

Yet quickly it becomes evident that the object of the narrator's desire is not as anxious as the narrator to pursue such a social rupture. At their second meeting, the young woman tells the narrator about her newfound love, a young boy with a "delicious, expert mouth" who she claims loves her (14). This announcement recasts the significance of the female body for the narrator, shifting the certainties of her body onto the grounds of a much more mundane relationship: "We became friends. The promise of female rituals enraged me. We met weekly, then monthly, then not at all. Her boy became her cause" (15). The narrator feels the young woman is consciously denying the feelings she holds, making heterosexual choice a political figuration, her "cause." The young woman begins to repress her own passion, suppressing her passion out of "fear, a reproach against me" (ibid.). All that remains is to follow scripted roles within a homosocial order that seeks to erase homosexuality. The narrator feels a betrayal that stands in opposition to the certainties of her body: an undeniable though transgressive queer desire. Her sexual desire becomes confounded by a socially sanctioned deception, substituting pain for pleasure. Ultimately, this substitution will become a dangerous training in which her sense of desire walks hand in hand with pain and violence. The processes of socialization that seek to circumscribe her body come, ultimately, to nearly destroy it as she substitutes bodily pain for feelings of sexual desire.[13]

## A Double Helix

The twin issues of trust and deception become central to the narrative. While the desire that arises from her body makes clear to the narrator one certainty, the color of her skin and eyes betrays another. Lighter than the rest of her siblings, she is left to struggle with the conflicts of racial and ethnic identity that is a legacy of colonial encounters: "Bronze in the summer with hair and eyes so light that I could pass through doors that shut out my sisters and brother. Their color and brown eyes, I envied. I grew to resent the colors that set me apart from my family" (1996, 15). The lightness of her mestiza body does nothing to free her from the pained contradictions inherent to racial hierarchy. This pain she internalizes, even at a young age. Upset at the difference in skin tone and how it seems to separate her from her family, she describes her early self-destructive drive: "At five, I took a butcher knife, sat calmly, sadly, on the pink chenille bedspread, threatening to slice away at tanned skin" (ibid.). The image of innocence is horrible, the juxtaposition of the pink chenille that surrounds the girl's body to the threat to flay her own flesh.

This internalized violence against racial difference manifests itself as well through language. The introduction of English ("strange foreign words, immigrant sounds") to the narrator's life in school underscores divisions already felt on the level of race: "Pronunciation divided worlds" (16).[14] These divisions manifest themselves not just between the narrator and the outside world. The function of language as a disciplining regime is felt at home as well. She recollects her younger brother who, in childhood, was such a constant companion to her that their family took to calling them the twins, *los cuates*. As she and her brother grow older, they begin to drift apart for reasons the narrator does not quite understand, even now, reflecting on the past as she writes the narrative. She discusses the mutual resentment they began to feel for each other: "I, bigger, lighter-skinned, had caught up with him in school, made friends and passing grades. Maybe I reminded him too much of the white world outside our home. Maybe in mastering the language of survival, I too became an outsider. He no longer allowed me to share his hopes. Long before, I had ceased listening" (20). The narrator's struggle to learn the language that "divided worlds" leaves her, perhaps, on the other side of a divide for which the racialized body serves as a marker of difference.

The narrator internalizes the very hierarchies of identity she knows to be destructive. Clearly, when she denies the desire her body makes certain—the meaning her body makes—she destroys the most liberating elements of her self. The image of a little girl threatening to cut her own body becomes emblematic of her own understanding of a self betrayed by the social discourses that surround and construct it. Yet, as she grows older, in order to protect herself, she succumbs to the very racial and gender hierarchies that place her in positions of disempowerment. She acquires a white boyfriend, a boy from Alabama whose "white skin stood like armor between me and an unjust town." This protection serves to encircle her in new constraints. She is forced to assume the role of the proper heterosexual high school girl: "We became lovers who kissed on Friday nights at drive-in theaters, where I avoided sex" (25). The sexual frustration leads the Alabama boy to become more demanding, to begin giving orders, to assert his male privilege, "so convinced of its superiority to the feminine" (22). Eventually, this game bores the narrator, and her eyes wander "to neighborhood boys, to *pachucos*, so coolly sexy, so dangerously off-limits" (26). Although she is attracted to the mestizo boys of her own neighborhood, they remain for her unobtainable Others. She internalizes the colonial structures of racial and ethnic hierarchy. The very mestizo bodies that surround her are those that, though coolly sexy, remain off-limits.

The narrator's relation to the feminine becomes double-edged. On the one hand, feminine beauty and friendship become the quintessence of unity. On the other, the feminine represents a separate physical/spiritual presence made dysfunctional by social propriety. The young girl of her desire metaphorically merges with the narrator and they become a kind of platonic whole:

We merged before birth, entwined in each other's souls, wrapped together like a bubble of mist, floating freely, reflecting rainbows. This was before flesh, before bones crushed each other foolishly trying to join mortal bodies, before the outline of skin shielded us from one another. We both knew this, that we came from the same place, that we were joined in a place so uncommon that this world, which bound and confined us, could not understand the bond that flesh frustrated. (27)

This vision of a prelinguistic bond evokes a kind of Kristevan chora, a connection to the maternal (here sororal) bond. The free-floating mist of this Edenic conjoining represents an ideal for the narrator, what she feels her heart tells her. A romantic vision of feminine bliss informs how she understands her body's desire.

This desire, when enacted in the complex web of social constraint, manifests itself as a destructive, self-perpetuating replay of patriarchal oppression. The evident attraction between the two women upsets their respective boyfriends: "I risked inviting her to my home every day, despite the moodiness she provoked. Her boyfriend grew more threatened each time I appeared. His hostility sharpened. Mine became silent when she approached. She and I, trapped in social circumstances. Propriety kept us apart" (28). Male power manifests itself through the imposition of social restraint. Although the narrator makes clear that the young woman finds her sexually attractive, the patriarchal formations that undergird social space here create a kind of separation, a sexual segregation that keeps the young women apart in the very moment of their mutually recognized desire.

The body begins as a site of yearning and passion, a location that produces meaning through the certainties of desire. Where these desires run against acceptable social roles for the body, the certainties once felt are forced to submit to patterns of behavior born of unequal power. The narrative highlights the power inherent in the distorting effects of a colonial legacy marked by asymmetries of gender, race, class, and ethnicity. As desire and social propriety are intertwined, the knowledge that the body produces is first silenced, then erased.

## An Impossible Tongue

The body is forced to deny its desire, to play roles that are detrimental and destructive. Grown, the narrator leaves El Pueblo for a time in order to get away from the self-destructive behavior she has internalized as a part of her life: "I instigated suicide with cheap wine and diet pills. When the pills weren't enough, I used needles" (46). Yet her time away from El Pueblo does not erase the memory of the young woman who has been so central in developing the forbidden knowledge of anticolonialist desire for the narrator.

Interestingly, the narrator comments only obliquely and in passing about her time away from El Pueblo, a suggestion of drug abuse, and stripping "for men whose power robbed my integrity" (25). Later the narrative returns to this time away in Los Angeles, recalling the "many women, many lovers, many nights" that helped "sedate" but never replace the memory of the missing young woman (70). ("There were men too," she recounts, some of whom "were friends, but never lovers" [71].) Although she was gone almost ten years, the focus of the narrative remains clearly in the coastal Texan town and the role that the young woman plays in the narrator's life. The young woman and the town stand as two polarities, one the object of desire, the other the social network that prohibits the fulfillment of desire. Both women have been taught that their love can never be realized. It is clear, however, that their forbidden desire represents for the narrator the dream of a life beyond the restrictive bonds of rigidly defined social relations.

With her return, the narrator finds that the young woman has bound herself even more tightly to the socially sanctified bonds of homosocial exchange by marrying a young lawyer, Pelón, whom she had met in college. The marriage serves to further confine the young woman, confirming for the narrator the pervasive power of male domination. The young woman's husband, Pelón, "owned her, sapping her, wanting every piece of her, expecting what he'd had as a child. He held her frantically. His possession. Always within sight of him, she mirrored him back to him. He was her purpose" (46). Patterns of male privilege, the narrative suggests, begin in childhood and return repeatedly in the relations between men and women. Women become mere reflections of men's desires.

Where Pelón views the young woman as his possession always within the specular power of his gaze, the narrator has a different view of her. For Pelón, his gaze controls the young woman. The narrator, by contrast, gazes "into a mirror at an aging face pronouncing her name clearly, succinctly. She is me, fused, when we're apart. I couldn't look into my own eyes without her mirrored back" (49). The narrator pronounces her name, recognizes the young woman's identity as she gazes into the reflection of her own eyes, the mirrors that reflect each's woman's identity back to the other, giving each other back to themselves. A process of self- and mutual recognition takes place in these moments of reflexivity, in many ways echoing the reflexive quality of the narrative itself. The story and images spun by the narrator become another reflection of her identity in the Other, the mutually constituted connection between narrator and young woman that is perpetually refused them. "With her," the narrator writes, "I have courage." And just as she allows herself the dream to imagine a future "in which I and the young woman from El Pueblo live alone, away from her gluttonous husband, her hollow baby crib, this infertile life" (50), Pelón "stalks through the door like a rupture" (51). Ever vigilant, the male gaze disrupts even tentative steps toward the unity the narrator feels is natural for her and the young woman. What the women can feel for each other does not even register as desire, but as the dream for desire.

Desire has become displaced for the narrator. The socially illicit attraction the women feel for each other must be expressed through others. The narrator recalls how, in college, the two friends spent Friday nights telling stories about their week, the "evening's back seat brawl with some boy. She confessed details, delightfully" (52). The delicious and salacious details cause the narrator to open up to the young woman's "seductive words, wanting more particulars to bond us intimately." Consequently, the narrator considers the erotics of language:

> Intimacies of the flesh achieved through words. That was our affair. Years later, I rediscovered my compulsion to consummate intimacy through dialogue—to make love with a tongue that spewed desire, that pleaded for more words, acid droplets on my skin. With her, I learned to make love to women without a touch. I craved intimate, erotic dialogue. I was addicted to words and she had spawned the addiction. (Ibid.)

Physically denied to the narrator, the world of desire becomes displaced into language. The ability of words to connect and entice—as well as create the narrative universe woven by the narrator's own story—provides a kind of power and ability to transcend the bonds of social constraint. The body's certainties can, for the narrator, become enacted through the power of words. The social sanctions against lesbian desire lead the two friends to exchange stories as the only acceptable mode of intimate exchange. Although this displaces the locus of desire from the body to language, it does enable an articulation of passion that inflects the form of the novella's narrative.

Throughout *Gulf Dreams*, language represents a site of delight, a tool for survival—as the narrator notes on numerous occasions—and the means by which she recollects her experiences. Language enables her to make sense of her conflicted memories. The disjuncture between what her body knows and the social repression of her desires becomes mediated through the language of narrative. Language is a means of envisioning the possible, describing what can never be achieved on the level of social constraint. Simultaneously, the narrator makes clear that language is part of the colonial condition that divides worlds: those who manage to master a language of survival and those caught in positions of subjugation. Language is always a type of mask or a means of performance, acting as a tool to erase or displace bodily differences of race, gender, and sexuality. As we have seen in relation to her family, however, this means for the narrator a familial dislocation, a distancing of her self from her family. Language—the means of recollection, reenvisioning, and reimagining what could have been possible regarding desire—also plays a role in the repressive systems that deny the possibility of desire.

Language serves to imagine and express the inexpressible and repressed. But language has its limits in relation to the knowledge the body produces. The opening of the novella addresses the narrator's need to fall back on weak metaphors ("the sun so hot, the trees so full, the earth pressed beneath me" [11]) in order to express her body's lesbian desire. Similarly, the structural center of the narrative is organized around an event inadequately represented through language. The narrator recalls an afternoon her mother took her as an infant of "two or three, maybe younger but speaking" (59) to the local seamstress. Left alone with the seamstress's young boys, the narrator remembers being taken into a back bedroom: "An older brother stands at the doorway, guarding those who play harmless children's games. A boy pulls down his pants, holds a hard penis in his hand, rubs it against a baby girl's flesh. The baby's eyes track a thin, cinnamon cockroach slithering against a wall, it finds a crack and slips through an opening that was invisible, nonexistent. She is numb" (60). In order to describe the rape she endures as a child, the narrator must rely on metaphor, suggesting that language fails to convey the power and significance that this moment of violation represents.

Narratively, the rape takes on an importance impossible to convey through language. In terms of narrative structure, the moment occupies a central position in the novella. Thematically, it represents a point of origin for the emotional conditions with which the narrator must contend as she later experiences intimacy and sexuality. Indeed, this moment creates the narrator's conscious awareness of sexuality when she becomes aware of the "opening that was invisible." Because of this violation, the narrator develops into "a woman who craved mixed sensations, that which would never satisfy her, to not be satisfied was her satisfaction, chasing an unconscious memory. She would long for a stinging slap on tender skin. A soothing roughness" (60). The dynamics of her relation with the young woman become clear: the mixing of pain and pleasure, the deceitful game of hurtful rage and soothing reconciliation are all part of a "soothing roughness." These dynamics are anchored in a moment of origin, a moment of violation. The narrator states bluntly: "This is betrayal I've been speaking about" (74). The betrayal not only colors all that follows, but it also represents a violation repeated over and over. Patriarchal privilege protects this type of violation, a violation that ultimately engenders this very same privilege.

### Duplication and Duplicity

The narrative turns to take up the aftereffects of another rape, one unlike the highly secretive rape of the narrator as a child. This second rape leads to a sensational trial in El Pueblo. The case gains notoriety because the woman against whom the crime is committed, Ermila, demands that justice be done. Rather than remain silent, Ermila seeks public redress by bringing the five young rapists to trial. The legal system, as will soon become apparent, represents those who in the narrator's estimation espouse truth but in reality distort the actual events of Ermila's violation. The defense attorney for the five men is, in a not unexpected irony, the young woman's husband, Pelón. His representation of the rape becomes a distortion of Ermila's experience as he argues his clients are being subjected to media-driven stereotyping.

In his defense of the five accused rapists, Pelón relies on binary constructs of elementary identity politics: "Pelón defended the rapists, accusing a white media of framing innocent young men, making them a gang of barrio punks. He was so sure of himself that when he spoke about gringo enemies, he forgot who Ermila was and where she came from" (89). As used by Pelón, the legal system produces meaning that displaces and erases the mestiza body as a site of knowledge. Ermila's experience of violation gets lost in the racial binary that pits victimized Chicano youth against racist white society. These constructions, as the narrative reveals, do not provide a proper vindication for the wrongs suffered by Ermila, a young Chicana whose identity and claim for redress is lost amid the male rhetoric of racial/ethnic identity. In this sense, another form of violence is enacted upon her. The discourse of racial discrimination overtakes the gendered discourse of rape. The demand for (male) racial equality silences the mestiza voice demanding justice as the object of intraethnic violence. The trial thus replicates and distorts the events of the rape in order to deny Ermila both voice and agency, duplicating the processes of disempowerment first experienced physically through rape.

For the narrator, the rape signifies part of the repeated violation that is the foundation of patriarchal privilege. The process that thwarts justice for Ermila represents the institutional enactment of this privilege. For Ermila, the gang rape represents something more devastating, more immediate, and more destructive. The violence Ermila endures not only makes her body "scarred inner flesh" but also makes her incapable of feeling intimacy: "Her flesh deadened, could not respond to contact anymore. How do you recreate loving touch in memory when repulsion ruptures the body, the psyche?" (78). The body as a locus of knowledge and certainty loses something more than innocence through sexual violence. It loses the ability to convey its knowledge, those primordial certainties that make the body a text on which meaning is imposed and from which meaning is created. The rupture of the body and psyche represents a violation that disrupts the connection between the mestiza body, memory, and desire. A body in dissolution replaces the body as a locus of meaning. Mestiza desire, destroyed, becomes a sign of emptiness.

The only means of redressing such a violation is in the realm of the law. Yet the social mechanisms for justice are one of the very means by which patriarchal power is produced, codified, and protected. As the narrator knows too well, the violation Ermila endures at the hands of her rapists and at the hands of the law cannot be escaped. Only the imagination can provide a type of solace, one indebted to a forging and duplicity of the real: "There can be no happy ending, only in fantasy, what the mind chooses to make up to hold on to as real. The imagination will dodge cruelty, escaping the crime—how the body has been pillaged, scarred—pretending this never happened, fooling memory with another meaning" (92). The role of the narrative in many respects plays this fantasy role, imaging the possible while asserting the inevitable. The injustices inflicted on Ermila—the rape, the accusations of promiscuity—coexist with the violation endured by the narrator both in her thwarted love for Pelón's wife and in her rape as a child that forms a kind of perverse origin story. "What happens here," the narrator writes, opening the second half of the book and the treatment of Ermila's rape, "began long ago. The story began in a hot, steamy room where three boys groped a baby's body" (77). Both the narrator and Ermila experience disempowerment as the result of a sexual violation. This underscores again the process of doubling repeated throughout the narrative. The narrator reveals that the oldest of the five men who raped Ermila is Inocencio—nicknamed Chencho—the boy who had sexually violated the narrator when she was a toddler.

The narrator's moment of original violation leads her to identify with Ermila: "She resurrects a puzzle daily. Surveying the courtroom, before me, appears the angelic face of the boy who had harmed me. Pelón calls the rapist a victim. The woman is absent, a consequence" (93). The narrator sees in Ermila's rape a doubling of her own violation. In both cases, the sexual violence enacted upon the female body robs it of agency.

The woman is absent precisely to the degree that she plays a part in both the Mexican and Chicano national imaginary as, herself, a site of origin: "Ermila, *la malinchista, la chingada*, a betrayer, her own people called her" as a result of the trail (ibid.).[15] Mestiza agency gets associated with dishonor and betrayal, placing an empowered mestiza identity outside the realm of the community. Mestiza agency, associated with La Malinche— the foundational figure of mestizaje—is equated with placelessness.

There is a doubling here, one where violation stands as the ideological root of Mexican and Chicano identity: the woman as betrayer, as the victim/victimizer, as the mother forcibly opened, violated, or deceived. For the narrator, her sense of violation turns this nationalist discourse of victimization inside out, asserting her own violation as a locus for identity. Only by overcoming the sense of separation and alienation imposed on her and the women around her can the narrator envision a wholeness that overcomes the scarring and violence inscribed by this violation. Yet, as we see, this reconnection is impossible within the social constraints that establish well-defined lines of demarcation between normative and transgressive sexual and gender identifications. Only the narrative can offer even a glimpse of other possibilities.

The narrative makes clear, however, that these ephemeral possibilities are constructed in the face of overwhelming pressures. As the narrator reviews the tempestuous life of Ermila ("the drunken father who couldn't hold a job; the mother who beat her two younger sons in frustration and cherished her oldest son. . . . Her mother neglected an only daughter" [98]), it becomes clear that the patterns of violence and violation in relation to sexuality and mestiza identity are as much a part of Ermila's life as they are of the narrator's. The town is quick to judge Ermila for her "arrogant air" and for exhibiting "strength and sexuality. . . . Women weren't supposed to be that sure of themselves, that lustful and proud" (97). Social judgment serves to constrain Ermila's willful sexuality. Her assertion of a sexual self flies in the face of a social propriety that disempowers the female body by robbing and constraining its sexuality.

Chencho's sexual violence against Ermila and the narrator is itself a type of doubling, the duplication of the violation committed against him as a child. Chencho is exposed early on in life to a world of sexuality for which he is not ready: "An older brother showed Chenchito things about sex, things not for a little boy, not yet. As he grew older, an uncle, his mother's brother, would frequent their house. . . . But the uncle became too familiar. He raped the boy, kept raping him until the boy was strong enough to beat up the old man and spit in his face" (103). The patterns of violation that crisscross the narrative are again located at a matrix where the mestizo/a body endures a moment of originary violence. This violence ensures the repeated cycles of violence and violation that scar the lives of many of the characters. Thus, though the narrative seeks to make present the possibility of a world in which true love, desire, and connection are possible, it also makes clear that practices of enforced gender and sexual roles bind victims in violent and deeply ingrained patterns of behavior. Indeed, the pattern of violation within the family is a symbolic mirroring of betrayal by the larger community.

The town views Ermila's rape as her responsibility, the inevitable result of her enticing the five young men. As a result, in a perverse twist of logic necessary to maintain patriarchal structures, the rapist becomes the victim. Pelón exploits this view in defending Chencho: "Sympathetically, he spoke, 'We all suffer, we're all victims.' The rapist looked grim for the jurors as Pelón cross-examined a court-appointed psychologist, asking about a rapist's temper. The psychologist described rapists, repeat offenders, repeating what they had learned as children" (105–6). The narrator, too, represents Chencho as a victim, not only because of the sexual violation he repeatedly endured as a boy, but because of the sexually repressive way he must experience his body's own desires. Chencho ends up frequenting gay bars, "fooling himself, convincing himself he was there to spy on men from El Pueblo, 'to check on queers,' he'd lie" (103). Yet the narrator makes clear that he "frequented men's bars to assuage his pain, but he couldn't quell the memories" (112). The narrator is, in a sense, forced to understand the dynamics driving Chencho's violent rage because she, too, is haunted by memories burned into the flesh and impossible to forget.

These memories all deal with how the certainties of the narrator's body are denied, thus casting her into a position of abject disempowerment. This disempowerment leads her to assert a type of masculine privilege: "I took risks in public, fighting with people I didn't like, barking orders and requests no one could meet. I became someone to hate. I hated myself" (126). The narrator assumes a masculinist prerogative, asserting her will and imposing her power in ways that make her the object of her own self-loathing. In part, the only way she can assert power is to duplicate the destructive forms of male privilege she has seen enacted throughout her life.

For this reason, the narrator knows that she has to escape the destructive patterns of violence and role-playing. She does this through storytelling. She addresses the young woman of her long-lasting desire directly, telling her: "The way I love you remains an act of language. Words, narrative, myth—all my dreams convey the way I would have loved you" (137). The narrativization of desire represents the only means of fulfilling her love. However, she knows that this act of language can occur only in the imagination. The felt, physical reality proves that there is no overcoming behavior the body has learned too well. This is especially true of the violence unleashed against transgressive desires. The main narrative closes with the realization that "for those of us who track the pleasure of pain" because of patriarchal and colonial power dynamics, "repression is learned; one prays for passion to fade, for dreaded obsessions to dissipate, that's the only comfort. Or act again. Fall victim to selfishness. Again. Ache again so much that death would be easier, softer. You will welcome death, its peace" (150). The narrator acknowledges that the mixture of pleasure and pain is a learned response, one inscribed in the flesh because the mestiza body inherits the lasting legacies of male privilege and racial oppression. Pleasure can only be felt through pain, because the certainties of the body are denied it when the queer mestiza body expresses its desires. The body is thus taught to perceive itself only through pain and denial.

As with Cuadros's text, the disruption of queer mestizo desire leads to an embrace of death. If death in Cuadros represents a kind of spiritual awakening, in Pérez it represents a form of forgetting. In both cases, all that remains are highly conflicted narratives. The epilogue to Pérez's novella recounts rather flatly that Chencho is sentenced to thirty years in prison for the rape of Ermila. The other defendants are set free, but the leader and instigator must face his punishment. Of course, Pelón claims that this is an outrage against his client and promises an extensive appeal.

A year after the trial, the narrator finds Chencho, presumably free on appeal, drinking a beer in a Los Angeles bar. She observes him for weeks as he prowls the bar's parking lot waiting to make contact with older men. Finally, one morning, his beaten and mutilated body is found in the alley behind the bar. The police, uninterested in a single murder behind a "pervert bar," generally ignore the case.

Ermila, too, is lost. She disappears, nobody knows where, until the bones of a woman's corpse are dug up in a cove on the beach. The people of El Pueblo identify the remains as Ermila's: "Everyone had wanted her silent. They wished her silence in decaying bones. For me, Ermila lives happily in her grandmother's village in Mexico. Children surround her as she weaves stories about el norte and how it makes some men evil, others greedy" (155–56). In both cases, the narrator serves to complete the narrative arc. Yet the horror accompanying the description of Chencho's beaten body ("Flattened, pale testicles with dried cakes of blood were jammed into Inocencio's mouth" [154]) is offset by the imagined idyll that Ermila lives. Both endings provide a sense of narrative closure and completeness, even if it is an imagined ending.

Thus the narrator draws her story to a close with a meditation on the powers of the imagination. Similar to Cuadros's narratives, imagination is all that is left in terms of redemption. Pérez's narrator thinks: "I choose this past—my mother's strong arms as she bent to pick cotton, my father's fried chicken when we came home from *la pisca* [the fields]. I remember my sisters dressing and painting their faces, my brothers strolling beside me" (156). This remembered past is a part of her imaginative recasting, a reenvisioning of her familial reality essential for a sense of wholeness and identity; for it is imagination—not the quotidian reality that makes of the body a site of pain and pleasure—that remains the central allure for the narrator and her mestiza body. She states, finally:

"This part of the story has to be over, even though I don't believe in endings. I believe in the imagination, its pleasure indelible, transgressive, a dream" (157). In the end, the narrator asserts the power of the imagination to conjure pleasure, to transgress the quotidian. At the same time, this signals a submission to the injustices and inadequacies of social systems working to ensure the perpetual disempowerment and dispossession of a queer mestizaje. Although the close of the story does not mark a true ending, in essence suggesting that closure is never possible given the endlessly creative and restless connections made by language, the narrator does suggest that the only sense of fulfillment possible can be found in the imaginative, the creative, the unreal. She evacuates queer agency from the realm of the social and, as does Cuadros's text, thus signals a capitulation to social injustice.[16]

As with the stories by Gil Cuadros, *Gulf Dreams* suggests that the mestiza body is marked and conditioned by the circuits of power through which it moves. The legacies of patriarchal privilege and colonial history ensure that the body is ceaselessly overwritten with meaning. At the same time, the mestiza body produces meaning, expressing the certainties of desire and longing that serve as a new formation of meaning, a meaning often at odds with socially sanctioned understandings of identity and propriety. In both Cuadros's stories and Pérez's novella, others read the significance of the mestiza/o body in numerous ways. The mestizo/a situates himself or herself in relation to new and unfolding identities, some that are destructive, others that promise new possibilities.

One of the reasons my discussion has dwelled at length and in detail on these narratives is that—beyond their aesthetic appeal—each reveals the richly embroidered complications of queer mestizaje. These are complications that, if it is to be of any use, a critical mestizaje must engage.

In the end, the texts by Pérez and Cuadros address how the socially denigrated crossing of an unvalued racial identity with an illicit sexuality leads to a profound struggle. These struggles serve to move the characters into new spaces and bring them to new—though not always satisfying—understandings of self-identity. The narratives trace a problematic journey, one that involves emotional, spiritual, and physical transformations at the expense of social change or queer political agency. A mestizaje of both a racial and a sexual nature makes manifest a belief in the transgressive possibilities of pleasure, even if that pleasure can occur only on the level of narrative and imagination. These narratives make clear the need for a new and empowered mestiza/o agency as an integral component of Chicano identity. The work by Cuadros and Pérez makes equally clear that, as configured in their narratives, that agency—crossing sexual and racial borders—has yet to find a home within the social worlds of Chicano/a reality.

CHAPTER 6

# Narrative and Loss

Philosophy is really homesickness, it is the urge to be at home everywhere.

—Novalis

As the sexualized and gendered crossings of the preceding chapter illustrate, mestizaje implies a powerful sense of loss, a gulf between the potential and the possible. Where the critical uses of mestizaje aver the flexible potency of new Chicana/o subjectivities, the enactment of mestizaje proves complex, both empowering and compromising. The uneven distribution of power that is part and parcel of a colonial legacy restricts new relational configurations of identity. The social and historical exigencies of the mestizo body bind it to inequitable discourses about racial, class, gender, and sexual hierarchies. These restrict the sense of free movement implicit in the most transformative and innovative performances of mestizaje.

Mestizaje often serves as an empowering thematic in Chicano expressive culture, one echoed in the formal hybridity so characteristic of that culture. The power to explain the meaning of lives lived in the racial and social margins of the national finds its correlative in the mixture of styles, languages, forms, and genres.[1]

However, the value granted hybridity and border crossing within a cultural arena becomes attenuated when that crossing takes place in terms of gender and sexuality. We have seen how the writings of Gil Cuadros and Emma Pérez weave narratives that expose the contradictory and often violent ways in which mestizo and mestiza bodies are disciplined for not following prescribed scripts of gender and sexual, class and racial identifications.

The present chapter considers the nature of loss inherent in the movement between identities that is part of Chicano mestizaje. The innovative potentiality of new subjectivity is offset by a profound sense of dislocation and absence that forms a dark shadow cast by the hybridity of identity. This shadow implies an absence, a loss in the process of developing one position of identification from another. This absence gets transfigured in a number of Chicano narratives into a missing ethical center often associated with the figure of an elder family member now gone.

Tey Diana Rebolledo has noted that loss forms one common theme in Chicana/o writing. She notes that this writing articulates "the nostalgia for a world lost, a world that signified spontaneity and comfort. The mythology of the past takes place spatially and emotionally: the past acquires enhanced meaning. These images contrast sharply with the stresses and ambiguity of the present moment. The past then must be recorded to safeguard it, to preserve it, to re-enact it. The retelling of the text, the documenting of tradition, the creation of a myth in time past creates the history of the self, modifying and expanding it" (1987, 153). The lost world of comfort and spontaneity, Rebolledo argues, is often associated with the figure of the grandmother, the *abuela*, who stands as a connection to a distant geography and history.[2] This sense of comfort derives from an apparent ethical wholeness located in a world that no longer exists. The seeming order of another place and another time forms a powerful myth of selfhood, one that undoubtedly holds a strong appeal in times of moral and social ambiguity to the mestiza/o subject in transition.

The present seems troubling because of the numerous dislocations with which Chicano/a subjects must grapple. The body represents—as we have seen most clearly in the narratives by Cuadros and Pérez—a site of contention. The racial mixture evoked by mestizaje highlights the relational quality of Chicana subjectivity, yet it also means that the body is always a compromised site of multiple identities. In the same way, home always represents a conflicted space of multiplicity. Home is located in an ambiguous present marked by highly conflicted colonial legacies. The idea of home resonates not just with an ambiguous present but with an absent past. This past is often associated with Mexico, which represents an ever-absent homeland. In the Chicano cultural imaginary, Mexico as homeland forms a site of origin well mapped as an ethical center. Meaning and moral clarity seem to be located in a time long past, though it is equally clear that the moral certainties of that past time can be terribly contradictory and damaging. Patriarchal privilege, rigid racial and social hierarchies, and embedded class distinctions are all part of a world in which moral certainties are possible. In short, a profound sense of dislocation lies at the dark heart of Chicano identity.

## Homeless

This book has regularly returned to how the racialized body in Chicano/a culture evokes a kind of historical consciousness. The body is the physical manifestation of a long, difficult, and constantly evolving colonial history. It suggests as well that there exists a relationship between ethics and aesthetics. In this regard, ideas of home and homelessness serve as touchstones for the articulation of self-identity. In the preceding chapter, we looked at the ways in which loss has been expressed through the struggles of the queer mestizo/a body to find a sense of home and place within a community that values heteronormative identities. The mestiza/o body experiences in the flesh this sense of homelessness, and thus the body serves as a site of authority and knowledge, though this authority and knowledge is premised upon loss.

In the literary realm, a similar recognition takes place at the level of the aesthetic. Chicana/o literary innovation often derives from a recasting of storytelling and other forms of oral literacy, forms of narrative that imply lost or attenuated cultural exchange. These aesthetic evocations serve to affirm, interrogate, or decry cultural values perceived as traditional. Often, the narratives arise from a history related to colonization or exploitation, to enslavement or genocide, to some insight that comes from deep reflection on how individuals and groups experience the world depending on the twin accidents of genetics and politics.[3] These stories assert that some special knowledge is born among those dispossessed by history, those discriminated against and excluded from power, those taught to hate themselves for their very physical presence. Words, of course, fail to convey the rage and exhaustion that this history engenders. Hatred carves pain deep in the flesh. Yet hate is not the end result of those lessons. Rather, like the trickster figure in Native

American and African traditions, the mestizo body gives voice to an observation and identity that turns a destructive image inside out.

In the introduction to his edited collection *Mixed Race Literature*, Jonathan Brennan notes the importance of mixed-race identity in undoing configurations of social convention:

> Perhaps one of the reasons behind the mixed race subjects' appropriation or assumption of the trickster role is their constant struggle to act in response to the enforcement of identity. In essence, the outside actor, slave owner or other oppressive figure, attempts to define the mixed race subject according to hypodescent, placing them at a political or psychological disadvantage, which can be overcome by the mixed race subject's assumption of the trickster role. In their constant struggle to maintain and define identity, they are thrust again and again into the role of trickster in order to overcome tragedy. (2002, 44–45)

The role is one of creation and destruction, a doing and undoing meant to hedge against oppressively inscribed roles. Rather than succumb to the crippling script of the "tragic mulatto" so evident in the popular imagination of the U.S. racial order, the mixed-race subject asserts a subversive agency that channels outrage into both self-creation and resistant irony. Chicano/a expressive culture represents mestizos and mestizas as tricksters who simultaneously make and unmake self, create and undo community, weave and unravel identity, mold and dissolve culture. Yet there are forces that configure and constrain the mestizo from assuming a free hand in his ironized construction of self-identity.

The family serves as one location where the doubled position of self-creation and identity-containment makes itself most clearly manifest. The family as a site of biological and ideological reproduction is an institution that preserves and passes on knowledge, knowledge that can be both liberatory and oppressive. Although conceptualizations of the Chicano family are changing and becoming more inclusive, as an institution it maintains both the productive and repressive elements of a heteronormative past. It in itself is a conflicted and contradictory institution.[4]

The family thus serves as an appropriate site of knowledge, one in which are maintained the vestiges of a history that has not fully been told.[5] The underside of history often runs through the family secrets and lore conveyed during late-night discussions over crises and cups of coffee, births and deaths, funerals and weddings. Forms of being and knowledge—some empowering, others repressive—passed down from the misty tunnels of the past, ideas generated generation to generation come down into the glaring light of history. Metonymically, the mestizo body serves as the repository of this knowledge, often neither cataloged nor collected.

## Chicano Melancholy

Chicano and Chicana fiction has sought to give voice to the mestiza body, articulating this vestigial knowledge. The fiction seeks to return what is absent, make present the invisible. Deeply ingrained, both in a sense of the mixed-race body and in mestizo literature, is a deep-felt awareness of loss.[6] Loss, as Chicana/o literature makes clear, is irrevocable. Thus Chicano narrative represents a paradox, investing its energies in a struggle to reclaim what can never be regained. The process of storytelling is one whereby the ambivalence and melancholy about loss find expression through culture.

Melancholy, understood most simply, is sorrow over a displaced sense of loss. In this sense Chicano melancholy resonates with the well-drawn line of thinking that finds in the Mexican character an epitome of the melancholic temperament, a human consciousness powerfully formed as a result of a double loss of innocence. As we have seen, Mexican national ideology places at the center of Mexican identity the Spanish violation of the Indian mother and the inevitable abandonment by the Spanish father. To graft this psychosocial dynamic onto the Chicano psyche in the United States does not take a great leap of imagination. The loss implicit in Chicano discourse within this frame is compounded by the sense of distance experienced by the orphaned Chicano left bereft of both a national fatherland and a native language. Betrayal and abandonment are compounded in the experiences of Mexican-descended populations north of the border. This elision of melancholic conditions is, ultimately, simplistic.

Discussions of melancholy, within a Freudian paradigm, center on the loss that arises from a child's sense of disconnection from the mother. This disconnection represents a moment of painful origin when the self is discovered only as it is forever cut loose from the comforting bonds of maternal wholeness. In the case of the melancholic, a complete individuation does not take place. The individual suffering from melancholy is ever caught between a desire and hatred for the object of love and loss. The loss of place, home, language, a loved one, a location, an object can evoke the unresolved loss of the mother's body as a matrix of meaning and completeness.

Julia Kristeva follows this line of analysis to a position where the loss of the maternal represents a loss of the semiotic, a loss of connection before the imposition of the symbolic order associated with the law and language of the father. Melancholy arises from our awareness of a lost time in which we possessed a prelinguistic understanding of the world, when the world and we seemed as one. This oneness results from the baby's bond with its mother that exists before—indeed, beyond—language. The ordering system of symbolic language serves as a weak substitution for a connection to the thing itself. Language is an ever poor substitute where symbols stand in for the object of our desires. Thus language reminds us that we are forever left floating in a world of meaning we ourselves have created, a world that separates us from the very things we attempt to understand.

Kristeva notes that the "child king becomes irredeemably sad before uttering his first words; this is because he has been irrevocably, desperately separated from the mother, a loss that causes him to try to find her again, along with other objects of love, first in the imagination, then in words" (1989, 6). In this way, melancholy becomes a form of unnamable mourning. That which is lost can never be articulated, and so a sense of loss is felt over both that which can never be understood and that which can never be named. We live, in Kristeva's view, ever melancholic over the failure of language.

Critics engaged with issues of racial, sexual, gendered, and ethnic identities have taken up the issue of melancholy in an effort to address not only the loss of maternal but the loss of social bonds. In her study

*The Melancholy of Race,* Anne Cheng traces the way in which loss among racial and ethnic groups in the United States leads a subject from feeling grief to expressive grievance. Reading Freud's analysis of melancholy through a social lens, Cheng situates her analysis within "the peculiar and uneasy dynamic of retaining a denigrated but sustaining loss that resonates most acutely against the mechanisms of the racial imaginary as they have been fashioned" in the United States (2001, 10). The sense of a simultaneous exclusion and retention of racial Others generates a type of melancholic bind between incorporation and rejection that permanently inflects America's ability to deal with racialized subjects.

The ensuing tension—one experienced by Chicanos/as as "strangers in their own land"—leads, potentially, to a type of productive engagement with new forms for understanding self. José Muñoz suggests, for example, that melancholy is part of the process by which America's sexual and racial Others deal with the crises and catastrophes endured because of their (mis)identification. Muñoz proposes that melancholia not be seen "as a pathology or as a self-absorbed mood that inhibits activism. Rather, it is a mechanism that helps us (re)construct identity and take our dead with us to the various battles we must wage in their names—and in our names" (1999, 74). Melancholy—the inability to let go of a loss, becomes a productive and necessary strategy for the assertion of a self working against the constraints of social control. In a similar vein, David Eng and David Kazanjian find in melancholia's persistent struggle with loss not simply a paralyzing fixation with the past "but rather a continuous engagement with loss and its remains. This engagement generates sites for memory and history, for the rewriting of the past as well as the reimagining of the future. While mourning abandons lost objects by laying their histories to rest, melancholia's continued and open relation to the past finally allows us to gain new perspectives on and new understandings of lost objects" (2003, 4). This potentiality, as well as perpetual struggle with the shadow of the past, informs the dynamics that make up Chicano culture and its continual engagement with identity and loss.

The Chicano cultural imaginary seems a site where the interaction between absence and presence elemental to the dynamic of melancholy and identity is always at play. The unnamable (suggestive of the modernist sublime but more evasive) and the representable create an unending tension. José Limón locates this tension in the form and thematic of Chicano expressive culture. He constructs a compelling argument about Chicano poetry as the manifestation of a "modernism of critical difference" (1992, 164). The poetry comes to terms with the paternal *corrido* as a strong but irrecoverable literary antecedent. The impulse of Chicano protest poetry derives from this particular literary strain. In so doing, the poetry comes to incorporate maternal voices as an equal, folkloric cultural endowment. Thus Chicano poetry can use dual folkloric inheritances to "make relevant a carefully and critically appropriated Anglo-American modernism to produce socially engaged and culturally instructive . . . poems that explicitly speak of class—and race—poems of our climate" (ibid.). In this view, Chicano poetry incorporates both the recognition of loss and an assertive reclamation of Chicana identity as key components of its critical, multiperspectival projection of subjectivity.

Throughout the history of Chicano/a cultural production, this multiperspectivity—part of mestizaje's legacy—instigates a paradoxical positionality. The relationship between loss, the articulation of new historical subjectivities, and the residual forces of well-established discursive power invest Chicano culture with a productive and problematic dynamic. For Ramón Saldívar, this paradoxical dynamic of construction and critique is central to the Chicano novel. The novel simultaneously creates and dissolves significance as it articulates new historical agency acting against established structures of meaning. "The Chicano novel's ideology of difference," he writes, "emerges from a . . . complex unity of at least two formal elements: its paradoxical impulse toward revolutionary deconstruction and toward the production of meaning" (1979, 88).[7] Chicano narratives (and other forms of Chicano expressive culture) work simultaneously to undo and remake forms of consciousness, very much in terms of Gloria Anzaldúa's Coatlicue state. Although Anzaldúa asserts that the disruption of the quotidian is necessary in order to achieve a new productive relation, there yet remains the quotidian. In terms of the novel, the absence of adequate cultural representations of mestiza subjectivity constitutes the conditions against which the novel writes mestiza identity. Implicit, then, in Saldívar's dialectical conceptualizations of the novel is the awareness of absence in terms of representation. The Chicano novel must work hard because it seeks to contest structures that do violence via their representations of Chicanos, and the novel seeks to fill the void left by this contestation over identity and representation.[8]

One source for loss within Chicano culture can be traced to the discursive configurations of solitude that Octavio Paz has posited as central to understanding Mexican national and cultural identity. Paz's infamous discussion about the Chicano in *The Labyrinth of Solitude* (1950) argues that the figure of the zoot-suited pachuco represents the apex of Chicano self-representation. Standing outside both U.S. and Mexican societies, the pachuco "actually flaunts his differences. The purpose of his grotesque dandyism and anarchic behavior is not so much to point out the injustice and incapacity of a society that has failed to assimilate him as it is to demonstrate his personal will to remain different" (1985, 14–15). Torn from the anchoring influence of nation, the pachuco flaunts his difference not as a form of social or political critique, but as willful spite. Paz implies that the pachuco imposes a self-willed alienation and isolation and consequently stands in contrast to the Mexican whose isolation derives from an elemental abandonment.

The influence of Paz on Chicano critical thought is undeniable. However, there is no single reason why loss should strike a dominant key in Chicano—or, for that matter, Mexican—cultural sensibilities. In *The Cage of Melancholy*, Roger Bartra has sought to demonstrate that no ontological basis exists for perceiving Mexican culture as one inevitably imbued with a sense of loss. On the contrary, he argues, the reliance on melancholy as a defining trait of Mexican national consciousness is a means by which a Mexican nationalist discourse reinscribes and reasserts relations of power. Bartra closes his book with the observation that there are agents at work who affirm the sense of loss and helplessness in order to define Mexican national culture:

> In Mexico, the suffering through melancholy and metamorphosis that I have described is precisely the strange medium through which the intelligentsia have revived and given form to popular sentiments. This process

activates a structure of mediation that serves as an imaginary bridge between the elite and the people. But it is clear that the result of this bridge
building is not an exact reflection of popular sentiments: it is a unification
and identification that, in its turn, must be accepted by the widest sectors
of the population as the national essence distilled by Mexico's intellectuals upon "reviving" and "appropriating" popular sentiments. (1992, 166)

The complex interaction between the intelligentsia and the people creates a condition in which popular sentiment is produced and distributed
in order to forge a nationalist consciousness and preserve an unequal distribution of power. This same condition does not apply (even by analogy)
to a Chicano context. Here there is no nationalist discourse of melancholy employed to delimit the social role of Chicanos.

The examples of Chicano melancholy and loss to which I now turn
do not seek to obfuscate relations of power in the service of national
identity. Quite the contrary, these examples help to reveal the multiple
ways in which power traverses self and place. The melancholic sense of
loss grants Chicano narratives a critical function that reveals the dynamics by which individuals transform and are transformed by their geographies. Yet this sense of loss remains, and no name can be given to
that loss.

## How the Quest Was One

Loss as one of the central tropes found in Chicano cultural expression
manifests itself in many aesthetic and critical texts that treat issues of
absence, search, and fulfillment. However, this fact may suggest that the
Chicano imaginary relies too easily on the location of an ontological
center. This lost center represents what Kristeva calls the "impossible
mourning for the maternal object" (1989, 9), the experience of "*object loss*
and of a *modification of signifying bonds*" (10). Within a Chicano framework, the loss of the maternal object can be read as a loss of a personal or
cultural identity, a loss of nation or language, a series (potentially unending) of losses leading inevitably to a profound anxiety in being.

In discussing the nature of Chicano identity, cultural critics often
translate this anxiety as a trope of search or location in the conceptu-

alization of their critical projects. Luis Leal, for example, has written on "The Problem of Identifying Chicano Literature" and has discussed Chicano culture "In Search of Aztlán." Marcienne Rocard is concerned with "The Chicano: A Minority in Search of a Proper Literary Medium for Self-Affirmation." Juan Rodríguez titles his article "La búsqueda de identidad y sus motivos en la literatura Chicana" (The search for identity and its motives in Chicano literature). Francisco Jiménez edits a collection called *The Identification and Analysis of Chicano Literature*. The titles of these works convey the loss that is the underlying premise of these discussions. Each expresses a concern with processes of search and identification. They help to strike a dominant (and decidedly dark) key in the realm of Chicano culture.

This tone is struck as Chicana and Chicano critics and writers respond to the often marginal conditions in which their sense of self has been configured. A profound awareness of displacement at the national, social, economic, political, and cultural level imbues Chicano consciousness. A nationally inscribed sense of identity—a configuration of self as either an American or Mexican citizen—stands as a normative center against which the Chicano is often compared.

This displacement of national identity becomes a common trope in one of the founding literary texts of the Chicano movement: Rodolpho "Corky" Gonzales's poem *Yo soy Joaquín/I Am Joaquín*, written in 1967 but published in 1972. The poetic voice asserts its identity in the first line: "I am Joaquín, / Lost in a world of confusion, / Caught up in a whirl of a gringo society" (lines 1–3). Against this world of neurosis and technology and "sterilization of the soul" (line 21), the speaker withdraws into the safety of his "own people" (line 36). Only after meditating on the multiple manifestations of self-identity as European and indigenous, as colonizer and colonized, the poetic voice asserts its decentered sense of self-identification:

> La Raza!
> Mejicano!
> Español!
> Latino!

> Hispano!
>
> Chicano!
>
> or whatever I call myself,
>
> I look the same . . . (lines 400–407)

The appellations serve to distinguish the Chicano hybrid self from the "American." There is an abjuring of identification with the United States.[9] The national separation the poem inscribes signals a continued separation from the United States and a simultaneous reconciliation with the lost Mexican national identity because, whatever Joaquín calls himself, he and his people "look the same" and are one. This statement asserts Chicano identity as a transnational one united by a common racial background. The grandiose and hyperbolic tone of Gonzales's self-consciously "epic" poem seeks to engender cultural pride and political action. It speaks to a displaced national identity by affirming racial and cultural forms of identification. The evocation of a lost Mexico forms one node where a sense of profound absence is made present. As with a melancholic loss, this missing national/cultural/racial connection produces a complicated anger and indignation. The elision of culture-race-nation marks an ethical center signified by the term *raza* and identified with the national geography of Mexico. The quest for identity leads to oneness that occurs only by embracing the collapse of an imagined Mexican unitary identity. This embrace does not, however, address the source of the actual loss itself.

## Displacement and Loss

Just as Corky Gonzales has, a number of writers have located loss within the framework of nation or national identity, revealing an anxiety about the Chicano/a condition as one that emerges from a lack: neither a Mexican nor an American identity. Moreover, this lack is often associated with an absent family member. As Gonzales's poem indicates, a sociocultural condition arises whereby the Chicano imaginary moves among sites of naming and loss. In the remaining discussion, I trace some of the ways in which loss is manifested in three texts dealing with the intimate domestic life of young Chicanas/os: Pat Mora's 1997 memoir, *House of*

*Houses,* Gary Soto's 1990 collection of stories, *A Summer Life,* and Victor Martinez's 1996 novel *Parrot in the Oven.* While only glancing here at some brief moments in these texts, it should become instantly evident that all three works engage with issues of displacement and absence in relation to mestizo identity. These texts all share a concern with the place of the individual in relation to larger family and community structures. They also all look at the small domestic details of daily life that compose a sense of personal and interpersonal identity. By paying attention to the quotidian and personal aspects of daily interaction, they reveal how—on a very intimate level—loss pervades self-identification.

Taking Ramón Saldívar's lead, I pay special attention to narrative as a cultural formation that clearly manifests the paradox of naming and loss implicit to the making of meaning within a Chicana/o context. I examine through these texts an attempt to identify that which gives Chicano culture and expression such a sense of loss; that is, I examine the ways in which they attempt to name a feeling of absence underlying the Chicano self. Melancholy lies heavy at the heart of Chicano literary production.

These Chicano/a narratives, in their representations of new historical subjectivities, help to crystallize some of the complexities inherent in the naming of loss in Chicano culture. What emerges from these texts is the awareness that loss ineluctably and inevitably informs mestizo consciousness, shaped as it is by notions of race, ethnicity, sexuality, class, and nationality in conflict. These texts not only identify a sense of absence and displacement, but they attempt, at the level of narrative, to fill that absence by creating—albeit provisionally and with a great deal of self-conscious artificiality—a sense of meaning and place. Even as these texts attempt to identify the loss at the heart of melancholy, they oscillate between replacing and reestablishing that unnamable loss.

The evocation of Mexico—or more specifically the Mexican past—as an ethical site manifests itself over and over in these narratives by Mora, Soto, and Martinez. Where Corky Gonzales's poetic recasting of this ethical center bases it on national and ethnic identification, these, like many Chicano/a narratives, employ the figure of a familial elder to embody a sense of connectivity between the present and the historical past.

This generational icon stands as the link to another place and another time that, in contrast to the present, seemed to afford a clearer sense of an ethical order. This holds true even if, ultimately, the narratives make clear that this order is not only problematic but impossible to reclaim.

In her book *House of Houses*, Pat Mora details the lives and interactions of the various members of her family present and past. Fairly early in the narrative, the narrator pays particular attention to her grandfather. This patriarchal figure represents for her all the courtliness and propriety of Mexican society, a figure who, for example, considers it bad manners for his American children to speak English in front of their parents. His is a strong presence manifesting law, manners, and nation: "One look from Papacito is enough. No one runs in the house if he sits in his chair reading his law books or newspaper. No one dares push past him even if late for school when he walks with slow steps down the hall. And all speak Spanish in those rooms that he considers Mexican territory. '*Cuando pisan en esta casa, hijos, pisan México*'" (When you step into this house, children, you step into Mexico) (1997, 57). Mora's grandfather manifests a sense of nationalist pride that is as powerful and threatening as it is romantic and ephemeral.

The narrative as recollection and memoir serves to evoke figures from Mora's past in order to situate herself and her family in a line of descent from a world ordered and whole. The book insists that the past is not lost so long as one maintains memories and thoughts of one's departed. The dead, in Mora's text, make themselves manifest, and no distinction is drawn between family members still present in this world and those who have passed on to the next.[10] These family members all interact and converse with each other as an extended, often funny, often sniping unit. The textual invocation of the grandfather (as well as with the rest of her family members) serves to make reference to an era and an ethos that are now lost, except in the memory of the narrator and the text of the narrative. In this sense, the book serves as a repository for family memory and the only utopian site where access to that memory can be manifest.

A similar sense of loss in relation to the past and, in particular, through the depiction of the Mexican patriarch is expressed in Gary

Soto's collection of stories, *A Summer Life*. In "The Grandfather," Soto recalls the attempt to plant an avocado tree in the family's backyard because his grandfather believed "a well-rooted tree was the color of money" (1990, 5). The patriarch, the narrator explains, "climbed" out of Mexico, settled in Fresno, California, and worked thirty years for Sun Maid Raisin. The avocado tree does poorly because, the grandfather believes, the mayor allowed the downtown office buildings to be built too high, thus blocking pollen from reaching his beloved planting. The grandfather informs the narrator that in Mexico, "buildings only grew so tall. You could see the moon at night, and the stars were clear points all the way to the horizon. And wind reached all the way from the sea, which was blue and clean, unlike the oily water sloshing against a San Francisco pier" (6). This idyllic recollection of Mexico constructs for the narrator a point of comparison by which to judge the United States. The naturalness and fecundity of the Mexican past stands in contradistinction to the impoverished present world of dust, urbanization, and economic necessity. Moreover, the sense of civic responsibility represents an ethical center lacking in the current conditions the narrator and his family must endure in their new homeland.

The narrator informs us that the tree his grandfather loved did indeed grow after twenty years of attention, even though "pollen never reached the poor part of town" (7). When he died, "all his sons standing on each other's shoulders, oldest to youngest, could not reach the highest branches. The wind could move the branches, but the trunk, thicker than any waist, hugged the ground" (7–8). The essay closes with an image that suggests the lasting influence and strength granted by the family patriarch. Even more clearly than in Mora's text (where the dead mix with the living in a narrative at once suggestive of magical realism and the power of familial memory), Soto's story makes clear the pained loss of an iconic connection to the past. Indeed, the remainder of the collection never again makes reference to Soto's grandfather or to the family's relation to Mexico. Rather, the grandfather stands as a figure of origin and loss, an image of past ethical and Edenic connections forever severed from the present generation.

Victor Martinez's 1996 novel *Parrot in the Oven* makes separation and loss equally evident. The young narrator, Manuel Hernández, recounts the difficulties of growing up under conflicted familial and economic conditions. He recalls seeking work as a picker in the chili pepper fields so he could earn enough money to buy a baseball glove. This makes him feel he was part "of my grandpa Ignacio's line of useful blood. All his life, no matter what the job, my grandpa worked like a man trying to fill all his tomorrows with one solid day's work" (1996, 6). Even as he got old and infirm, the elder patriarch would putter around the house fixing up things, "although the finished chore was always more a sign of how much his mind had gotten older than anything else" (6–7). This is the only description of grandpa Ignacio in the narrative. Yet his extremely brief mention signals the power of his work ethic, an ethic passed on to his grandson Manny as the narrative traces Manny's struggle to assert the ethical lessons his grandfather taught him.

In these narratives by Mora, Soto, and Martinez, the sense of loss that provides the basis for melancholy is named as the lost ancestral connection—in each of these three cases represented by a patriarchal figure—who most immediately connects the present with the past, the United States with Mexico, the American with the mestizo, actions with ethics. These texts are haunted by the image of an ever-present (though often mediated) image of an always-absent homeland. Mexico becomes an imaginary construct in these texts—part ethical center, part historical site of descent—that suggests another geography in the Chicano imaginary: Aztlán. These evocations of loss may seem to signal some ontological matrix represented by an ancestor who stands as a now lost source of ethical certainty. There is, however, a greater elasticity in the melancholy asserted by Chicana/o narratives. This elasticity is represented in a complex and ambiguous process of aesthetic representation. In addition to linking the figure of the missing grandfather with a missing ethical center, the narratives by Mora, Soto, and Martinez share a common concern with the function of the aesthetic text. They all, in various ways, indicate that Chicana/o narratives emerge from an attempt to overcome the melancholic condition, to name the loss that engenders melancholia, and therefore to address the sense of displacement and absence that informs these texts.

## Ancestral Ethics

*House of Houses, Parrot in the Oven,* and *A Summer Life* weave worlds in which the narrators—through memories of an older family member—seek to make sense of themselves in an alien space. The calling up of the past helps the narrators understand themselves in a process of growth and transformation. All three texts consider how radically different and alienating are the new worlds the narrators must confront. The texts all make clear that the past itself is lost but can be tentatively recaptured through storytelling. Similar to the texts by Gil Cuadros and Emma Pérez, these three books assert the centrality of textualization, in this case for reclaiming and understanding the connection to an ethical center. This center exists only in relation to the aesthetic and only as part of a larger portrait of Chicano and Chicana subjectivity as a new and conflicted agent in history.

In *House of Houses,* for example, each chapter of the book is named after a month, opening in January and closing in December.[11] The book ends with the narrator wandering through her father's old house, the house of houses, returning because she "needed a place to put the stories and the voices before they vanished like blooms and leaves will vanish on the wind outside, voices which, perceived as ordinary, would be unprotected, blown into oblivion" (1997, 272). The narrator re-establishes the house as a site where the memories of family, place and belonging can be evoked and collected. The home created in Mora's text is the site where loss is held at bay: "Since the family isn't together geographically, using the tools I know, I created a place welcoming to our spirits, a place for communion and reunion, no invitation necessary; a space, like all spaces, as real as we choose to make it . . . the past, our present in the house and garden" (272–73). The speaker here refers to the narrative evocation of the house as she uses the tools of language she has at hand to create a space inviting and sustaining, to also build a house of houses. The narrator informs us that she has been brought to the house through stories: "words, as words can, transporting us" (289). Through words, the narrator seeks to overcome displacement and loss, and names a return to a center where, gradually, as the last line of the book explains, "our breaths become one" (291). The narrative creates a world in which the spirit of each family member becomes part of a larger whole.

The evocation through words of the past, of the family, of an ancestral geography that encompasses and accepts all, is a soothing vision. Yet this evocation can only occur within the narrative itself, and it can only be made present through its evocation of absence. The re-membering of the family in this manner takes place as a result of its displacement from home, its geographic dislocation. Thus, even the narrative evocation of place and connection is premised on loss and absence.

This same sense of fulfillment and loss is present in *Parrot in the Oven* as the narrator—who had taken on the work ethic of his grandpa Ignacio—undergoes his first challenge of maturity as he moves out of boyhood. When the narrator's friend, Eddie, snatches a woman's purse, Manny chases after him. Although Manny had previously looked up to his friend—an object of cool danger in the neighborhood gang—the moment of ethical decision for him comes when he realizes that he does not want to be like Eddie. Instead, it dawns on him that he wants to lecture his friend "about how to treat people, how to be somebody who knows how to treat people" (1996, 210). This (perhaps overly neat) epiphany leads Manny to see his house and his family with new eyes.

Returning home, sitting in the living room on his father's cushioned chair, Manny does not know why ("because there's no way of explaining why") he realizes: "I'd never again see anything so wondrous as my two sisters lying on the couch. And it wasn't just them, but the whole room. . . . And it was wondrous, like a place I was meant to be. A place, I felt, that I had come back to after a long journey of being away. My home" (215). The insight is momentous for the young Manny. All the pieces of his life seemed to fall into place, evincing a newfound joy in domestic ordering. The new sense of place can only be manifest after his conflict over wanting to belong and be admired. The ethical lessons taught him by his grandfather return in order to provide not just a sense of proper behavior for the boy but a means of making a new home, a sense of belonging premised on an ancestral and ethical center.

This moment of perceived wholeness can only be textualized in hindsight as the narrator notes his epiphany from a distance. And that sense of distance imbues the moment with the shadow of its own absence. The narrative itself exists only because the moment of epiphany is instantaneous and fleeting. Manny knows (and he tells this in reflection via the narrative) that he will never again see anything so wondrous as he does just then. Indeed, the novel closes with this image as Manny sits in his father's chair feeling weary and sleepy. The closing lines of the book describe how the image "was dissolving and shifting in through my eyelashes in thin, filtered streams, and then there was only the dull blood under my eyelids, then dark, then sleep" (216). Manny assumes the patriarchal position, dozing contentedly in his father's armchair after this trial of his youth. The evocation is shadowed by its loss, textualized as a moment already gone. The narrative seeks to dispel—albeit in a complicated and incomplete way—the ethical loss that opened the book and haunts it throughout.

Gary Soto's *A Summer Life* likewise addresses the function of loss in the process of a boy's growth and maturation. In "The Buddha," the narrator locates himself in relation to the geography that helps to situate and compose him: "I killed ants here, and pulled puncture vine there. *There* was a small rise of earth and oily weeds at the junkyard at Van Ness and Braly. At the young age of five, I could not go far, maybe to the side of the house" (1990, 3). The sights are familiar, giving the narrator a sense of belonging linked to the recollection of his own boyish activity.

A seemingly pedestrian but quite complex act of violence disrupts this connection between recollection and event. The narrator recounts the time his uncle's collie got hit by a car: "I watched him pant on the side of the road, his eyes quiet with the dusk that had captured the street. I couldn't see what was wrong with the dog. No blood flowed, no tears streamed, no protruding bone made the dog curl his lips. He just seemed tired, and Uncle seemed tired as he lifted him into his arms and told us kids to get the hell away" (5). The narrative conveys an elemental loss that does not disrupt the seeming order of the world—there is nothing to see that would reveal the dog's injuries—yet the dusk has "captured the street" and clouded the dog's eyes. Walking back to his home, the narrator passes by a spot where earlier he had found a statue of the Buddha. He tells himself: "that there was where the Buddha had been. But I didn't know this place. The grass had sprung back where the Buddha had rested" (ibid.). The disruption signaled by the collie's accident manifests itself in the narrator's consciousness as a sense of dislocation and unfamiliarity. That which had before revealed a connection between self and place now registers as emptiness and a strong sense of alienation.

The recollection of the past, which forms the thematic core of Soto's collection, does not lend the present a sense of completion or of fulfillment. On the contrary, the past serves to evoke only absence. As the narrator notes in "The Rhino": "I was four and already at night thinking of the past. The cat with a sliver in his eye came and went. The blimp came and went, and the black smudge of tire. The rose could hold its fiery petals only so long, and the three sick pups shivered and blinked twilight in their eyes" (33). The recollection of the past already manifests the inconstancy of the narrator's young life. The blimp, the mark of a tire, the ephemeral rose all evoke the fleeting nature of human existence. Rather than serve as a source of connection, memory in these stories instead reveals the gaps and absences surrounding the world of the narrator.

Although Soto's work does not overtly foreground the role that the aesthetic plays in compensating for a melancholic absence and loss, it does focus on the process that memory, reflection, and recollection play in locating the conscious self within its surroundings. In large part, the stories focus on how the narrator locates himself in his own life. In so doing, they reveal that this process of location is highly ambiguous and inevitably rife with contradiction. At each moment that memory is evoked and the past recalled, the narratives foreground the ephemeral and temporally bound nature of the narrator's life. The highly elliptical, imagistic, and fragmented narrative—characteristic of Soto's prose— underscores the sense of loss that haunts the narrator's perceptions. The narration identifies the absences felt and so helps bring to the fore the process of evacuation (of self, of consciousness, of meaning, of identity) detailed by the narrative action. The narrative plays a contradictory role in that it asserts meaning, but only to the extent that the narrative serves as a representation of the unrepresentable: the unnameable loss of being.

## The Winnowing Fan of Odysseus

As told in Homer's *Odyssey*, the blind seer Tyreseus, after lapping at the pool of blood offered him by Odysseus, foretells Odysseus's tormented journey. Deep in the shadowy world of Hades, Tyreseus recounts how the son of Laertes will wash ashore his land alone, bereft of companions, left to defend his home, to which—struggling against man and god—he has, across the vast expanse of ocean, finally returned. Upon slaying the insolent suitors courting his wife's favor and reestablishing proper order in his household, Odysseus is to carry a great oar overland on one last journey. He is to walk farther and farther from the sea until he comes to a place where men, having known neither sea nor ship, confuse the oar for a winnowing fan. There, he is to plant the oar in the ground and make a final sacrifice to Poseidon. Only then will he be spared further torment and find a gentle death in a peaceful old age.

Throughout his life, Odysseus has served as the disrupter, he who brings knowledge of the unknown to others. He gives voice to new forms of thought, offers a different vision of the world, and takes action in order to accomplish a transformation in the world around him.

So too, mestizo bodies—those who inherit the legacy of European colonization in the flesh—bring forth a kind of knowledge that disrupts and disturbs. The body itself becomes something of a winnowing fan, an unrecognized (and misrecognized) sign. Mestizo subjects carry their body through globalized circuits of exchange. As part of this process, new identities are forged, new relations founded, new epistemologies undertaken in an innovative and inventive process creating new knowledge. Simultaneous with this project, the movement across unfamiliar terrain means that the mestiza subject learns to live with a sense of productive gain modified by the realization of loss. In order to move to new spaces, older ones must be left behind. Chicano culture seeks to index the significance of those gains and losses. It fills those losses with new formulations of understanding and expression. It teaches one to live with the inescapable loss that the mixed legacy of mestizaje has brought into the contemporary world.

Julia Kristeva observes in *Black Sun*: "art seems to point to a few devices that bypass complacency and, without simply turning mourning into mania, secure for the artist and the connoisseur a sublimatory hold over the lost Thing" (1989, 97). Artistic expression affords a space whereby an inexpressible connection to loss is, if not quite overcome, made at least manageable. A central concern of the narratives I have here discussed is their drive to recapture and rename the loss that seems everywhere to haunt the narrators. Yet the texts (viewed only sketchily in this chapter) reveal that this drive proves at once elusive and illusive.

Loss and melancholy form a register made manifest through these and numerous other articulations of Chicano/a cultural identity. Why this sense of loss is relevant to discussions of Chicano culture has to do with the complex discussions about the subjectivities of Chicanas and Chicanos understood within a transnational and translational arena. Both as "Others" against dominant Euro-American conceptions of identity and as subjectivities that configure Euro-American society as an "Other," Chicana/o identification opposes and internalizes its alterity. There is a double reclamation and a double sense of loss. The discourses of Chicano identity claim a form of subjectivity that rejects both American and Mexican national identities. Yet Chicano culture also seeks to make intelligible another identity, seeks to translate for others the experiences and knowledge produced through restless processes of rejection and reclamation.

This dynamic of Chicana and Chicano identity as transnational/translational runs parallel to the mixed-racial condition of the mestizo and mestiza body. The loss implicit in mestizaje is not the tragic loss of the Indian now remembered only as part of a nebulous past forever severed from the complexities of contemporary history. Rather, the loss implicit in a critical mestizaje is one that actively propels mestizo bodies through the ruptured terrain of a historical present. Melancholy and nostalgia mark a condition of genuine loss. As such, both melancholy and nostalgia may prove to be the affective legacy of a history under critique. But the ennui associated with these conditions is anathema to the condition of mestizaje I have explored in this book. The mestiza body as a body-in-becoming represents not the passive inheritor of a disempowered past, forever severed from the utopian possibility of some always-evasive authenticity or authority. Rather, the mestiza body moves—aware of the power dynamics in which it functions—in a constantly negotiated process forging new relational identities. As empowering as this process may prove, implicit is an awareness of loss as well.

At several levels of the social interactions that compose Chicana/o experience, the dynamics of displaced loss emerge. Consciousness of loss on the level of the linguistic, the religious, the familial, the economic, and the educational informs the articulation of Chicano/a subjectivity.[12] Quite simply, the process of naming oneself and one's identity within a Chicana/o context is overwritten by vying discourses. The self forms an ever-evasive site of naming and unnaming traversed by numerous discourses of inclusion and exclusion created and disseminated through an uneven distribution of power. The focus of this book, metaphorized in terms of racial mixture, addresses the numerous dislocations produced through the as yet unfinished naming and unnaming of Chicano and Chicana subjectivity.

While the aesthetic space of Chicano narrative offers some reprieve from an unendurable loss, it also re-creates loss. Similarly, Chicano/a critical discourse responds to this sense of loss and develops a sense of melancholia that paradoxically helps to generate movement across a vexed social, historical, and political terrain. This movement elicits the fluid and dynamic quality of Chicano culture, the transformative and ever-shifting process of identification that characterizes Chicana and Chicano subjectivity. Finally, the place of melancholy in Chicano culture—emerging from the movement of hybrid subjectivities across a troubled terrain—is multiple, overcoded, elusive, problematic, and persistent.

As I have sought to elucidate in the different sections of this book, issues of voice, vision, and agency complicate Chicano culture's naming and unnaming of the self. The racialized body in Chicano culture represents the site about which an important voicing takes place, where the experiences of the dispossessed become articulated. This voicing engages the various and often competing discourses that vie to name Chicano/a subjectivity. At the same time, this voicing offers a vision of identity that situates the racialized body within a historical context. The deployment of a mestizo voice seeks to forge out of the vexed legacy of colonial displacement and racial hierarchies new relational connections and political alliances. Finally, in seeking to give voice to what social agency might mean, the mestizo voice articulates the loss implicit in the reach for new historical subjectivities.

In part, this discussion has been a meditation on the condition of Chicana and Chicano studies at this historical juncture. After twenty-five years of pathbreaking scholarship, much has been done to name and explain the various realms and significances of Chicana and Chicano experiences. One important lesson of this extensive body of work is that Chicano/a studies must call upon and move beyond many of the antagonistic oppositions that have marked the field: nationalists versus assimilationists, men versus women, Spanish speakers versus English speakers, indigenous versus mestizo, aesthetic versus political, Texan versus Californian, queer versus straight. A comprehensive Chicana/o criticism needs to acknowledge the many advancements in knowledge, compassion, and comprehension offered by those made to feel alien from the term "Chicano": women, gay men, lesbians, all those who have questioned the normalcy of some static and self-contained notion of identity. This criticism also needs to recognize the relational condition of Chicano and Chicana identities, one that embraces the diverse and distinct experiences that help to compose what we come to term Chicana and Chicano. Those terms must prove flexible enough to name an increasingly broader range of interests, needs, and desires.

Chicano critical discourse has helped to illustrate how Chicana/o culture bases itself on a complex and doubled dance of acceptance and rejection, of displacement and relocation, of loss and reclamation. This doubled movement allows for a renaming and regeneration of identity. As such, Chicano culture does not necessarily rely on an ontological base by which to explain itself. And it disrupts any normative processes by which identity might be understood. The Chicano cultural imaginary reconceives of the mestiza/o body as a transitional and translational site that maneuvers through extant channels of power linked to the legacies of our colonial past. Loss is inescapably integral to these legacies. Yet dealing with these legacies allows mestiza and mestizo subjects to form spaces in which the self and others can be understood in relation to one another, a relation often mediated through the overt deployment of discourses that define and distribute social and political power unequally. At its most productive, Chicano culture seeks to make present a moment of insight, an ethical awareness. This critical awareness may, in the end, prove the most enlightening legacy of our conflicted and tenebrous colonial past.

# Notes

## Introduction

1. In order to avoid using the clunky term "Chicana/o" or "Chicano/a" over-much, I employ the terms "Chicano" and "Chicana" almost interchangeably. I am aware all the time that the identities they index are not coterminous. Try as we might, differences between gendered identities in a Chicana/o context as everywhere else remain entrenched in patterns of inequality. Discursively, the interchangeability in this study of Chicana and Chicano is an attempt to undo erasure beneath the term "Chicano" while by and large trying to avoid the clumsiness of "Chicana/o" or the increasingly popular "Chican@" construction. Nevertheless, at moments I do rely on the slashed term. In addition, I recognize that the terms "Chicano" and "Chicana" have a particular currency within academic discussions of people of Mexican descent in the United States that is not always matched in daily social uses. Although the term was first employed in the 1960s and 1970s as a name of self-affirmation and empowerment, its current use is much more problematic. In California and Arizona, the term has a political and social charge that it does not have in places like New Mexico or even Texas, where individuals may reject the term "Chicano" in favor of "Hispano" or "Mexicano" or "Tejano." There are generational differences as well in the power of the term: more recent immigrants often reject identifying as Chicana or Chicano and prefer that their children avoid the term as well. The terminology, in short, is vexed and I acknowledge the conundrum of identification and naming that is Chicano or Chicana.

2. For a cogent comparative discussion of the relationship between black, white, and indigenous racial identities and literary representation, see Suzanne Bost's *Mulattas and Mestizas*. Her study focuses on the insistence of race in producing identities always racially inflected by the socially discursive power of racial mixture. She argues that mixed-race texts trace a memory of oppression and exploitation at the root of racial formation, one that reflects how colonization and conquest embody in the Americas a racial, sexual, and national memory.

3. For studies that situate the importance of race for Chicano studies, see Neil Foley's *The White Scourge*, Tomás Almaguer's *Racial Fault Lines*, and Ian Haney-López's *White by Law* and *Racism on Trial*. Although race has not yet played a pivotal role in Chicana/o cultural criticism, there has been an increasing interest in the relation between race and culture. María Herrera-Sobek has undertaken a series of conferences at UC Santa Barbara with the University of Guerrero in Acapulco in order to address issues concerning the Afromestizo population of Mexico. In addition, several scholars interested in nineteenth-century Chicano/a literature have examined the evolution of racial identity in Chicano subjectivity. For example, both John González and Jesse Alemán explore the problem of race in the nineteenth-century novel. See González's essay "The Warp of Whiteness," on Helen Hunt Jackson's romance *Ramona*, and Alemán's comparison of *Ramona* with María Ruiz de Burton's *The Squatter and the Don*. In a more contemporary context, Theresa Delgadillo has traced the manner in which Mexican and Chicano/a cultures manifest an identification with the struggle for black rights and the effects of the African diaspora in the Americas.

4. Elise Lemire's book *"Miscegenation": Making Race in America* demonstrates clearly how the fear of race mixture in the eighteenth and nineteenth centuries produced in the United States a culture of racial segregation, one in which the legal separation of races ultimately became unnecessary as populations incorporated the view that racial separation was not just necessary but natural. Her study traces the means by which the idea of race mixture—whether understood as preference, amalgamation, or miscegenation—served to naturalize American conceptualizations of race as essentially biologized and binary.

5. In the 2000 U.S. census, to cite one example, about half of the Hispanic respondents identified themselves as white, and at the same time almost as many labeled themselves not black, Asian, or Native American but "other race"

(Richardson and Fields 2003, A25). This finding bolsters the results of a 1990 Public Use Micro Sample of 1 percent in which 52.1 percent of respondents self-classified as white, while 43.5 percent identified as "other race" (Rodríguez 2000, 9). Both findings suggest that a substantial portion of the U.S. Latino population recognizes its mixed-racial condition. At the same time, the relation between race and culture in the minds of the respondents may be quite complicated. A small case study of sixty Latinos living in the northeastern United States conducted by Clara Rodríguez reveals that 11.5 percent chose the category "other race" based on a biological understanding of race and 15.4 percent based on both physical and cultural considerations. Sixty-three percent based their response entirely on cultural reasons (ibid., 132). In other words, the respondents view the self-assignation of "other race" as simply a choice that reflects cultural practices, not necessarily personal identity. It is significant that the sample, besides being quite small, was geographically very circumscribed and did not include any respondents of Mexican origin (ibid., 47).

## 1. The Critical Mixture of Race

1. *Casta* paintings created under colonial conditions in Mexico represent one example of the anxiety surrounding racial categorization. The paintings formed a genre in which social caste and ability were represented in relation to both racial stratification and mixture. See Ilona Katzew's *Casta Painting: Images of Race in Eighteenth-Century Mexico* for an extensive discussion of the style and uses of this genre.

2. Winant writes: "There was a long period—centuries—in which race was seen as a natural condition, an essence. This was succeeded although not entirely superseded by a shorter but potent way of thinking about race as subordinate to supposedly more concrete, 'material' relationships; during that period, down to now, race was understood as an illusion, an excrescence. Perhaps now we are approaching the end of that racial epoch too" (1994, 21).

3. In particular, Franco analyzes Vasconcelos's efforts to maintain a patriarchal front in chapter 5 of *Plotting Women*.

4. Florencia Mallon's article "Indian Communities, Political Cultures and the State in Latin America, 1780–1990" (1992) provides a detailed analysis of this issue as well.

5. Cognizant of this, Raymund Paredes notes: "The great divide in Chicano history is the year 1848 when the Treaty of Guadalupe Hidalgo ended twenty-one months of warfare between Mexico and the United States" (1982, 36). Luis Leal and Pepe Barrón argue that the period between 1848 and 1910 "was the time during which Chicano literature laid the basis on which it was later to develop" (1982, 18). Chicano critics locate, in retrospect, the preconditions for Chicano consciousness in the political and national chasm created by the open warfare between the United States and Mexico.

6. Chávez goes on to explain: "These multiple occurrences of discrimination coupled with the 'lure of whiteness' have ensured that Mexican Americans are (1) not a unified group, and (2) have primarily waged battles for inclusion and parity" (2002, 2). One of the conundrums of modern Chicano political history has been the fact that although the rhetoric of political change has ostensibly been revolutionary, in practice—as historian Juan Gómez-Quiñones notes—Chicano leaders of the 1960s were impeded by the contradictions between their assertive, often separatist, rhetoric and their conventional reformist demands and programs involving educational reform and voter-registration drives (1990, 141–46).

7. Their Web site notes that the establishment of the D-Q University "represented the first time that the diverse groups of Native races on the American continent successfully worked together on a project, despite vast language barriers, geographical differences and outside pressures." The Web site http://www.dqu.cc.ca.us/ provides information on the university and its history. Unfortunately, the university lost its accreditation just before the start of the 2005 spring term. After a court battle, the university reopened for the following fall term.

8. In her study of multicultural art, Lucy Lippard notes that the San Diego group Los Toltecas en Aztlán joined other Chicanos in attending Native American gatherings, "committing themselves to treaty rights and national sovereignty by supporting the Alcatraz occupation and going on caravans to Indian reservations. Made easier by some common bloodlines and harder by the history of Mexican invasion and enslavement of Native peoples, these coalitions eventually diffused. Yet Chicanos and Native Americans remain the two peoples who are the most closely interwoven in the United States" (1990, 173).

9. Tomás Rivera provided a pointed critique of Rodriguez's views in "Richard Rodriguez's *Hunger of Memory* as Humanistic Antithesis."

10. Norma Alarcón's article "Traddutora, Traditora: A Paradigmatic Figure of Chicana Feminism" presents a cogent overview of the Malinche/Malintzín myth and addresses rape as a trope in the articulation of Chicana cultural identity. Tey Diana Rebolledo looks at the feminist literary reconfiguration of La Malinche in what she sees as a revision of negative mythology (1995, 62ff.).

11. For a discussion of Rodriguez and his writing on miscegenation and culture, see Juan E. de Castro's chapter on Richard Rodriguez in his study of mestizaje, *Mestizo Nations*. Although Rodriguez envisions what de Castro calls a "new, brown U.S. reality" (2002, 116), it is one that delinks the relationship between racial/cultural hybridity and a progressive political agenda. This distinguishes Rodriguez from other Chicano and Chicana writers who employ the position of hybridity as one that challenges repressive social conditions.

12. In "Challenging Colonial Histories," Fernando Coronil examines how Ortiz constructs an anticolonial representation of Cuban identity, arguing that *Cuban Counterpoint* "challenges colonial histories and prefigures contemporary concerns with the politics and poetics of representation" (1993, 77). Ortiz helps to create a vocabulary for the flux and flow of representational power and cultural transformation. His model calls into question simple conceptions of domination and control.

13. This multiplicity of influence extends even beyond these familiar categories. When it comes to culture, the term "American," for example, cannot be understood outside of the powerful influence of African and African American cultural production. The term must be understood as well with regard to the influences by Native American and Asian cultures. Moreover, the terms "Chicano" and "Chicana" are being transformed by the influence of Central American immigrant cultures and communities. There is a continuing mutability within the terms that form primary components of Pratt's contact zones.

14. In this regard, one thinks of Roger Rouse's essay "Mexican Migration and the Social Space of Postmodernism." He addresses the complex relation a migrant community from Aguililla, Michoacán, has to time and space as its members negotiate social relations in both Aguililla and Redwood City, California. The Aguillans, he writes, "see their current lives and future possibilities as involving simultaneous engagements in places associated with markedly different forms of experience. Moreover, the way in which at least some people are preparing their children to operate within a dichotomized setting spanning

national borders suggests that current contradictions will not be resolved through a simple process of generational succession" (1991, 14). For an extensive and insightful view of how these contradictions viscerally affect transnational communities and families, see Rubén Martínez's *Crossing Over: A Mexican Family on the Migrant Trail* (2002). To understand how these migrations are affecting other established Latino communities—and the asymmetrical experiences even among migrant communities—see Arlene Dávila's *Barrio Dreams: Puerto Ricans, Latinos, and the Neoliberal City* (2004).

15. It is important to note that the "riots" were also a part of a wave of racist violence by civilians against communities of color across the United States. There were attacks by whites on blacks in Detroit, Mobile, and Beaumont, Texas, in 1943, as well as "hate strikes" where white workers refused to work with blacks and walked off the job even in the midst of wartime production. I thank George Lipsitz for pointing out these important historical ruptures in race relations.

16. "Es evidente que categorías como mestizaje e hibridez toman pie en disciplinas ajenas al análisis cultural y literario, básicamente en la biología, con el agravante —en el caso del mestizaje— que se trata de un concepto ideologizado en el extremo" (all translations are mine unless otherwise stated).

17. In an added irony, Polar says: "En lo que toca la hibridez la asociación casi espontánea tiene que ver con la esterilidad de los productos híbridos, objección tantas veces repetida que hoy día García Canclini tiene una impresionante lista de productos híbridos y fecundos. [ . . . ] De cualquier manera esa asociación no es facíl de destruir. [In the case of hybridity, the almost spontaneous association has to do with the sterility of hybrid products, an objection repeated so many times that now García Canclini has an impressive list of products that are hybrid and fecund. . . . In any case, this association is not easy to destroy]" (1998, 7). Polar reads hybridity within a biological frame and carries forward the metaphor.

18. "el concepto de mestizaje, pese a su tradición y prestigio es el que falsifica de una manera más drástica la condición de nuestra cultura y literatura. En efecto lo que hace es ofrecer imágenes armónicas de lo que obviamente es desgajado y beligerante, proponiendo figuraciones que en el fondo sólo son pertinentes a quienes convene imaginar nuestras sociedades como tersos y nada conflictivos espacios de convevencia."

19. "la idea de transculturación se ha convertido cada vez más en la cobertura

más sofisticada de la categoría de mestizaje. Después de todo el símbolo del 'ajiaco' de Fernando Ortiz que reasume Rama bien puede ser el emblema mayor de la falaz armonía en la que habría concluido un proceso múltiple de mixturación."

20. Moreiras does note that these dreams "are also the metacritical dream as it informs this essay that I am writing, here and now—and thus the dream of a critical Latin Americanism" (2001, 70). Within the terms of his essay, however, that metacritical dream remains at the level of dream and offers no genuine political expression.

## 2. The Mestizo Voice

1. On May 17, 1954, the Supreme Court unanimously declared that separate educational facilities violate the Fourteenth Amendment to the U.S. Constitution, which guarantees all citizens "equal protection of the laws." In delivering the opinion of the Court, Chief Justice Earl Warren wrote: "Does segregation of children in public schools solely on the basis of race, even though the physical facilities and other 'tangible' factors may be equal, deprive the children of the minority group of equal educational opportunities? We believe that it does." He went on: "We conclude that, in the field of public education, the doctrine of 'separate but equal' has no place. Separate educational facilities are inherently unequal. Therefore, we hold that the plaintiffs and others similarly situated for whom the actions have been brought are, by reason of the segregation complained of, deprived of the equal protection of the laws guaranteed by the Fourteenth Amendment." The ruling is posted on the Web site for the National Center for Public Policy Research: http://www.nationalcenter.org/brown.html.

2. Mark Rappaport, the director of *Rock Hudson's Home Movies*, addresses Hudson's hidden sexuality in his films: "Rock Hudson was a prisoner, as well as a purveyor, of sexual politics and stereotypes. He is a prism through which sexual assumptions, gender-coding, and sexual role-playing in Hollywood movies and, therefore, by extension, America of the 1950s and 1960s can be explored. In a sense, it is Hudson's sexuality that is the real auteur of his movies—just as his closeted-ness was the icon all America was worshipping" (1996, 16). This closetedness proved costly in numerous ways. Hudson kept his HIV status secret from even his partner of three years, Marc Christian. According to a suit filed by Christian seeking damages, he and Hudson had high-risk sex 160 times

during their relationship. Hudson continually blamed his wasting condition on anorexia nervosa. A jury, in awarding Christian $21.7 million, called Hudson's deception "outrageous conduct." Christian did not get HIV (*U.S. News & World Report* 1989, 16).

3. The song, a top-ten hit in its day, celebrates the beauty of a multiracial African American woman: not the "white" but the "yellow" rose of Texas. As a cultural text, the music serves to underscore the national political battle being waged over the role of race in a new postwar America.

4. In his response to my essay "Chicano Ethnicity, Cultural Hybridity, and the Mestizo Voice," an earlier version of the present discussion, José Limón critiques my reading of the movie and its representation of Mexican characters. In his spirited and thoughtful response, Limón argues: "Dr. Guerra's character and actions do receive close and focused attention, and this representation must always be referenced to the real-life activity of Dr. Hector García at that moment in Texas" (1998, 122). Dr. García was instrumental in founding the G.I. Forum, one of the powerful political organizations advocating for Mexican Americans in the postwar era. Similarly, Limón argues that though Angel is killed in World War II, his character has symbolic import "regarding the profound and affirmative social outcomes for Mexican-Americans after the war, paradoxically as a result of such deaths but even more as a consequence of the enlarged status and opportunities of those veterans who returned" (ibid., 123). Although I disagree with a few of his conclusions, I acknowledge and thank him for his engaging reading of my work.

5. In his review of the movie, screened for its fortieth anniversary at New York's Lincoln Square, Gary Arnold notes the smug moral tone the film assumes: "*Giant* settles into a kind of rocking chair of virtue and self-congratulation while isolating Jett as the exclusive bad apple of the Lone Star State" (1996, 37).

6. Manuel Luis Martinez notes that Acosta's sense of a divided self is part of his struggle "to negotiate among the individualist strains of his brown buffalo identity—the misunderstood misfit uneasy with the assimilation of the Mexican American generation, the alienating Anglo-directed counterculture, and the call . . . to forsake the self for communal identity" (2003, 172). This struggle leads toward a greater isolation and separatism that ultimately leaves him unable to foster a new and radical sense of agency.

7. Acosta enacts the kind of dysfunctional desire required by colonization.

As Homi Bhabha asserts in his analysis of Frantz Fanon's writing: "the black man wants the objectifying confrontation with otherness; in the colonial psyche there is an unconscious disavowal of the negating, splitting moment of desire" (1994, 51). See Bhabha's 1989 essay "Remembering Fanon: Self, Psyche, and the Colonial Position" for an earlier version of his discussion.

8. Adelitas were the women of the Mexican Revolution who helped feed and care for their male counterparts. Elizabeth Salas notes that although these women were in fact active insurrectionary agents, they were subject to representation within a strongly patriarchal order. See "Soldaderas: New Questions, New Sources," *Women's Studies Quarterly* 23 (fall–winter 1995): 112–16.

9. See Brady's "Sandra Cisneros's Contrapuntal 'Geography of Scars'" in *Extinct Lands, Temporal Geographies* for a cogent and influential reading of *Woman Hollering Creek and Other Stories*.

10. Rosa Linda Fregoso responds to José Limón's reading of "Woman Hollering Creek" in his book *American Encounters*. Limón criticizes the way Cisneros represents Cleófilas's husband as brutal and animalistic, adding fuel to the fire of colonialist anti-immigrant attitudes. Fregoso notes that Limón's "desire for alternative (humanized) portrayals of Chicano masculinity involves imposing a gag order on Chicana feminists" (2003, 32) and observes that this pattern of empowerment and silencing along gender lines within communities of color is part of a conspiracy of silence. The drive to resist colonialist disempowerment of men of color takes priority over the need to discuss violence against women of color. A critical mestizaje seeks to overcome this type of intracommunity silencing.

11. The issue of voice is indeed complex in the story. Although several critics argue that it is the company of women that gives Cleófilas her first shot at developing her voice, we might keep in mind, as Jacqueline Doyle notes, that the first moment in which Cleófilas voices opposition to her husband represents a kind of ventriloquism. Doyle argues that Cleófilas "mobilizes another discourse of power to break free from [her husband]: 'Because the doctor has said so' (53). Deploying the American doctor's voice to counter her husband's voice, she secures permission to cross the arroyo and journey to San Antonio" (1996, 61). The voice Cleófilas adopts to assert power is not hers, but rather the (false) evocation of the doctor's male authority to counter her husband's. That she knows to wield this power demonstrates agency, but not voice.

## 3. Popular Music and Postmodern Mestizaje

1. As a *Newsweek* article on Martin notes, his "songs are less Latin workouts than frothy cocktails of global pop styles" (Chambers and Leland 1999, 72). Martin stands as an excellent example of the global mass culture critiqued by Stuart Hall. Mass culture as one of the tools of globalized economies has, according to Hall, two main characteristics: it remains centered in the West, and it is particularly homogenizing. The driving powerhouse of this global mass culture lies in "Western technology, the concentration of capital, the concentration of techniques, the concentration of advanced labor in the Western societies, and the stories and the imagery of Western societies" (1991a, 28). Moreover, although its homogenizing drive makes it enormously absorptive, it does not work for absolute completeness. It is, Hall argues, "powerfully located in the increasing and ongoing concentration of culture and other forms of capital. But it is now a form of capital which recognizes that it can only, to use a metaphor, rule through other local capitals, rule alongside and in partnership with other economic and political elites" (ibid.). The global, in order to better manage and subsume the local, negotiates the specificity of local cultures not to fully destroy, but to reshape, recast, re-form in the service of further capital expansion. In order to hold the whole framework of globalization in place and simultaneously police that system, global mass culture must, in Hall's phrase, stage-manage independence within it. The argument I posit in this chapter is that, despite how actively mass culture seeks to stage-manage independence, eruptions of difference and historical and political consciousness occur at both the level of consumption and, consequently, production. This hedges the overwhelming control that global mass culture seeks to enact.

2. This chapter in very different form appears as "Mestizaje in the Mix: Chicano Identity, Politics, and Postmodern Music" in *Music and the Racial Imagination*, edited by Ronald Radano and Philip Bohlman. I would like to thank Ron and Phil as well as Angie Chabram-Dernersesian for their invaluable help and suggestions with the present, though yet flawed, discussion of my ideas.

3. Much of this information is taken from the Del-Fi CD *The Ritchie Valens Story* (Del-Fi R271414). See also Ernesto Lechner's article "Short Career, Long Shadow."

4. The term *pocho* has had a highly negative connotation to it, meaning spoiled or ruined, and was used by Mexicans to refer to their brethren north of

the border. José Antonio Villarreal used the word as the title of his 1959 book, set in Depression-era California, that focuses on a young Mexican American experiencing conflicts over loyalty to the traditional values of his family and the new conditions of his American life. The term has been reappropriated as part of a stitched-together *rasquache* aesthetic, even serving as the name for the satiric online magazine www.pocho.com ("Satire, News y Chat for the Spanglish Generation").

5. "Postmodern" here includes those stylistic features that Richard Shusterman lists in his essay "The Fine Art of Rap": "recycling appropriation rather than unique originative creation, the eclectic mixing of styles, the enthusiastic embracing of the new technology and mass culture, the challenging of modernist notions of aesthetic autonomy and artistic purity, and an emphasis on the localized and temporal rather than the putatively universal and eternal" (1991, 614).

6. Rosaura Sánchez notes that the origins of caló "have been traced back to Spain where the gypsy language (of Indic origin) had become heavily hispanicized and mingled and greatly blended with *germanía*, the speech of Spanish delinquents. In Spain *caló* generally means 'language of the Gypsies' but is now used by the Gypsies to refer to themselves" (1983, 84–85). Used in the El Paso underworld in the early part of the twentieth century, it has spread throughout the Chicano world as a form of linguistic demarcation. From its inception, the term "caló" has been associated with marginal constituencies.

7. Code-switching is the borrowing or substitution of a word in one language for the corresponding word in the other language. Incorporated borrowing or lexicalization occurs where the dialect has taken the particular word from another language. This type of linguistic interpenetration on the sociodiscursive stage forms a type of bilingualism (more precisely polyglossia) in which speakers use code-switching to establish a social relation. Fernando Peñalosa notes: "Chicano code switching can . . . be a verbal strategy for conveying social information, such as a sociopolitical identity marker or intimate relationship, for signalling social distance from an Anglo role, and for implying that one's own interlocutor will not be offended by language mixture" (1980, 68).

8. For a brief discussion of Chicano musicians such as Kid Frost drawing on African American musical forms, see Peter Watrous, "Bilingual Music Is Breaking Down Cultural Barriers."

9. See Renato Rosaldo for a discussion of Chicano subjectivity as being "crisscrossed by multiple identities" (1989, 216). This is, he argues, a type of transculturated identity of the borderlands. For a discussion of the ways in which border theory has supplanted liminal studies as advocated by Victor Turner, see Donald Weber, "From Limen to Border," especially pp. 530–33.

10. The clumsy term "deterritorialization" implies not simply an alienation or estrangement, but also a dissolution of system, stratification, and order. As Gilles Deleuze and Félix Guattari explain, deterritorialization is marked by an expression that "must break forms, encourage ruptures and new sproutings. When a form is broken, one must reconstruct the content that will necessarily be part of a rupture in the order of things" (1986, 28). For a cogent discussion of linguistic deterritorialization, see Roland Bogue, *Deleuze and Guattari*, especially pp. 116–21. In evoking Deleuze and Guattari, I do not mean to imply a complete embrace of their perspective. Their view seems to remove too easily processes of deterritorialization from the exigencies of historically bound necessity, a view that I argue a critical mestizaje makes clear.

11. In his article "The Verse of the Godfather," Richard T. Rodríguez discusses the manner in which family and nationalism are two terms that play a foundational role in Chicano rap and hip-hop. The terms often evoke an uncritical linkage to paternalism, heterosexuality, and male dominance. He concludes, quite rightly, that although "we must continue to critique the inequalities and contradictions inherent within the tradition from which it emerges, we can also highlight Chicano rap's strands of resistance and potential for personal and community empowerment" (2003, 118). At the same time, Rodríguez encourages attention to the ways that empowerment can maintain positions of disempowerment for gendered and sexualized Others.

12. For a discussion of the development of Chicano music in Los Angeles, see Steven Loza, *Barrio Rhythm: Mexican American Music in Los Angeles.* For a discussion of the development of rap music in Los Angeles, see Brian Cross, *It's Not about a Salary: Rap, Race, and Resistance in Los Angeles.*

13. In a well-quoted passage, Fredric Jameson defines postmodern pastiche: "Pastiche is, like parody, the imitation of a peculiar mask, speech in a dead language: but it is a neutral practice of such mimicry, without any of parody's ulterior motives, amputated of the satiric impulse, devoid of laughter and of any conviction that alongside the abnormal tongue you have momentarily borrowed,

some healthy linguistic normality still exists. Pastiche is thus blank parody, a statue with blind eyeballs: it is to parody what that other interesting and historically original modern thing, the practice of a kind of blank irony, is to what Wayne Booth calls the 'stable ironies' of the 18th century" (1984, 65). Although I disagree with Jameson's blanket characterization of postmodernistic pastiche, in this case his discussion of blank parody seems particularly apt.

14. In an interview with Cheo Hodari Coker, Kemo says of the song: "It's straight-up hip-hop to us. We didn't try to do something special 'cause we're Latino. This is just our form of expression" (1996, 60). Yet clearly the desire to strike a "Latin" note is evident, and Coker notes that "the music juxtaposes the soothing, mariachi-tinged strains of Herb Alpert & the Tijuana Brass' 'Lonely Bull' with a hard-core rap aesthetic" (1996, 60).

15. Of course, as a young band Delinquent Habits undoubtedly could not control every aspect of its marketing. In 2001 they were attempting to start their own record label in order to maintain greater control over production and marketing. By 2004 Kemo the Blaxican had left the band. For information about the band at these points, refer to a 2001 European interview with the band on the Web site Toazted.nl (http://www.toazted.nl/artistinfo.php?artist=419), and a 2004 interview with Kemo on Latinrapper.com (http://www.latinrapper.com/featurednews10.html).

16. Just because de la Rocha is Chicano—son of the troubled visual artist Roberto de la Rocha who, with Carlos Almaraz, Gilbert Luján, and Frank Romero, formed the exhibiting group known as "Los Four" in 1974—does not unequivocally make Rage Against the Machine producers of Chicano music. Guitarist Tom Morello, drummer Brad Wilk, and bassist Tim Bob form a multiracial band with numerous musical influences and interests. However, without dwelling on biography or racial categorization, the political stances articulated by the lyrics de la Rocha pens as well as the hybridization of musical forms and reliance on hip-hop and rap as both an African American and a Latino art form compel me to classify the band as producers of Chicano music.

17. In an interview with Simon Price, Zack de la Rocha cites as musical influences Minor Threat, Public Enemy, Led Zeppelin, Run DMC, The Clash, Bad Brains, "from hardcore to hip hop to heavy rock" in a seamless combination (1993, 7). Culturally and politically, if the liner photo on *Evil Empire* is any indication, the band's influences range from *The Age of Reason* by Jean-Paul Sartre

to *Guerrilla Warfare* by Che Guevara, from *Play It As It Lays* by Joan Didion, to *The Wretched of the Earth* by Frantz Fanon. A complete list of the photographed books appears on the Web page www.RATM.com.

18. Jon Pareles's review of the band's 1993 New York City concert is a prime example: "In classic rock-rebel syle, the paradoxes of disseminating its ideas via the mass-media machinery of Epic Records and Sony Music, alongside Michael Jackson, go unexamined" (1993, C14).

19. Linda Hutcheon discusses this process as "inside yet outside, inscribing yet contesting, complicitous yet critical" (1989, 158).

20. For an insightful review of the album, see Carola Dibbell, "Found in Translation."

## 4. Land and Race in Chicano Public Art

1. A significantly different version of this chapter appeared as "Remapping Chicano Expressive Culture," part of the exhibition catalog *Just Another Poster? Chicano Graphic Arts in California*.

2. The date is highly symbolic for Mexicans because it marks when the struggle for independence from Spain crystallized around Father Miguel Hidalgo's famous *grito*. On September 16, 1810, Father Hidalgo summoned the people of Dolores in the state of Querétaro and urged the Indians and mestizos to rise up against the *gachopines*, the native Spaniards who had exploited and oppressed Mexicans for generations.

3. As the political and social landscape changed over time, and as the production of Chicano lithography became more established, Romo argues that the imagery shifted to reflect "individual aesthetics and/or personal interpretations" (2001, 110). One of the key transformations in the iconographic form of the poster was the insatiable hunger for multiculturalism in the art market of the 1980s and 1990s, forever changing the role of the poster, fueling an explosion of imagery and contributing "to the continuing redefinition of 'Chicano Art'" (ibid., 112).

4. Chicano intellectuals (often political scientists) have argued that Chicano culture becomes an essential salve to heal the pain of historical dispossession. As Eugene García puts it, Chicano literary arts "provided the road to recovery, as a type of spiritual reconquest of our ethos from which a fuller appreciation of our cultural heritage was regained. The first issue at hand was to establish

an operational identity of personal dignity to serve as a rallying point" (García, Lomelí, and Ortiz 1984, 99).

5. It was not until 2004 that curators sought to explore how the Los Angeles County Museum of Art could become one of the first major art institutions to permanently incorporate Latino artists into its exhibitions and acquisitions. Relying on the advice of Chon Noriega, the museum launched its five-year Latino Arts Initiative to develop exhibitions and collections of local Latino artists (Gurza 2004, E1).

6. We might think here of Peter Bürger's *Theory of the Avant-Garde* and his assertion that postmodernism emerges out of and against the failure of the modernist project. One impulse of the aesthetic avant-garde in the 1960s, he notes, was to reinvigorate the project of the early-twentieth-century avant-garde. Both sought to reintegrate the aesthetic and quotidian planes, politicizing the aesthetic and aestheticizing life practices. In many respects, Chicano artists who reformulate historically bounded discourses in the aesthetic realm make this impulse strongly manifest. The attempt to form a new aesthetic syntax is integrally related to the general cultural condition of postmodernism.

7. Lucy Lippard has noted: "Artists often act in the interstices between old and new, in the possibility of spaces that are as yet socially unrealizable" (1990, 8). Chicano poster art locates itself in this interstitial space, commenting on present social conditions while envisioning new potential identities and political possibilities.

8. Karen Mary Davalos notes that graffiti, or urban calligraphy, "is a claim to public space, an individual signature written across a public domain. Urban calligraphers legitimate their own signature and disregard legal claims to ownership. They invest their own meaning and power in the objects they sign. If their signature is not crossed out or mutilated, they gain status and prestige in the eyes of other urban calligraphers. Of if they can return again and again to the place, their signature makes history and they can claim authenticity" (2001, 188). For an extensive discussion of gangs, graffiti, and urban self-identification, see Susan Phillips, *Wallbangin': Graffiti and Gangs in L.A.*

9. The poster was originally published as the cover for the July 6, 1916, issue of *Leslie's Weekly* with the title "What Are You Doing for Preparedness?" The portrait of "Uncle Sam" went on to become—according to its creator, James Montgomery Flagg—"the most famous poster in the world." Between 1917 and

1918, as the United States was mobilizing for World War I, more than four million copies were printed. For further information, see the Web site for the American Treasures of the Library of Congress: www.loc.gov/exhibits/treasures/trm015.html.

10. Carol Wells discusses the role that Chicano poster art has played in expressing political solidarity in a national and international context. Although the posters expressed ethnic pride and promoted multicultural coalition from the beginning (with the United Farm Workers and the organization of Filipino and Mexican laborers), "[i]nternational solidarity began appearing in Chicano posters as the Cuban Revolution, the Viet Nam War, and other Third World liberation struggles generated political consciousness that crossed class, race, and ethnic boundaries" (2001, 173). Strikingly, as Wells notes, Chicano activism found support in a number of quarters, also expressed through the poster art form (2001, 191ff.).

11. Because of a legal dispute unrelated to this book, *La Ofrenda* could not be reproduced here.

12. In addition to Fregoso and Chabram, both Angie Chabram's "Chicana/o Studies as Oppositional Ethnography" and Norma Alarcón's "Chicana Feminism: In the Tracks of 'The' Native Woman" discuss the ways in which a male-dominated Chicano identity came to be established. Chabram, for example, quotes comments by a female colleague about her involvement in the Chicano movement: "I was aware from the very beginning that the establishing of a Chicano intellectual tradition was very male dominated—androcentric, if you will. It was often the case that women were only being included in this tradition if their point of view fit under the cultural nationalist banner" (1990, 229). And Alarcón notes: "Though the formation of the new political Chicano class was dominated by men, Chicana feminists have intervened from the beginning. The early Chicana intervention is available in the serial and journals that mushroomed in tandem with the alternative press in the United States in the 1960s and 1970s. Unfortunately much of that early work by Chicanas often goes unrecognized which is indicative of the process of erasure and exclusion of raced ethnic women within a patriarchal cultural and political economy" (1990, 249). There has been some attempt to undo this process of erasure and re-collect Chicana voices once unrecognized. See, for example, Alma García's edited collection *Chicana Feminist Thought: The Basic Historical Writings.*

13. I have discussed the variety of uses to which Aztlán has been put in "Refiguring Aztlán."

14. Tomás Ybarra-Frausto writes: "Rasquachismo is a vernacular system of taste that is intuitive and sincere, not thought out and self-conscious. It is a way of putting yourself together or creating an environment replete with color, texture, and pattern; a rampant decorative sense whose basic axiom might be 'too much is not enough.' Rasquachismo draws its essence within the world of the tattered, shattered, and broken: lo remendado (stitched together)" (1991, 156).

Alicia Gaspar de Alba takes up the discussion in her analysis of the CARA Exhibit in *Chicano Art*. She argues that *rasquachismo* serves as a dominant aesthetic in Chicano cultural expression and is manifest in three ways: "first-degree *rasquachismo*, or icons, objects, and practices that are rooted in the oral and popular traditions of Chicano/a culture; second-degree *rasquachismo*, which is appropriated from its original context by mainstream commercial enterprises such as stores that sell 'ethnic' paraphernalia . . . ; and third-degree *rasquachismo* that informs the work of Chicano and Chicana artists" (1998, 14). Gaspar de Alba's degree system is provocative by suggesting a measurement of the extent to which these different uses of *rasquachismo* are revolutionary or transformative.

## 5. The Transgressive Body and Sexual Mestizaje

1. José Limón argues that the sexualized and scatological expression of Chicano working-class social interactivity serves as a type of nonrepressive sublimation, "anticipatory sites of the free social play of sexuality and desire, framed always in forms of humor and artistic patterns that are not themselves part of the established civilization." As such, the "theme of homosexuality may be the initial articulation of a movement beyond conventional heterosexuality toward the expanded realm of sexuality and full eroticization of culture" (1998, 98). Although his analysis fails to take into account the aggressive homophobia rampant in such social interactions, it does point toward the shared liberatory desire that participants in marginal social situations express.

2. Brief reviews of Cuadros's work in *Library Journal* by Thomas Tavis and in *Publishers Weekly* provide some key information on his career.

3. This formation parallels somewhat the characterization present in Tomás Rivera's seminal novel *...y no se lo tragó la tierra*. Ramón Saldívar notes about Rivera's novel that the "narrator protagonist is not actually present as a main

character in all of the sections of the novel but rather serves as . . . a chronotopic point—a figural intersection of time and space—around which the collective subjective experiences" of the characters coalesce (1990, 75). In many ways, the characters of Cuadros's collection—which is highly autobiographical—might be thought of as coalescing around a chronotopic point that is the narrator/protagonist.

4. In this regard, Tomás Ybarra-Frausto's analysis of the origins of Chicano poetry is instructive. Ybarra-Frausto argues that the Chicano movement relied on a coalescence of urban and rural experiences, but that the rural world of the farmworkers was elemental in politicizing and forging a sense of political and cultural unity. "At the grass-roots level," he observes, "as Chicano workers began to understand the farm workers' plight, they often shared a common vision of oppression. Gradually both urban workers and rural campesinos recognized that the many forms of social, political and cultural oppression which they suffered were determined as much by class and economics as by cultural conflict" (1977, 84). Ybarra-Frausto notes that the publication of *El Malcriado*, an organizing tool used by the farmworkers, also functioned as a vehicle promoting unity by building class, cultural, and political awareness. The poetry and stories, in addition to the journalistic works printed by the broadsheet, encompassed "not an individual drama but the experience of a collective protagonist: the rural working class" (ibid.).

5. In his essay on Chicano homosexuality, "Chicano Men: A Cartography of Homosexual Identity and Behavior," Tomás Almaguer argues that there are three models of Chicano homosexual identity: men who consider themselves gay and participate in an emergent gay Latino subculture, those who consider themselves gay but maintain a primary identity as Chicano, and those fully assimilated into the white gay male community. In Cuadros's stories, the characters seem to struggle most with the contradictions inherent in these last two positions, unable to find or identify any emergent community that allows for both a Chicano and a gay identity.

6. Cuadros, quoted in Robert Drake and Terry Wolverton's edition of gay fiction *His2*, says: "I want to write about AIDS spiritually, symbolically, out of context of time and reality" (1997, 290).

7. I am referring, of course, to Louis Althusser's "Ideology and Ideological State Apparatuses." He observes that ideological state apparatuses, like the

family, schools, and churches, "function secondarily by repression, even if ultimately, but only ultimately, this is very attenuated and concealed, even symbolic" (1971, 145). The queer body within the Chicano context detailed by Cuadros's narratives reveals how overt the repressive qualities of the family unit are.

8. Although Pérez's essay deals primarily with the dynamics of a racialized heterosexuality, she goes on to argue: "Both women and men are addicted to the very thing that destroys them—the patriarchy within capitalist constructs in the late twentieth century. And the social sexual relations between men and women condoned by the patriarchy are inherently unhealthy and destructive most of the time. Of course, gay men and lesbians who mimic the heterosexual arrangement inherit patriarchy's problems" (1991, 173). The patterns of abusive power made present through sexual desire can be manifested through homosexual relations. This is premised on control of the symbolic order that has been racialized by a history of colonization.

9. The concern with the relation between physical suffering and spiritual awakening is evident in Cuadros's other work. See, for example, the online story "Hands" posted in the summer of 1996. The main character of that story, also suffering from AIDS, finds himself working in the garden of a church as he waits for his lover to get off work at the nursery across the street. Digging in the flower beds, the narrator becomes aware of a transformation: "I start to notice the meditative quality of working this soil, how there is something like a warm charge I receive from the earth, that I become more spirit than being" (http://www.echonyc.com/~meehan/Soil/Medium/cuadros.html). The concern with the body and the renewal of spiritual growth despite physical suffering and emotional loss echoes the direction taken in the stories in *City of God*. For information on the hard copy and virtual publication of "Hands" and other stories dealing with soil in the journal *xxxfruit* see http://www.echonyc.com/~meehan/Soil/credits/htm.

10. This tension is evident still in Cuadros's last published work, "Birth." This short story treats a man living with AIDS who imagines he carries a child inside him. He tells his partner, Marcus, that the child will be born at the moment of the narrator's own demise: "I do not know if the little one will appear launched from my head, or emerge from the muscles of my legs. But when the moment happens it will be as if a part of me dies. When I release him to the river I will surely crumble to the ground, crying out for Marcus, my body

disintegrating into the stuff of protons, neutrons, quarks, shattering back into the dark matter of an unforgiving universe" (1997, 122). The story continues the thematic and narrative issues developed in *City of God*, the concern with spiritual renewal in the face of physical decay and, more generally, the interaction between destructive and creative forces.

11. See Leon Roudiez's introduction to Kristeva's *Revolution in Poetic Language* for a further discussion of these possibilities. Roudiez argues that poetic language, for Kristeva, "stands for the infinite possibilities of language, and all other language acts are merely partial realizations of the possibilities inherent in 'poetic language.' From such a point of view, 'literary practice is seen as exploration and discovery of the possibilities of language; as an activity that liberates the subject from a number of linguistic, psychic, and social networks; as a dynamism that breaks up the inertia of language habits and grants linguists the unique possibility of studying the *becoming* of the significations of signs'" (1984, 2) (quoting Kristeva from *Recherches pour une sémanalyse* [Paris: Seuil, 1969], 178–79). Literary practice is liberating precisely when it frees one from the constraints of established linguistic, psychic, and social networks.

12. In her essay "Sexuality and Discourse," Pérez notes: "Consciousness is born out of one's intimate awareness of one's oppression" (1991, 160). I argue that *Gulf Dreams* stands as a narrative representation of the protagonist coming into consciousness. It traces the intimacy of oppression in relation to the narrator's queer mestiza body.

13. Mary Pat Brady's discussion of Cherríe Moraga is instructive in this regard. Brady notes that Moraga's writing focuses on the wounds caused by obedience to and defiance of the cultural injunction to put men first. "For Moraga," Brady writes, "it is this injunction, jealously guarded, that orders Chicana sexuality, that establishes it as secondary, largely despised, and always marked deficient. It is this injunction that undergirds heterosexism and that marks lesbian desire as monstrous, outrageous, prohibited, and a betrayal of the cultural order" (2002, 159). In Pérez's narrative, the wounds the narrator experiences occur because of her inability to act on a desire that defies the cultural order.

14. As I have noted, in "Sexuality and Discourse" Pérez discusses the role language plays for mestizos and mestizas within a colonial dynamic: "Mestizos/as master the conqueror's language as the language of survival, but it never belongs to the conquered completely" (1991, 168). Pérez argues that it is through lan-

guage that one seizes sociosexual power, a language of white and male privilege. Employing the work of Luce Irigaray, especially her 1974 book *Speculum: Of the Other Woman*, she argues that (phallocentric) language is used as a speculum, an invasive observation, against women. And the loss of a woman's language Pérez equates with the loss of memory, of a pre-oedipal (perhaps prelinguistic) connection to the maternal.

15. A *malinchista* is one who betrays her people. The term derives from the name Malinche, the disparaging name for Malintzín, the Aztec woman who served as translator (and rumored lover) of Hernán Cortés. *La chingada* means literally "the fucked one," a derogatory term for Malintzín. Octavio Paz discusses the sense of violation inherent to Mexican self-identity in *The Labyrinth of Solitude*: "The *Chingada* is the Mother forcibly opened, violated or deceived. The *hijo de la Chingada* is the offspring of violation, of abduction or deceit. If we compare this expression with the Spanish *hijo de puta* (son of a whore), the difference is immediately obvious. To the Spaniard, dishonor consists in being the son of a woman who voluntarily surrenders herself: a prostitute. To the Mexican it consists in being the fruit of violation" (1985, 79–80). See also María Herrera-Sobek's "The Politics of Rape" (1988) and Norma Alarcón's "Traddutora, Traditora" (1989) for a discussion of rape as a trope in the articulation of Chicano (and particularly Chicana) cultural identity. See also Alarcón's "Chicana's Feminist Literature: A Re-Vision through/*or* Malintzín: Putting Flesh Back on the Subject" (1983) for an example of how Chicana critics have reclaimed the figure of Malintzín as part of a politics of liberation.

16. For a more positive and politically assertive reading of Pérez's book, see Ellie Hernández's essay "Chronotope of Desire."

## 6. Narrative and Loss

1. Gabriele Pisarz-Ramírez's analysis of the work by Alfredo Véa and Francisco Alarcón provides a good example of how critics understand the intermixture of cultural, linguistic, and social mestizaje. She writes that Véa and Alarcón "are just two out of many Chicano/a writers who functionalize interlingualism to textualize the hybrid in Chicano/a texts and to invest Chicano/a literary discourse with an alternate consciousness. However, not only interlingual, but also bilingual and even monolingual texts by Chicanos/as participate in the production of a polyglossic discourse that is affirmative of a mestizo/a identity

permanently in the making" (2000, 74). The polyglossia evident in Chicano writing becomes, for Pisarz-Ramírez and others, a component of Chicano subjectivity as a category-under-construction.

2. Genaro Padilla discusses the general sense of dislocation evident in Chicano writing. He argues that the texts make evident how "Chicano writers have . . . suffered from an 'orphan complex' that led, in past generations, to an idealization of the Spanish forebearers, and more recently to a nostalgia for the Mexican homeland, especially as it has been imagined in that mythical realm of Aztlán. This impulse has manifested itself intensely in the last two decades, a period during which the Chicano, feeling deeply alienated from the foster parent United States, wished to maintain a vital spiritual link with Mexico, the model of language, culture and social behavior" (1989: 126). The draw to the national space of Mexico is based on an imagined recognition of Mexico as an ethical center, what Padilla calls "a vital spiritual link."

3. The work of Ramón Saldívar, in particular *Chicano Narrative: The Dialectics of Difference*, has been germinal in establishing the connection between narrative and the history of dispossession that has made up the cultural mythology of Chicano/a identity. See as well Héctor Calderón's essay "To Read Chicano Narrative: Commentary and Metacommentary."

4. Richard T. Rodríguez's forthcoming book *Next of Kin* brilliantly treats the discourse of the Chicano family and its attachment to masculinity and nationalism. See also his essay "Serial Kinship: Representing La Familia in Early Chicano Publications."

5. In a particularly moving chapter of her book on film and the borderlands, Rosa Linda Fregoso discusses how she collected the memories her grandmother had about growing up in Corpus Christi in the early twentieth century. Her grandmother's memories of discrimination and resistant readings to movies serve as a kind of ethical center and repository of historical countermemory evident in Fregoso's own exceptional intellectual work. See "Ghosts of a Mexican Past" in *MeXicana Encounters*.

6. For an ingenious reading of melancholy as a response to colonial legacies of race evidenced in texts by Che Guevara and Jack Kerouac, see Josefina Saldaña's "'On the Road' with Che and Jack: Melancholia and the Legacy of Colonial Racial Geographies in the Americas."

7. Saldívar provides a splendid example of how Chicano and Chicana critical discourse has appropriated and formed a dialogue with dominant critical discourses. He points to the "differential structure" of the Chicano novel based on Jacques Derrida's notion of *différance*: "Différance is what makes the movement of signification possible only if each element that is said to be 'present,' appearing on the stage of presence, is related to something other than itself but retains the mark of a past element and already lets itself be hollowed out by the mark of its relation to a future element. . . . From Derrida's concept I wish to retain the two ideas of difference as a *differing* (in kind) and as a *deferring* (in time)" (1979, 75).

8. In his introduction to Mikhail Bakhtin's *The Dialogic Imagination*, Michael Holquist notes that Bakhtin's concept of language "has as its enabling *a priori* an almost Manichean sense of opposition and struggle at the heart of existence, a ceaseless battle between centrifugal forces that seek to keep things apart, and centripetal forces that strive to make things cohere. This Zoroastrian clash is present in culture as well as nature, and in the specificity of individual consciousness; it is at work in the even greater particularity of individual utterances. The most complete and complex reflection of these forces is found in human language, and the best transcription of language so understood is the novel" (1981, xviii). For Georg Lukács, the novel is an expression of philosophical inquiry about human existence. Philosophy, as Novalis noted, is the "urge to be at home everywhere," which is why, for Lukács, philosophy "as a form of life or as that which determines the form and supplies the content of literary creation, is always a symptom of the rift between 'inside' and 'outside,' a sign of the essential difference between the self and the world, the incongruence of soul and deed. That is why the happy ages have no philosophy" (1985, 29). The a priori that is for Bakhtin the battle between totalization and molecularization in the work of Lukács is the drive for an impossible wholeness between self and the world. Both theorists consider struggle as a central component of human experience and the novel's representation of it. However, the distinction of the Chicano novel (perhaps the U.S. ethnic novel as a genre) is the manner in which it contests structures of representation that do violence to Chicano/a subjectivity and agency.

9. In his study of Chicano literature and American counterculture, Manuel

Luis Martinez argues that in Gonzales's poetry, Chicano identity "must be forged, free of the dross that is 'Anglo' culture—read here as 'American.' Separatism and a nostalgia for *la patria*, an idealized Mexico, and a nascent indigenism *(indigenismo)* begin to shape the parameters and identity of Aztlan. . . . [This indigenism] was a form of countererasure" (2003, 200). The rejection of American identity forms the underpinning of a Chicano counterdiscourse.

10. This evokes Anne Cheng's observation that "the melancholic ego is a haunted ego, at once made ghostly and embodied in its ghostliness, but the 'object' [of loss] is also ghostly . . . because its image has been introjected or incorporated within the melancholic psyche" (2001, 9–10). The idea of the haunted ego calls up as well Gil Cuadros's story "Reynaldo" and its protagonist yearning for a lost familial love. For a discussion of how absense and haunting inflect modern social dynamics, see Avery Gordon's *Ghostly Matters: Haunting and the Sociological Imagination* (1997).

11. This device may very well be inspired by the structure of one of the foundational Chicano novels, Tomás Rivera's 1971 *...y no se lo tragó la tierra*. That novel is divided into twelve main stories, alternating with brief narrative fragments, in order to form the twelve months of the year. This suggests both the cyclical nature of the narrative and the growth of the unnamed protagonist who comes into agency by the end of the novel, paralleling the seasonal changes that determine the lives of the fieldworkers, the primary subject of the novel.

12. As Alvina Quintana notes, when Chicanos and Chicanas assert an identity, "we involve ourselves in a self-fashioning process that engages someone else's political agenda. Renaming oneself, in this situation, represents a symbolic act of resistance that requires imagination, fluidity, and finesse" (1996, 8–9).

# Works Cited

Acosta, Oscar "Zeta." 1987. *The Revolt of the Cockroach People.* Introduction by Hunter S. Thompson. New York: Vintage.

———. 1989. *The Autobiography of a Brown Buffalo.* Introduction by Hunter S. Thompson. New York: Vintage.

Acuña, Rodolfo. 1972. *Occupied America: A History of Chicanos.* New York: Harper & Row.

———. 1996. *Anything but Mexican: Chicanos in Contemporary Los Angeles.* New York: Verso.

Alarcón, Daniel Cooper. 1997. *The Aztec Palimpsest: Mexico in the Modern Imagination.* Tucson: University of Arizona Press.

Alarcón, Norma. 1983. "Chicana's Feminist Literature: A Re-Vision through/*or* Malintzín: Putting Flesh Back on the Subject." In *This Bridge Called My Back: Writings by Radical Women of Color,* ed. Cherríe Moraga and Gloria Anzaldúa, 182–90. New York: Kitchen Table.

———. 1989. "Traddutora, Traditora: A Paradigmatic Figure of Chicana Feminism." *Cultural Critique* 13 (fall): 57–87.

———. 1990. "Chicana Feminism: In the Tracks of 'The' Native Woman." *Cultural Studies* 4.3: (248–56).

———. 1994. "Conjugating Subjects: The Heteroglossia of Essence and Resistance." In *An Other Tongue: Nation and Ethnicity in the Linguistic Borderlands,* ed. Alfred Arteaga, 125–38. Durham, NC: Duke University Press.

Aldama, Arturo J. 2001. *Disrupting Savagism: Intersecting Chicana/o, Mexican*

*Immigrant, and Native American Struggles for Self-Representation*. Durham, NC: Duke University Press.

Alemán, Jesse. 2002. "Historical Amnesia and the Vanishing Mestiza: The Problem of Race in *The Squatter and the Don* and *Ramona*." *Aztlán* 27.1 (spring): 59–93.

Almaguer, Tomás. 1991. "Chicano Men: A Cartography of Homosexual Identity and Behavior." *Differences*. 3.2: 75–100.

———. 1994. *Racial Fault Lines: The Historical Origins of White Supremacy in California*. Berkeley: University of California Press.

Althusser, Louis. 1971. *Lenin and Philosophy and Other Essays*. Trans. Ben Brewster. New York: Monthly Review Press.

Anzaldúa, Gloria. 1987. *Borderlands/La Frontera: The New Mestiza*. San Francisco: Spinsters/Aunt Lute.

Archibald, Priscilla. 2002. "Gender and *Mestizaje* in the Andes." In *Mixing Race, Mixing Culture: Inter-American Literary Dialogues*, 103–21. Austin: University of Texas Press.

Arnold, Gary. 1996. "Giant (Movie Reviews)." *Insight on the News* 12.45 (December 2): 37.

Arteaga, Alfred. 1997. *Chicano Poetics: Heterotexts and Hybridities*. New York: Cambridge University Press.

Bakhtin, Mikhail Mikhailovich. 1981. *The Dialogic Imagination*. Ed. Michael Holquist. Trans. Caryl Emerson and Michael Holquist. Austin: University of Texas Press.

Bartra, Roger. 1992. *The Cage of Melancholy: Identity and Metamorphosis in the Mexican Character*. Trans. Christopher J. Hall. New Brunswick, NJ: Rutgers University Press.

Berg, Charles Ramírez. 1992. "*Bordertown*, the Assimilation Narrative, and the Chicano Social Problem Film." In *Chicanos and Film: Representation and Resistance*, ed. Chon A. Noriega, 29–46. Minneapolis: University of Minnesota Press.

Bhabha, Homi K. 1989. "Remembering Fanon: Self, Psyche, and the Colonial Position." In *Remaking History*, ed. Barbara Kruger and Phil Mariani, 131–48. Seattle: Bay Press, 1989.

———. 1994. *The Location of Culture*. New York: Routledge.

Bogue, Roland. 1989. *Deleuze and Guattari*. New York: Routledge.

Bohlman, Philip V. 1993. "Musicology as a Political Act." *Journal of Musicology* 11.4 (fall): 411–36.

Bost, Suzanne. 2003. *Mulattas and Mestizas: Representing Mixed Identities in the Americas, 1850–2000*. Athens: University of Georgia Press.

Brady, Mary Pat. 2002. *Extinct Lands, Temporal Geographies: Chicana Literature and the Urgency of Space*. Durham, NC: Duke University Press.

Brennan, Jonathan, ed. 2002. *Mixed Race Literature*. Stanford, CA: Stanford University Press.

Bürger, Peter. 1984. *Theory of the Avant-Garde*. Trans. Michael Shaw. Foreword by Jochen Schulte-Sasse. Minneapolis: University of Minnesota Press.

Calderón, Héctor. 1983. "To Read Chicano Narrative: Commentary and Metacommentary." *MESTER* 11 (May): 3–14.

———. 1990. "At the Crossroads of History, on the Borders of Change: Chicano Literary Studies Past, Present, and Future." In *Left Politics and the Literary Profession*, ed. Lennard J. Davis and M. Bella Mirabella, 211–35. New York: Columbia University Press.

Canclini, Néstor García. 1995. *Hybrid Cultures: Strategies for Entering and Leaving Modernity*. Trans. Christopher L. Chiappari and Silvia L. López. Foreword by Renato Rosaldo. Minneapolis: University of Minnesota Press.

Carbonell, Ana María. 1999. "From Llorona to Gritona: Coatlicue in Feminist Tales by Viramontes and Cisneros." *MELUS* 24.2 (summer): 53–74.

Cervantes, Lorna Dee. 1981. *Emplumada*. Pittsburgh: University of Pittsburgh Press.

Chabram, Angie. 1990. "Chicana/o Studies as Oppositional Ethnography." *Cultural Studies* 4.3 (October): 228–47.

Chabram-Dernersesian, Angie. 1997. "On the Social Construction of Whiteness within Selected Chicana/o Discourses." In *Displacing Whiteness: Essays in Social and Cultural Criticism*, ed. Ruth Frankenberg. Durham, NC: Duke University Press.

Chambers, Veronica, and John Leland. 1999. "Lovin' La Vida Loca." *Newsweek* 133.22 (May 31): 72.

Chávez, Ernesto. 2002. *"¡Mi Raza Primero!" ("My People First"): Nationalism, Identity and Insurgency in the Chicano Movement in Los Angeles, 1966–1978*. Berkeley: University of California Press.

Chávez, John R. 1984. *The Lost Land: The Chicano Image of the Southwest*. Albuquerque: University of New Mexico Press.

Cheng, Anne Anlin. 2001. *The Melancholy of Race: Psychoanalysis, Assimilation, and Hidden Grief*. New York: Oxford University Press.

Cisneros, Sandra. 1991. "Woman Hollering Creek." In *Woman Hollering Creek and Other Stories*, 43–56. New York: Vintage.

Coker, Cheo Hodari. 1996. "Stirring It Up with Latino Hip, Hip-Hop." *Los Angeles Times*, June 9, calendar section, 60+.

Coronil, Fernando. 1993. "Challenging Colonial Histories: *Cuban Counterpoint/* Ortiz's Counterfetishism." In *Critical Theory, Cultural Politics, and Latin American Narrative*, ed. Steven M. Bell, Albert H. LeMay, and Leonard Orr, 61–80. Notre Dame: University of Notre Dame Press.

Cross, Brian. 1993. *It's Not about a Salary: Rap, Race, and Resistance in Los Angeles*. London and New York: Verso.

Cuadros, Gil. 1994. *City of God*. San Francisco: City Lights Books.

———. 1996. "Hands." *xxxfruit* 2 (June). http://www.echonyc.com/~meehan/ Soil/Medium/cuadros.html.

———. 1997. "Birth." In *His2: Brilliant New Fiction by Gay Writers*, ed. Robert Drake and Terry Wolverton, 120–22. Boston: Faber and Faber.

Davalos, Karen Mary. 2001. *Exhibiting Mestizaje: Mexican (American) Museums in the Diaspora*. Albuquerque: University of New Mexico Press.

Davíla, Arlene. 2001. *Latinos, Inc.: The Marketing and Making of a People*. Berkeley: University of California Press.

———. 2004. *Barrio Dreams: Puerto Ricans, Latinos, and the Neoliberal City*. Berkeley: University of California Press.

de Castro, Juan E. 2002. *Mestizo Nations: Culture, Race, and Conformity in Latin American Literature*. Tucson: University of Arizona Press.

Deleuze, Gilles, and Félix Guattari. 1986. *Kafka: Toward a Minor Literature*. Trans. Dana Polan. Foreword by Réda Bensmaïa. Minneapolis: University of Minnesota Press.

———. 1987. *A Thousand Plateaus: Capitalism and Schizophrenia*. Trans. and foreword by Brian Massumi. Minneapolis: University of Minnesota Press.

Delgadillo, Theresa. 2004. "'Angelitos Negros' and Transnational Racial Identifications." In *Rebellious Reading: The Dynamics of Chicana/o Cultural Literacy*, ed. Carl Gutiérrez-Jones, 129–43. Santa Barbara: Center for Chicano Studies at the University of California, Santa Barbara.

Dibbell, Carola. 1996. "Found in Translation." *Village Voice*, April 16, 57, 62.

Doyle, Jacqueline. 1996. "Haunting the Borderlands: La Llorona in Sandra Cisneros's 'Woman Hollering Creek.'" *Frontiers* 16.1: 53–70.

Drake, Robert, and Terry Wolverton, eds. 1997. *His2: Brilliant New Fiction by Gay Writers*. Boston: Faber and Faber.

Eng, David L., and David Kazanjian, eds. 2003. *Loss*. Berkeley: University of California Press.

Fitz, Earl E. 2002. "From Blood to Culture: Miscegenation as Metaphor for the Americas." In *Mixing Race, Mixing Culture: Inter-American Literary Dialogues*, ed. Monica Kaup and Debra J. Rosenthal, 243–72. Austin: University of Texas Press.

Foley, Neil. 1997. *The White Scourge: Mexicans, Blacks, and Poor Whites in Texas Cotton Culture*. Berkeley: University of California Press.

Franco, Jean. 1989. *Plotting Women: Gender and Representation in Mexico*. New York: Columbia University Press.

Fregoso, Rosa Linda. 2003. *MeXicana Encounters: The Making of Social Identities on the Borderlands*. Berkeley: University of California Press.

Fregoso, Rosa Linda, and Angie Chabram. 1990. "Chicana/o Cultural Representations: Reframing Alternative Critical Discourses." *Cultural Studies* 4.3 (October): 203–12.

García, Alma M., ed. 1997. *Chicana Feminist Thought: The Basic Historical Writings*. New York: Routledge.

García, Eugene E., Francisco A. Lomelí, and Isidro D. Ortiz, eds. 1984. *Chicano Studies: A Multidisciplinary Approach*. New York: Teachers College Press.

García, Guy. 1994. "Extending Chicano Roots into Polyglot Textures." *New York Times*, April 3, national edition, H27.

Gaspar de Alba, Alicia. 1998. *Chicano Art: Inside/Outside the Master's House*. Austin: University of Texas Press.

Gilroy, Paul. 1993. *The Black Atlantic: Modernity and Double Consciousness*. Cambridge: Harvard University Press.

Gómez-Quiñones, Juan. 1990. *Chicano Politics: Reality and Promise, 1940–1990*. Albuquerque: University of New Mexico Press.

Gonzales, Rodolpho. 1972. *Yo soy Joaquín/I Am Joaquín*. New York: Bantam.

González, John M. 2004. "The Warp of Whiteness: Domesticity and Empire in Helen Hunt Jackson's *Ramona*." *American Literary History* 16.3 (fall): 437–65.

González, Rafael Jesús. 1977. "Chicano Poetry/Smoking Mirror." *New Scholar* 6: 127–37.

Gordon, Avery F. 1997. *Ghostly Matters: Haunting and the Sociological Imagination*. Minneapolis: University of Minnesota Press.

Gurza, Augustin. 2004. "LACMA to Put Spotlight on Local Latino Artists." *Los Angeles Times*, October 27, E1.

Hall, Stuart. 1988. *The Hard Road to Renewal*. London: Verso.

———. 1991a. "The Local and the Global: Globalization and Ethnicity." In *Culture, Globalization and the World-System: Contemporary Conditions for the Representation of Identity*, ed. Anthony D. King, 19–39. Binghamton: Department of Art and Art History, State University of New York at Binghamton.

———. 1991b. "Old and New Identities, Old and New Ethnicities." In *Culture, Globalization and the World-System: Contemporary Conditions for the Representation of Identity*, ed. Anthony D. King, 41–68. Binghamton: Department of Art and Art History, State University of New York at Binghamton.

———. 1996. "Introduction: Who Needs Identity?" In *Questions of Cultural Identity*, ed. Stuart Hall and Paul du Gay, 1–17. London: Sage Publications.

Haney-López, Ian F. 1996. *White by Law: The Legal Construction of Race*. New York: New York University Press.

———. 2003. *Racism on Trial: The Chicano Fight for Justice*. Cambridge: Belknap Press of Harvard University Press.

Haraway, Donna. 1991. "A Cyborg Manifesto: Science, Technology, and Socialist-Feminism in the Late Twentieth Century." In *Simians, Cyborgs, and Women: The Reinvention of Nature*, 148–81. New York: Routledge.

Hernández, Ellie. 2001. "Chronotope of Desire: Emma Pérez's *Gulf Dreams*." In *Chicana Feminisms: A Critical Reader*, ed. Gabriela F. Arredondon, Aida Hurtado, Norma Klahn, Olga Najera-Ramírez, and Patricia Zavella, 155–77. Durham, NC: Duke University Press.

Herrera-Sobek, María. 1988. "The Politics of Rape: Sexual Transgression in Chicana Fiction." In *Chicana Creativity and Criticism: Charting New Frontiers in American Literature*, 171–81, ed. María Herrera-Sobek and Helena María Viramontes. Houston: Arte Público Press.

Hutcheon, Linda. 1989. "The Post-Modern Ex-centric: The Center That Will Not Hold." In *Feminism and Institutions: Dialogues on Feminist Theory*, ed. Linda Kaufman, 141–65. Cambridge: Basil Blackwell.

Huyssen, Andreas. 1984. "Mapping the Postmodern." *New German Critique* 33 (fall): 5–52.

Irigaray, Luce. 1985. *Speculum: Of the Other Woman*. Trans. Gillian C. Gill. Ithaca, NY: Cornell University Press.

Islas, Arturo. 1991. *The Rain God*. New York: Avon Books.

Jameson, Fredric. 1984. "Postmodernism, or The Cultural Logic of Late Capitalism." *New Left Review* 146 (July/August): 53–93.

Jiménez, Francisco, ed. 1979. *The Identification and Analysis of Chicano Literature*. New York: Bilingual Press/Editorial Binlingüe.

Katzew, Ilona. 2004. *Casta Painting: Images of Race in Eighteenth-Century Mexico.* New Haven: Yale University Press.

Kaup, Monika. 1994. "Reterritorializing the Border in Chicano/a Fiction." *Amerikastudien/American Studies* 39.4: 579–95.

———. 2002. "Constituting Hybridity as Hybrid: Métis Canadian and Mexican American Formations." In *Mixing Race, Mixing Culture: Inter-American Literary Dialogues,* ed. Monica Kaup and Debra J. Rosenthal, 185–210. Austin: University of Texas Press.

Kristeva, Julia. 1980. "Ellipsis on Dread and the Specular Seduction." Trans. Dolores Burdick. *Wide Angle* 3.3: 42–47.

———. 1984. *Revolution in Poetic Language.* Trans. Margaret Waller. Introduction by Leon S. Roudiez. New York: Columbia University Press.

———. 1989. *Black Sun: Depression and Melancholia.* Trans. Leon S. Roudiez. New York: Columbia University Press.

Leal, Luís. 1979. "The Problem of Identifying Chicano Literature." In *The Identification and Analysis of Chicano Literature,* ed. Francisco Jiménez, 2–6. New York: Bilingual Press/Editorial Bilingüe.

———. 1981. "In Search of Aztlán." Trans. Gladys Leal. *Denver Quarterly* 16 (fall): 16–22.

Leal, Luis, and Pepe Barrón. 1982. "Chicano Literature: An Overview." In *Three American Literatures,* ed. Houston A. Baker Jr., introduction by Walter J. Ong, 9–32. New York: Modern Language Association.

Lechner, Ernesto. 2001. "Short Career, Long Shadow." *Los Angeles Times,* March 18, calendar section, 4, 77.

Lemire, Elise. 2002. *"Miscegenation": Making Race in America.* Philadelphia: University of Pennsylvania Press.

Limón, José E. 1992. *Mexican Ballads, Chicano Poems: History and Influence in Mexican-American Social Poetry.* Berkeley: University of California Press.

———. 1998. *American Encounters: Greater Mexico, the United States, and the Erotics of Culture.* Boston: Beacon Press.

Lippard, Lucy R. 1990. *Mixed Blessings: New Art in a Multicultural America.* New York: Pantheon Books.

Lipsitz, George. 1991a. *"Buscando América* (Looking for America): Collective Memory in an Age of Amnesia." In *Time Passages: Collective Memory and American Popular Culture,* 257–71. Minneapolis: University of Minnesota Press.

———. 1991b. "Cruising around the Historical Bloc: Postmodernism and Popular Music in East Los Angeles." In *Time Passages: Collective Memory and American Popular Culture,* 133–60. Minneapolis: University of Minnesota Press.

———. 1994. "We Know What Time It Is: Race, Class and Youth Culture in the Nineties." In *Microphone Fiends: Youth Music and Youth Culture*, ed. Andrew Ross and Tricia Rose, 17–28. New York: Routledge.

Lomelí, Francisco A. 1984. "An Overview of Chicano Letters: From Origins to Resurgence." In *Chicano Studies: A Multidisciplinary Approach*, ed. Eugene E. García, Francisco A. Lomelí, and Isidro D. Ortiz, 103–19. New York: Teachers College Press.

Lowe, Lisa. 1996. *Immigrant Acts: On Asian American Cultural Politics*. Durham, NC: Duke University Press.

Loza, Steven. 1992. "From Veracruz to Los Angeles: The Reinterpretation of the Son Jarocho." *Latin American Music Review* 13.2 (fall/winter): 179–94.

———. 1993. *Barrio Rhythm: Mexican American Music in Los Angeles*. Urbana and Chicago: University of Illinois Press.

Lukács, Georg. 1985. *The Theory of the Novel*. Trans. Anna Bostock. Cambridge: MIT Press.

Mallon, Florencia E. 1992. "Indian Communities, Political Cultures and the State in Latin America, 1780–1990." *Journal of LatinAmerican Studies* 24 (spring): 35–53.

Manuel, Peter. 1995. "Music as Symbol, Music as Simulacrum: Postmodern, Pre-Modern, and Modern Aesthetics in Subcultural Popular Musics." *Popular Music* 14.2: 227–39.

Martinez, Manuel Luis. 2003. *Countering the Counterculture: Rereading Post-war American Dissent from Jack Kerouac to Tomás Rivera*. Madison: University of Wisconsin Press.

Martínez, Rubén. 2002. *Crossing Over: A Mexican Family on the Migrant Trail*. New York: Picado.

Martinez, Victor. 1996. *Parrot in the Oven: Mi Vida*. New York: Joanna Cotler Books.

Mazón, Mauricio. 1984. *The Zoot-Suit Riots: The Psychology of Symbolic Annihilation*. Austin: University of Texas Press.

McKenna, Teresa. 1997. *Migrant Song: Politics and Process in Contemporary Chicano Literature*. Austin: University of Texas Press.

Meyer, Richard. 1991. "Rock Hudson's Body." In *Inside/Out: Lesbian Theories, Gay Theories*, ed. Diana Fuss, 259–88. New York: Routledge.

Mignolo, Walter D. 2000. *Local Histories/Global Designs: Coloniality, Subaltern Knowledges, and Border Thinking*. Princeton, NJ: Princeton University Press.

Mohanty, Chandra Talpade. 1989/90. "On Race and Voice: Challenges for Liberal Education in the 1990s." *Cultural Critique* 14 (winter): 174–208.

Monteagudo, José. 1995. *Lambda Book Report* 4.8 (January–February): 34.

Mora, Pat. 1997. *House of Houses*. Boston: Beacon Press.

Moraga, Cherríe. 1993. "Queer Aztlán: The Re-formation of the Chicano Tribe." In *The Last Generation*, 145–74. Boston: South End Press.

Moreiras, Alberto. 2001. *The Exhaustion of Difference: The Politics of Latin American Cultural Studies*. Durham, NC: Duke University Press.

Muñoz, José Esteban. 1999. *Disidentifications: Queers of Color and the Performance of Politics*. Minneapolis: University of Minnesota Press.

Nancy, Jean-Luc. 1994. "Cut Throat Sun." Trans. Lydie Moudileno. In *An Other Tongue: Nation and Ethnicity in the Linguistic Borderlands*, ed. Alfred Arteaga, 113–23. Durham, NC: Duke University Press.

Nash, June. 1978. "The Aztecs and the Ideology of Male Dominance." *Signs* 4 (winter): 349–62.

Noriega, Chon. 2001a. "Fashion Crimes." *Aztlán: A Journal of Chicano Studies* 26.1 (spring): 1–13.

———. 2001b. "Postermodernism, or Why This Is Just Another Poster." In *Just Another Poster? Chicano Graphic Arts in California*, ed. Chon Noriega, 19–23. Santa Barbara: University Art Museum, University of California, Santa Barbara.

Oboler, Suzanne. 1995. *Ethnic Labels, Latino Lives: Identity and the Politics of (Re)Presentation in the United States*. Minneapolis: University of Minnesota Press.

Ortiz, Fernando. 1947. *Cuban Counterpoint: Tobacco and Sugar*. New York: Knopf.

Padilla, Genaro M. 1989. "Myth and Comparative Cultural Nationalism: The Ideological Uses of Aztlán." In *Aztlán: Essays on the Chicano Homeland*, 111–34. Albuquerque: Academia/El Norte Publications.

Paredes, Américo. 1958. *"With His Pistol in His Hand": A Border Ballad and Its Hero*. Austin: University of Texas Press.

Paredes, Raymund A. 1982. "The Evolution of Chicano Literature." In *Three American Literatures*, ed. Houston A. Baker Jr., introduction by Walter J. Ong, 33–79. New York: Modern Language Association.

Pareles, Jon. 1993. "Rage Against the Machine: Roseland." *New York Times*, November 8, national edition, C14.

Paz, Octavio. 1985. *Labyrinth of Solitude*. Trans. Lysander Kemp, Yara Milos, and Rachel Phillips Belash. New York: Grove Press.

Peña, Manuel H. 1985. *The Texas-Mexican Conjunto: History of a Working-Class Music*. Austin: University of Texas Press.

Peñalosa, Fernando. 1980. *Chicano Sociolinguistics: A Brief Introduction*. Rowley, MA: Newbury House.

Pérez, Emma. 1991. "Sexuality and Discourse: Notes from a Chicana Survivor." In *Chicana Lesbians: The Girls Our Mothers Warned Us About*, ed. Carla Trujillo, 159–84. Berkeley: Third Woman Press.

———. 1996. *Gulf Dreams*. Berkeley: Third Woman Press.

———. 1999. *The Decolonial Imaginary: Writing Chicanas into History*. Bloomington: Indiana University Press.

Pérez-Torres, Rafael. 1997. "Refiguring Aztlán." *Aztlán: A Journal of Chicano Studies* 22.2 (fall): 15–41. Reprinted in *The Chicano Studies Readers: An Anthology of Aztlán 1970–2000*, 213–39. Los Angeles: Chicano Studies Research Center Publications, 2001.

———. 1998. "Chicano Ethnicity, Cultural Hybridity, and the Mestizo Voice." *American Literature* 70.1 (March): 153–76.

———. 2001a. "Mestizaje in the Mix: Chicano Identity, Politics, and Postmodern Music." In *Music and the Racial Imagination*, ed. Ronald Radano and Philip Bohlman, 206–30. Chicago: University of Chicago Press.

———. 2001b. "Remapping Chicano Expressive Culture." In *Just Another Poster? Chicano Graphic Arts in California*, ed. Chon Noriega, 151–69. Santa Barbara: University Art Museum, University of California, Santa Barbara.

Phelan, James. 1998. "Sandra Cisneros's 'Woman Hollering Creek': Narrative as Rhetoric and as Cultural Practice." *Narrative* 6.3 (October): 221–35.

Phillips, Susan A. 1999. *Wallbangin': Graffiti and Gangs in L.A.* Chicago: University of Chicago Press.

Pisarz-Ramírez, Gabriele. 2000. "Language and Identity Construction in Mexican American Literary Discourse." In *Holding Their Own: Perspectives on the Multi-Ethnic Literatures of the United States*, ed. Dorothea Fisher-Hornung and Heike Raphael-Hernandez, 67–75. Tübingen: Stauffenburg Verlag.

"Plan de Delano." 1973. In *Aztlán: An Anthology of Mexican American Literature*, ed. Luis Valdez and Stan Steiner, 197–201. New York: Knopf.

"Plan Espiritual de Aztlán." 1973. In *Aztlán: An Anthology of Mexican American Literature*, ed. Luis Valdez and Stan Steiner, 402–6. New York: Knopf.

Polar, Antonio Cornejo. 1998. "Mestizaje e hibridez: los riesgos de las metáforas." *Revista de Crítica Literaria Latinoamericana* 24.47: 7–11.

Pratt, Mary Louise. 1992. *Imperial Eyes: Travel Writing and Transculturaltion*. London: Routledge.

———. 1993. "Criticism in the Contact Zone: Decentering Community and Nation." In *Critical Theory, Cultural Politics, and Latin American Narrative*, ed. Steven M. Bell, Albert H. LeMay, and Leonard Orr, 83–102. Notre Dame: University of Notre Dame Press.

Price, Simon. 1993. "Rage Against the Machine." *Melody Maker*, August 28, 6–7.

*Publishers Weekly*. 1994. Review of *City of God*. 241.44 (October 31): 59.

Quintana, Alvina E. 1996. *Home Girls: Chicana Literary Voices*. Philadelphia: Temple University Press.

Radway, Janice A. 1991. *Reading the Romance: Women, Patriarchy, and Popular Literature*. Chapel Hill: University of North Carolina Press.

Ramírez, Catherine S. 2002. "Crimes of Fashion: The Pachuca and Chicana Style Politics." *Meridians: Feminism, Race, Transnationalism* 2.2: 1–35.

Rappaport, Mark. 1996. "Mark Rappaport's Notes on 'Rock Hudson's Home Movies.'" *Film Quarterly* 49.4 (summer): 16–22.

Rebolledo, Tey Diana. 1987. "Abuelitas: Mythology and Integration in Chicana Literature." In *Woman of Her Word: Hispanic Women Write*, ed. Evangelina Vigil, 2d ed., 148–58. Houston: Arte Público Press.

———. 1995. *Women Singing in the Snow: A Cultural Analysis of Chicana Literature*. Tucson: University of Arizona Press.

Richardson, Lisa, and Robin Fields. 2003. "Latino Majority Arrives—among State's Babies." *Los Angeles Times*, February 6, A1, A25.

Rivera, Tomás. 1987. *...y no se lo tragó la tierra / . . . and the Earth Did Not Devour Him*. Trans. Evangelina Vigil-Piñon. Houston: Arte Público Press.

———. 1988. "Richard Rodriguez's *Hunger of Memory* as Humanistic Antithesis." In *Tomás Rivera, 1935–1984: The Man and His Work*, ed. Vernon Lattin, Rolando Hinojosa, and Gary Keller, 28–33. Tempe, AZ: Bilingual Press.

Rocard, Marcienne. 1986. "The Chicano: A Minority in Search of a Proper Literary Medium for Self-Affirmation." In *Missions in Conflict: Essays on U.S.–Mexican Relations and Chicano Culture*, ed. Renate von Bardeleben, 31–40. Tübingen: Gunter Narr Verlag.

Rodríguez, Clara E. 2000. *Changing Race: Latinos, the Census, and the History of Ethnicity in the United States*. New York: New York University Press.

Rodríguez, Juan. 1979. "La búsqueda de identidad y sus motivos en la literatura Chicana." In *The Identification and Analysis of Chicano Literature*, ed. Francisco Jiménez, 170–78. New York: Bilingual Press/Editorial Bilingüe.

Rodriguez, Richard. 1992. "India." In *Days of Obligation: An Argument with My Mexican Father*, 1–25. New York: Penguin.

———. 2002. *Brown: The Last Discovery of America*. New York: Viking.

————. 2003. "Dear Edna: Why Can't We Laugh Anymore?" *Los Angeles Times*, February 16, M1, M3.

Rodríguez, Richard T. 2002. "Serial Kinship: Representing La Familia in Early Chicano Publications." *Aztlán: A Journal of Chicano Studies* (spring): 123–38.

————. 2003. "The Verse of the Godfather: Signifying Family and Nationalism in Chicano Rap and Hip-Hop Culture." In *Velvet Barrios: Popular Culture and Chicana/o Sexualities*, ed. Alicia Gaspar de Alba, 107–22. New York: Palgrave Macmillan.

————. Forthcoming. *Next of Kin: Reconfiguring the Family in Chicano/a Cultural Politics.* Raleigh, NC: Duke University Press.

Romo, Tere. 2001. "Points of Convergence: The Iconography of the Chicano Poster." *Just Another Poster? Chicano Graphic Arts in California*, ed. Chon Noriega, 91–115. Santa Barbara: University Art Museum, University of California, Santa Barbara.

Rosaldo, Renato. 1989. *Culture and Truth: The Remaking of Social Analysis.* Boston: Beacon Press.

Rose, Tricia. 1994. "A Style Nobody Can Deal With: Politics, Style and the Postindustrial City in Hip Hop." In *Microphone Fiends: Youth Music and Youth Culture*, ed. Andrew Ross and Tricia Rose, 71–88. New York: Routledge.

Rouse, Roger. 1991. "Mexican Migration and the Social Space of Postmodernism." *Diaspora* 1 (spring): 8–23.

Rushdie, Salman. 1995. *The Moor's Last Sigh.* New York: Pantheon Books.

Sáenz, Benjamin Alire. 1997. "In the Borderlands of Chicano Identity, There Are Only Fragments." In *Border Theory: The Limits of Cultural Politics*, ed. Scott Michaelsen and David E. Johnson, 68–96. Minneapolis: University of Minnesota Press.

Salas, Elizabeth. 1995. "Soldaderas: New Questions, New Sources." *Women's Studies Quarterly* 23 (fall–winter): 112–16.

Saldaña-Portillo, María Josefina. 2001. "Who's the Indian in Aztlán? Re-Writing Mestizaje, Indianism, and Chicanismo from the Lacadón." In *The Latin American Subaltern Studies Reader*, ed. Ileana Rodríguez, 402–23. Durham, NC: Duke University Press.

————. 2002. "'On the Road' with Che and Jack: Melancholia and the Legacy of Colonial Racial Geographies in the Americas." *New Formations* 47 (summer): 87–108.

Saldívar, José David. 1991. *The Dialectics of Our America: Genealogy, Cultural Critique, and Literary History.* Durham, NC: Duke University Press.

————. 1997. *Border Matters: Remapping American Cultural Studies*. Berkeley: University of California Press.

Saldívar, Ramón. 1979. "A Dialectic of Difference: Towards a Theory of the Chicano Novel." *MELUS* 6.3 (fall): 73–92.

————. 1990. *Chicano Narrative: The Dialectics of Difference*. Madison: University of Wisconsin Press.

Saldívar-Hull, Sonia. 2000. *Feminism on the Border: Chicana Gender Politics and Literature*. Berkeley: University of California Press.

Sánchez, George. 1993. *Becoming Mexican American: Ethnicity, Culture and Identity in Chicano Los Angeles, 1900–1945*. New York: Oxford University Press.

Sánchez, Rosaura. 1983. *Chicano Discourse: Socio-Historic Perspectives*. Rowley, MA: Newbury House.

Sandoval, Chela. 2000. *Methodology of the Oppressed*. Minneapolis: University of Minnesota Press.

Savin, Ada. 1994. "Bilingualism and Dialogism: Another Reading of Lorna Dee Cervantes's Poetry." In *An Other Tongue: Nation and Ethnicity in the Linguistic Borderlands*, ed. Alfred Arteaga, 215–23. Durham, NC: Duke University Press.

Sedgwick, Eve Kosofsky. 1985. *Between Men: English Literature and Male Homosocial Desire*. New York: Columbia University Press.

Shusterman, Richard. 1991. "The Fine Art of Rap." *New Literary History* 22.3: 613–32.

Smith, Andrew. 1993. "Rage Against the Machine." *Melody Maker*, August 28, 10–11.

Soto, Gary. 1990. *A Summer Life*. Hanover, NH, and London: University Press of New England.

Spivak, Gayatri. 1991. "Theory in the Margin." In *Consequences of Theory*, ed. Jonathan Arac and Barbara Johnson, 154–80. Baltimore: Johns Hopkins University Press.

Streeby, Shelley. 2002. *American Sensations: Class, Empire, and the Production of Popular Culture*. Berkeley: University of California Press.

Tavis, Thomas. 1994. "Review *City of God*." *Library Journal* 119.18 (November 1): 80.

*U.S. News & World Report*. 1989. "Rock Hudson's $21.7 Million Secret." February 27, 16.

Valdes-Rodriguez, Alisa. 1999. "More Than a Single Voice." *Los Angeles Times*, May 4, F1+.

Valle, Victor M., and Rodolfo D. Torres. 2000. *Latino Metropolis*. Minneapolis: University of Minnesota Press.

Villanueva, Tino. 1993. *Scene from the Movie Giant*. Willimantic, CT: Curbstone Press.

Villarreal, José Antonio. 1959. *Pocho*. Garden City, NY: Doubleday.

Wade, Peter. 1997. *Race and Ethnicity in Latin America*. London: Pluto Press.

Watrous, Peter. 1990. "Bilingual Music Is Breaking Down Cultural Barriers." *New York Times*, September 2, national edition, H19.

Weber, Donald. 1995. "From Limen to Border: A Meditation on the Legacy of Victor Turner for American Cultural Studies." *American Quarterly* 47.3: 525–36.

Wells, Carol A. 2001. "La lucha sigue: From East Los Angeles to the Middle East." In *Just Another Poster? Chicano Graphic Arts in California*, ed. Chon Noriega, 171–201. Santa Barbara: University Art Museum, University of California, Santa Barbara.

Williams, William Appleman. 1972. *The Tragedy of American Diplomacy*. New York: Dell.

Winant, Howard. 1994. *Racial Conditions: Politics, Theory, Comparisons*. Minneapolis: University of Minnesota Press.

Wyatt, Jean. 1995. "On Not Being La Malinche: Border Negotiations of Gender in Sandra Cisneros's 'Never Marry a Mexican' and 'Woman Hollering Creek.'" *Tulsa Studies in Women's Literature* 14.2 (fall): 243–71.

Ybarra-Frausto, Tomás. 1977. "The Chicano Movement and the Emergence of a Chicano Poetic Consciousness." *New Scholar* 6: 81–109.

———. 1991. "Rasquachismo: A Chicano Sensibility." In *Chicano Art: Resistance and Affirmation, 1965–1985*, ed. Richard Griswold del Castillo, Teresa McKenna, and Yvonne Yarbro-Bejarano, 155–62. Los Angeles: Wright Art Gallery.

Young, Robert J. C. 1995. *Colonial Desire: Hybridity in Theory, Culture and Race*. New York: Routledge.

**Discography**

Aztlan Underground, 1999, *Sub-Verses*, Xican@ Records, 40003–2.

Cypress Hill, 1991, *Cypress Hill*, Columbia 47889.

Cypress Hill, 1993, *Black Sunday*, Columbia 53931.

Delinquent Habits, 1996, *Delinquent Habits*, RCA 66929.

Delinquent Habits, 1998, *Here Come the Horns*, RCA 67559.

Delinquent Habits, 2001, *Merry Go Round*, Ark 21 810066.

Delinquent Habits, 2004, *Freedom Band*, Ark 21 810085.

Kid Frost, 1990, *Hispanic Causing Panic*, Virgin Records 91377.

Kid Frost, 1992, *East Side Story*, Virgin Records 92097.

Latin Alliance, 1991, *Latin Alliance*, Virgin Records 91625.

Latin Playboys, 1994, *Latin Playboys*, Slash/Warner Bros. 45543.

Latin Playboys, 1999, *Dose*, Atlantic Records 83173–2.

Los Lobos, 1978, *Just Another Band from East L.A.*, Independent release.

Los Lobos, 1983, *. . . And a Time to Dance*, Slash 23963.

Los Lobos, 1984, *Will the Wolf Survive?*, Slash/Warner Bros. 25177.

Los Lobos, 1987, *La Bamba*, Slash/Warner Bros. 25605.

Los Lobos, 1987, *By the Light of the Moon*, Slash/Warner Bros. 25523.

Los Lobos, 1988, *La Pistola y el Corazón*, Slash/Warner Bros. 25790.

Los Lobos, 1990, *The Neighborhood*, Slash/Warner Bros. 26131.

Los Lobos, 1992, *Kiko*, Slash/Warner Bros. 26786.

Los Lobos, 1993, *Just Another Band from East L.A.: A Collection*, Slash/Warner Bros. 45367.

Los Lobos, 1996, *Colossal Head*, Slash/Warner Bros. 46172.

Los Punkeros, 1997, *Raza Punk y Hardcore*, Aztlan Records 08012.

Ozomatli, 1998, *Ozomatli*, Almo Sounds 80020.

Rage Against the Machine, 1992, *Rage Against the Machine*, Epic 52959.

Rage Against the Machine, 1996, *Evil Empire*, Epic 57523.

Rage Against the Machine, 1999, *The Battle of Los Angeles*, Epic 69630.

Rage Against the Machine, 2001, *Renegades*, Sony B000053EZW.

Ritchie Valens, 1993, *The Ritchie Valens Story*, Del-Fi R271414.

# Index

abuela: lost world of comfort and
spontaneity associated with, 196.
*See also* generational icon

abusive power, patterns of, 239n.8

Acosta, Oscar "Zeta," xvi, 53–54,
63–68, 228n.6–7; *The Autobiog-*
*raphy of a Brown Buffalo*, 53–54,
63–65; *The Revolt of the Cockroach*
*People*, 53–54, 64–68

Acuña, Rodolfo, 15–16, 146

Adelitas, 66, 229n.8

advertising: Hispanic identity propa-
gated in, 11–12

aesthetics: ethics and, 197

African American musical forms:
deployment of, 88

Aguililla, Michoacán, 225n.14

AIDS, 58, 157, 161, 164, 169,
239n.9–10

Alarcón, Daniel Cooper, 148–49

Alarcón, Francisco, 241n.1

Alarcón, Norma, 3, 49, 69–70, 156,
225n.10, 236n.12, 241n.15

Aldama, Arturo, 25

Alemán, Jesse, 222n.3

*¡Alerta!* (Cervántez), 128–31

alienation: *indigenismo* in 1980s in
response to, 16; simultaneous
feeling of home and, 152

Almaguer, Tomás, 9, 222n.3, 238n.5

Almaraz, Carlos, 233n.16

Alpert, Herb, 103

ALT, 98, 100–101

Althusser, Louis, 238n.7

amalgamation, 5

ambiguity: productive, 35; tolerance
for, 24

*American Encounters* (Limón), 229n.10

ancestral connection: ancestral
ethics, 196, 211–14; melancholy
based on lost, 207–10. *See also*
Aztlán

**Rafael Pérez-Torres** is the author of *Movements in Chicano Poetry: Against Myths, Against Margins* and, with Ernie López, the memoir *To Alcatraz, Death Row, and Back: Memories of an East L.A. Outlaw*. He is professor of English at the University of California, Los Angeles.